WILDMEN,
WARRIORS,
AND KINGS

WILDMEN, WARRIORS, AND KINGS

Masculine Spirituality and the Bible

Patrick M. Arnold

CROSSROAD • NEW YORK

1992

The Crossroad Publishing Company
370 Lexington Avenue, New York, NY 10017

Printed in the United States of America
Typesetting output: TEXSource, Houston

Library of Congress Cataloging-in-Publication Data

Arnold, Patrick M.
    Wildmen, warriors, and kings : masculine spirituality and the
Bible / Patrick M. Arnold.
      p. cm.
    Includes index.
    ISBN 0-8245-1105-0; 0-8245-1252-9 (pbk.)
    1. Men — Religious life.   2. Men (Christian theology).   3. Bible.
O.T. — Biography.   I. Title.
BV4843.A764   1991
248.8'42 — dc20   91-18347
                                                CIP

FOR MY JESUIT BROTHERS

Contents

Foreword

Patrick Arnold as he writes jumps into his subject almost at once. He states flatly that a positive era for men has come to a close, at least for now, and a positive era for women has arrived. "Western culture and the Christian church are becoming more feminine and less masculine; the great transformation has been underway for well over a century. Every major institution in the West, from the military to the academy and from politics to religion, is experiencing the change from static masculine (patriarchal) values to dynamic feminine ones." This is a disturbing and depressing time for most men. Male privilege is disappearing. The respect that our grandfathers took for granted has vanished, men cannot find the roles their fathers lived in easily or uneasily, gifts for which men used to be praised they are now despised. Men's ability to go to extremes — for example, their ability to travel to the ends of the earth or to the moon, expressed in "the road of excess leads to the palace of wisdom" (Blake's sally) — now seems dangerous, incorrect, and not charming.

Usually when a man writes of contemporary male distress, the reviewer assumes that the writer wants to go back to patriarchy. But Arnold says: "The dynamic feminine Age of Aquarius has begun, and nothing can or should be done to stop it."

Men and women today need to be able to talk about the pain of men without imagining that the writer is proposing a solution. Difficulty is difficulty, loss is loss, grief is grief, and it is important simply to describe it.

This book differs from other books on contemporary men in that it is addressed primarily to readers who are deeply concerned with the Christian church in America, whether Catholic or Protestant. Patrick Arnold remarks rightly that the churches come late to the men's crisis. The images for men's grief have not come from ministers or priests. He notes moreover that seminaries everywhere in the United States have filled up recently with feminized men. Many male students have entered the seminary, he speculates, to please their mothers, and by doing so have cut themselves off from fathers and brothers, and their own certainty. They feel little bond with other men. The women, however, feel themselves to be pioneers acting very much out of their centers, willing to fight for different gender language, and ready to battle for honor and self-esteem.

This warrior behavior in women Arnold believes to be part of the rise of Aquarian energy, but he wants to warn us that a psychic plague is approaching, some of the first symptoms of which appeared in the seminaries ten or fifteen years ago. The plague is a contempt for the masculine. Arnold prefers to call this plague "misandry," which is the Greek for man-hatred. He remarks that its practice "is by no means limited to women; many men, full of self-hatred and guilt, also purvey it." One leader of the men's movement in England recently set down a proud description of a ritual that he had invented, which went this way: Men and women at the workshop divide into gender groups. The women stand erect in a circle and imagine positive female energy in the center of the circle, holding out their hands to it, visualizing power, energy, and joy. The men go into an adjoining room, where their male leader tells them they should now imagine themselves passing through ten gateways; at each gateway they are to give up something masculine. For example, they are to give up the male attitude to emotions and feelings, the male attitude to children, to science and technology; then they were asked to give up the male ego, then the male body hair and beard, then their testicles, and at the tenth gateway their penis. Following this meditation, they crawl under the raised arms of the women and so enter the female circle.

It is important to remember that misandry cannot be imputed to women only. Men speaking out of misandry ask other men to give up their sexuality, their creativity, and basically their essence. Patrick Arnold remarks that where misandry prevails, "whether in the school, in the parish, or on the job, it presents a bizarre and Kafkaesque form of moral algebra to males who live under it. Their very masculinity attaches to them a negative value, no matter what they do to prove themselves, the best they can do is remove the 'minus' male sign and work themselves up to an even zero: inoffensive, harmless, and acceptable."

We know that where misogyny prevails, women find themselves precisely in the situation described. Change "male" to "female" and women recognize the algebra: the best they can do is to work themselves up to be inoffensive, harmless, and acceptable.

In the second part of Arnold's book, following the teaching of Robert Moore, he treats Old Testament figures such as Moses, Elijah, and Jonah as reservoirs for new information about masculine models such as the Warrior, the Wild Man, and the Trickster (his description of Jonah as a trickster is particularly brilliant), and he wisely adds to those the Prophet, Healer, and Pilgrim. I'm not so sure that it's right for the New Testament church to claim the Wild Man. The Wild Man seems to me profoundly pagan.

In the third part Arnold plunges into the debate on the gender of the Divine. Something inside us knows that "God is not a male. God is not even human. God has no gender." But human beings seem incapable of approaching the Divine without the comforting veil of masculine and feminine genders. Women now desire to hear the words "Mother" and "feminine" associated with the Divine, and I think women are right in their desire. Arnold remarks, however, that "the neutering of God is already well underway in liberal and mainline Christian churches in America." "The issue is whether the disappearing male metaphors possess indispensable and irreplaceable potentials for imaging and relating to God, which cannot be summarily dismissed without causing irreparable harm to the essentials of the Christian message." Too hasty excising of metaphor results in a soul that is simply stunned and cannot associate with Mother or Father, let alone the utterly impersonal Divine.

What we have here then is a brave, passionate, sometimes one-sided book that aims to bring the members of the church to a greater consciousness of the demoralization of masculine priests and ministers and the neutering of liturgical language as examples of the enormous changes taking place all around us.

ROBERT BLY

Acknowledgments

It is humbling and pleasurable to consider, after a writing project of almost three years' duration, how many people have contributed to the work in ways great and small.

I am especially grateful to those men who have offered moral support and strong encouragement to write this book: Asa Baber, Robert Bly, Michael V. Tueth, S.J., and William H. McNichols, S.J. The topic of this book is controversial and even offensive to some in the circles in which I work, and I have often very much needed the brotherly support of these men.

I would also like to acknowledge those men and women who have been such help over the years in contributing ideas, offering constructive criticism, suggesting books and articles, reading various drafts of the manuscript, and providing stimulating conversation on the subject of men's spirituality: Timothy Manion, John Staudenmaier, S.J., Kathleen Dugan, John Foley, S.J., Thomas F. Michel, S.J., Eugene August, Michael D. Barber, S.J., Edward T. Oakes, S.J., Keith Barton, M.D., Michael W. Swartout, Christopher L. Nickerson, Michael E. Breault, S.J., William J. Dobbels, S.J., Gary Macy, Rev. Ron Pachence, Hubie T. Alexander, Christopher Harding, Rev. Bob Kress, E. Edward Kinerk, S.J., Christopher Matthews, M.D., Richard D. Perl, S.J., Dr. John Platania, Michael Scott, Paul Sussman, James Glenn Murray, S.J., Sam Mackintosh, Gerry McKevitt, S.J., Ron Seminara, S.J., Michael Rolland, O.P., Rev. Ed O'Brien, Robert Hamma, Wilkie Au, S.J., Walter J. Ong, S.J., Art Gramaje, George Bryjak, John W. Padberg, S.J., and Kenneth H. Nickerson.

I would also like to thank the University of San Diego for a research grant that assisted in the production of this book, as well as the following USD students who contributed criticism, ideas, and research to the project: Robyn Dimino, Kevin Fisher, Charles T. Hanna, Kurt Hildebrandt, Tim Houston, Elizabeth Lanning, Ken Luther-Kashing, Nadine Naber, Lori Neary, Kendall Pasborg, Andrew Rounseville, and Jeffrey Compton.

Introduction

There's a new movement out there. Though it started at the grassroots level many years ago, this phenomenon has only recently begun to appear on the radar screen of America's media and the popular consciousness — an article here, a television interview there, a few books, a bunch of audio cassettes, and a flurry of newsletters and journals. It's the New Men's Movement, and it promises to become one of the strongest forces in American culture during the Decade of the 1990s.

The burgeoning New Men's Movement is many things to many people, and combines divergent interests. At its most extreme, it represents the angry reaction of a few men fed up with the excesses of feminism; these activists are suspicious of women's liberation in general and are determined to fight it. The vast majority of men in the movement, however, are driven not by a reactionary hostility against women, but by a host of concerns about the well-being of men. There is a lot to be concerned about. Statistics show that American men are stressed out. Compared to women, they die much earlier, suffer higher rates of suicide, fatal illnesses, and substance abuse, and are more likely to be murdered, robbed, and assaulted; some scholars say that black men in America are becoming an endangered species. Moreover, masculine values in our culture are gradually diminishing, and a new kind of prejudice called "misandry" (the hatred of males) is beginning to appear in many circles.

Men and masculinity in America are beginning to break down. This fact is of great concern to our whole society since most of our major cultural problems relate in some way to the collapse of masculinity: homelessness, crime, drug addiction, divorce, single-parent families, gang warfare, and so on. On an individual level, many men are also beginning to recognize the masculine spiritual crisis in their own lives in the form of father-wounds, alienation, emptiness in their work, collapsed relationships, and loneliness, to name a few. In the last few generations, these problems have grown too serious to deny or dismiss with a macho shrug of the shoulders. Men are beginning to face their challenges squarely.

That is what the New Men's Movement is really about. After two decades of gradual growth, this loose confederation of individuals and

1

groups offers a variety of newsletters, books, workshops, retreats, discussion groups, and even rituals to men seeking masculine energy and searching for the support and understanding of their fellow males. Some groups are concerned with legal issues (child custody, divorce, sexual discrimination) while others focus on problems of men in the family, the workplace, or society in general. But one vibrant wing of this movement focuses especially on what we are now calling "masculine spirituality," that is, the distinctive characteristics, gifts, and archetypes of the male spirit. Whether through old European fairy stories or Hindu myths, Native American rituals or African drumming, these men are gaining access again to the *animus*, the masculine soul. They are learning to feel emotions once more, bonding with kindred spirits again, and finding renewed energy and courage to go on with their lives.

This book is part of the movement that is trying to articulate a masculine spirituality. It is written in the conviction that the Jewish and Christian spiritual tradition contains powerful, challenging, and healing assets for men as they face the dangers, stresses, and vapidity of modern life. Though modern liberal religion has lost awareness of male spiritual needs and even grown hostile to them, great resources for men still lie buried in the biblical and historical tradition. It is long past time to do a little consciousness-raising through a spiritual archaeological expedition to find these treasures. The Bible is the locus where we shall undertake these psychological excavations.

This book originates in much more than lofty spiritual goals, however; it is an outgrowth of my own love, joy, and grief. Above all, I write because I love men — old men and young men, white men and black men, Muslim men and Catholic men; I love myself as a man, and I am proud of the men I know. Yet some unwritten rule in our culture seems to forbid the expression of such love and pride in masculinity. A positive, affirming attitude toward masculinity is frequently dismissed as "male chauvinism." This is a male-positive book; criticisms of men and their failures are given in the context of a much greater sense of respect and even awe for the masculine gender.

I write, too, out of grief and pain. I hurt inside as I see the great divorce that has developed over the generations between men and Christian spirituality. I hurt for the men that have lost the close contact with God that a healthy religiosity can nurture. This is an alienation that affects me personally as well as most men, and I'd like to share my life experience of it here to indicate better where I'm coming from.

Even in my childhood I was vaguely aware of what we now call masculine spirituality. My earliest memories record in a simple way the puzzling predicament of men and religion. At the altar where I served, in the *front* of the church presided the dashing and hearty Fr. Michael P. Thompson, an Irish immigrant with a booming voice and a clever mind. I idolized him. Yet at *back* of the church, that nether-world of the Christian religion, milled my father and most of the few men I knew who came to church at all. There weren't many men in between. Men, it seemed, either *ran* the church as the solitary priest, or watched it from afar between cigarette breaks at Christmas and Easter.

Though these door-huggers might sheepishly admit that they "should" be in church, they certainly didn't enjoy it. On the contrary, their arm-folding, wall-leaning, ceiling-gazing, and cigarette-smoking comportment communicated to everyone with clear passive-aggressive body language that they really didn't want to be there in the first place. The weekly repetition of these male behaviors etched in my heart the sense that real men more or less resist religion; at least, until they got old. My grandfather Martin M. Hassett, a convert, went to church not only every Sunday, but every First Friday, as well; in fact, he told me that after the first nine, you were guaranteed to go to heaven (he surpassed the two hundred mark). This seemed to a young boy like a very good deal. I suppose watching elders like my grandfather suggested to me that when you get old, religion was a pretty good thing. But until then, it wasn't cool to get too interested in it. In fact, for men, going to church seemed a lot like going to the dentist: if you were smart you went regularly, but nobody expected you to look forward to it.

In strong contrast to this diffidence to organized religion it began to dawn on me, even as a child, that the men I knew who spent a lot of time working, hunting, and fishing out in the Black Hills of South Dakota (where I grew up) almost always had a very appealing air of wisdom and spiritual strength about them, a sense of belonging to the earth and relatedness to its creatures. They said wise things about life. They were respectful of God. And they almost always would say something along these lines: "I'm not a religious man, I don't go to church, but up here in the Hills I feel close to God and I talk to him in my own words." These "unreligious" men made simple faith and prayer something personal and attractive.

As a teenager, I coasted toward a typical case of conflicted and alienated American male spirituality until two unexpected things happened. First, I encountered Jesuit teachers at Regis High School in Denver, Colorado. Until then, my religiosity had consisted entirely in arriving for weekly Mass just before the gospel (or else it didn't count — a mortal sin) and leaving right before communion. But I saw in my teachers men of a totally different spirit than the sin and guilt mongers of pre-Vatican II Catholicism, men of great generosity, intelligence, humor, and kindness who openly expressed their love of Christ and enthusiasm for faith. They completely belied my developing notion that church men were lugubrious and unctuous wimps; in fact, they were the most intensely alive, imaginative, and energetic men I'd ever met (or have since met).

I was hooked. I wanted to be like that when I grew up. Thus began my deliberately committed life in the Catholic Church, a community then buzzing with Vatican II excitement and alive with the promise of service to humanity according to the example of Christ. That is the church I'm committed to still, though wimpy, lugubrious, and unctuous men have since returned to it with sanctimonious vengeance.

Something even more wonderful happened a short time later, in the summer of my seventeenth year when I'd returned to the Black Hills to work. I began to have what can only be called "mystical" experiences, powerful and joyful feelings about God and nature. I had no idea what this all meant at the time; looking back on it, I could say now that, back home in that Lakota holy land, I had just experienced first-hand the male archetype of the Wildman. And though I couldn't have articulated it at the time, I'd stumbled into my first electric, personal encounter with genuine masculine spirituality.

The following autumn of 1968, I entered the Jesuit order and encountered there a spirituality rich with masculine myth, symbols, and lore. In long hours of silence, prayer, and reading, my Jesuit novice master, Vincent J. O'Flaherty, S.J., schooled us in the Spiritual Exercises with their themes of the Kingdom, the Two Standards, and the *magis*; we read the lives of the Don Quixote-like Ignatius of Loyola, followed the adventures of Francis Xavier to China, Roberto diNobili to India, and Peter DeSmet to America. We male-bonded in life-long friendships and dreamed of heroic lives in service to Christ, like our forebears.

And what of my Wildman? No one seemed to understand what in the world I was talking about when I spoke of God in nature; indeed one Jesuit hinted darkly of paganism and *pantheism*, an awful-sounding thing I had to look up in the dictionary. It must be bad — it wasn't Catholic. And so I suffered as one does when the thing most real to him in the world, the thing most important to his soul, is considered by those he respects as irrelevant and unimportant.

In the midst of profound depression and confusion I considered returning to the Black Hills, but a Jesuit friend's letter of encouragement to me in my darkness instantly catalyzed in me another archetype! With amazing ingenuity, my friend boldly suggested that I make a pilgrimage to Israel, to the Holy Land, to seek and find God's will in my life. Now, Jesuit novices simply did not do such things; wrapped in our black cassocks, we were expected to pray, do our chores, study our Latin, and get to bed by 9:00 P.M. But in a matter of seconds after finishing the letter, my inner Pilgrim flared to life, and I was going to the Holy Land come hell or high water. Astonishingly, my novice master and provincial approved of the idea, and in the summer of 1970 I left everything and everybody I knew and was off hitchhiking to New York to join a Jewish Youth Group leaving for a kibbutz in Israel. God did not ignore this bold gamble on his grace. In Jerusalem that summer, at age nineteen, I discovered clearly my life's vocation: to be a priest, an Old Testament teacher, and an archaeologist; and that is what I do today, twenty years later.

Over those years and mostly under the surface, I've felt a certain dull pain about being a man and living a life of faith. On the one hand, I have felt somehow odd, for the most real thing in the world to me — the life of the spirit — seems almost incomprehensible to most of the men I meet in everyday life. On the other hand, I've felt genuine sadness for many good men whose lives seem to lack a certain spiritual depth and direction, whose vision is solely focussed on the Reagan-era Star of the East, Opportunity.

All of these doubts and concerns simmered mostly below the surface of my consciousness in the 1980s as I pursued a theological education and began teaching biblical literature in liberal seminaries in Toronto, Atlanta, and Berkeley. These theology schools hummed with the energy of the Christian feminist movement as it sought full equality for women in the church. Like most of my male colleagues, I originally supported the movement wholeheartedly, but in time I began to recognize a dark undertow to the tide of feminist change that only later could I name: misandry. In the literature of the movement, in classroom lectures, and in informal conversations and comments, I began to hear both men and women feminists articulate openly my ugliest unspoken fears and concerns about men. At one time or another, it all came out: "men aren't naturally religious; men are spiritually superficial; men are naturally violent and dominating; the Mass is the ritual rape of women; if men could get pregnant, abortion would be a sacrament; white men are responsible for the ruin of the planet"; and so on. And no one objected to these outrageous sexist and racist claims; male-bashing had now achieved status as politically correct dogma from which no dissent was permitted. I began to object: it got my Warrior going.

Fortunately, what started rather negatively and defensively ten years ago has been transformed into a positive experience as I've read, conversed, reflected, and written about the male spirit. This present book is an outgrowth of that learning process, an attempt to share some ideas and stories about masculinity and its relation to spirituality. This work is also intended, frankly, as something of a celebration of the male spirit. It is, like Caesar's Gaul, divided into three parts. Part One, "Gender and Spirit," is devoted to a discussion of ideas and issues concerning the relationship between gender and spirituality. It tackles the concept of "masculine spirituality" by defining and describing it, and indicates how modern religion might better relate to it. Part Two, "Masculine Archetypes and the Bible," is a much more practical discussion of ten classic masculine psychological archetypes and how they directly affect men's lives. Based on the developing field of archetypal psychology, the chapters treat the Pilgrim, Patriarch, Warrior, Magician, King, Wildman, Healer, Prophet, Trickster, and Lover as they appear in the Bible. All of these archetypes lie dormant or unrecognized in most men; a discussion of them as they appear in the Bible, in literature, film, and real men's lives will help reveal the tremendous spiritual potentials that men possess, but may not experience consciously. Part Three is theologically oriented and discusses the necessity of a masculine theology if ever we are to relate to God. We shall see how, on close examination, Jesus is pictured in the Christian Scriptures as a stark male figure quite unlike the "bearded lady" that is often purveyed to us in modernity. Finally, we shall explore how the Bible reveals divine qualities in metaphorical language that depends on the masculine archetypes. Some truths about the biblical God cannot be communicated clearly except through the medium of masculine spirituality.

Caveats and Clarifications

The discussion of gender is an extremely sensitive and emotional one in our culture. An atmosphere of victimization (real and imagined) often poisons any conversation about sexuality, especially as it relates to spirituality. An unfortunate tendency to impute negative attitudes where none exist is also noteworthy. I would like, therefore, to be clear here regarding the intentions, methods, and assumptions that guide this book.

First, this work is not an overt or a covert attack on women or feminism; on the contrary, one will find many positive evaluations of the feminine in this book. I will be quite clear in stating at the outset, however, that this book is critical of a phenomenon in feminism that we are now calling misandry, or "male-bashing." In providing this critique in the past, I have been labelled a fool, overly sensitive, negative, reactionary, and covertly anti-feminist. None of this is surprising — exposing hatred always draws animosity in response. But I categorically reject the implication that criticism of misandry in the feminist movement's excesses regarding men constitutes a covert attack on the entire movement.

Second, this is a book about men. I do not deal in depth with women's issues. Yet I have found it amazing that attempts to raise issues regarding men are sometimes judged as oppressive, or viewed as important or valuable only to the extent that they reflect on the *women's* movement. Men have the right and duty to discuss their own spirituality without accusations of chauvinism, and without getting clearance or permission from anyone to do so. Indeed, the best Christian feminists among us, such as Rosemary Radford Ruether, have long urged men to do their own work.

Third, this book is written in *general* terms about *typical* masculinity for *most* males. There is, of course, no such thing as a "typical" man — such a claim would verge on sexism. Each man is as unique spiritually as he is physically. Nevertheless, one can speak generally about males and masculinity without pleading guilty to a charge of automatic stereotyping. Many men and women feel oppressed by discussions of sexual spirituality because they assume such conversations are in some way prescriptive. In describing classic masculine patterns or ancient male archetypes, however, I am only observing that, in fact, men tend to display certain psychological typologies and act and value in certain ways. I am neither condemning nor condoning the many men who are not typical, but am only articulating the classic characteristics that most men can identify with as they reflect on their manhood.

Fourth, I do not claim that men alone possess certain characteristics or archetypes. Nor do I hold that there are gender virtues or vices ("gentleness" = feminine, or "courage" = masculine). I am saying that there is a masculine and a feminine inflection to qualities such as courage and kindness, or evils such as violence and cruelty. It is a common strategy in the Gender Wars for combatants to twist an attempt to identify the sexual distinctiveness of one gender into an alleged claim of superiority. Our discussion of masculine spirituality is based on the fact that, throughout history, most men have tended to develop a masculine identity — a male spirituality — through the influence of inherited unconscious archetypes as well as biological conditioning, psychological patterning, and cultural stereotyping. To deny this truth is to blind oneself to valuable insights.

Finally, I am not saying that men or masculinity are superior — or inferior — to women or femininity. I am only saying that men are spiritually different, interesting, and wonderful to behold for all that.

PART ONE

Gender and Spirit

THE FIRST PART OF THIS BOOK is an issue-oriented discussion of the major questions involved in the relationship of gender to spirituality, particularly as related to males. The opening chapter raises general considerations of the role that sexuality plays in religion and how current discussions of this topic impact upon masculine spirituality. The second chapter specifically defines and describes what masculine spirituality is, and how it is expressed in the language of the classical male archetypes. Chapter 3 addresses an emerging cultural impediment to healthy men's spirituality: "misandry" or "male-bashing." The final chapter in Part One discusses historical issues that explain widespread male alienation from religion. It offers concrete suggestions as to ways the church could reach out to men more effectively.

Chapter 1

Sexuality, Gender, and Spirit

The term "masculine spirituality" may, to many, seem a strange or even vaguely threatening phrase. Traditional church conservatives find the words a bit trendy, an all-too-fashionable product of New Age spirituality. Some feminists, on the other hand, feel that the expression masks a hostile, reactionary riposte to the now well-established concept of feminine spirituality. Most of the rest of us merely find the term "masculine spirituality" somewhat unusual if not jarring, combining as it does two seemingly contradictory words in an oxymoron. For the word "masculine" usually connotes muscular physicality — the raucous *machismo* one might encounter in a locker-room, a motorcycle club, or on a Southern California beach. By contrast, "spirituality" normally suggests the highest reaches of the human soul — or the ethereal quiet one experiences in a cloistered convent or a medieval French cathedral.

Discomfort with the term "masculine spirituality" betrays some of the unconscious and widespread cultural attitudes toward both masculinity and spirituality that we will explore in these pages. Most of us are hardly aware that sexuality has anything positive to do with the life of the spirit in the first place; unfortunately, some people even strongly believe that the two are inimically opposed. For many among us, the pursuit of the spiritual life amounts to a flight from sexual concerns, or worse, an attempt to conquer the body and all the problems that our gender and sexuality present for us. We will see that our sexuality — our gender — is not an enemy but an ally, and influences our spirit in profound and powerful ways.

Real Men Aren't Spiritual

Our unfamiliarity with the role that masculine sexuality plays in spiritual matters is worthy of very close consideration. Most of us are likely to hold a severely stunted notion of masculinity. It is widely perceived in our culture, for example, that masculinity basically concerns itself with pragmatic and down-to-earth things; males, it is thought, are only interested in the so-called real world, the bottom line, and concrete results. We tend to think that while men might make the world go round, cut the deals, and bring home the bacon, they really aren't very good at spiritual or emotional things like religion. When males do get involved with their local church, it seems, they gravitate once again to practical affairs: church maintenance, administration and long-term financing. But the life of the spirit? That is not really in the purview of our culture's ideal Real Man. Spirituality, prayer, and worship belong somehow to the world of women; stained-glass windows, elaborate rituals, lacy weddings, and dainty sermons make a Real Man uncomfortable. So Real Men not only eschew quiche, they avoid church, too. And the only times a Real Man goes to church are at his baptism, wedding, or funeral: the "carried, married, and buried" syndrome.

Obstacles and Allies

If men would search more carefully and find a wider and deeper notion of masculinity than that purveyed by popular American culture, they would see that their native manhood actually stimulates, enriches, and energizes the life of their spirits in ways that they never imagined. Yet this search is impeded by a variety of stumbling-blocks. Every man on the quest for masculine spirituality needs to identify these obstacles quite deliberately and overcome them, as well as recognize the many opportunities and allies he has on his journey.

Male estrangement from spirituality in Western Christianity is an old and complicated phenomenon finding its roots in an intricate web of historical factors ranging from psychology to sociology to economics. Men are responsible for this alienation from their native religiosity and it is they who must do the bulk of the hard work in reconciling the split. Yet the church as an institution also bears responsibility for this great divorce, for it has failed to understand men and to speak to them in a language that they can comprehend. Except for isolated pastors and teachers, few Christian ministers seem to have a sympathetic notion of "what makes men tick," an empathy for their unique problems, or a clue how to solve those problems. If men are to find the way to a vibrant Christian spirituality, they will need help from mentors who have already blazed their own trails and learned the delights as well as the hazards of the road. The church is worthless if it is unwilling or unable to help such people find their paths to God.

Tragically, just as American men are beginning to experience a renewed desire for spirituality, an ugly sentiment is simultaneously developing among some of the very people who could help guide men along their journeys. It is the belief that men are somehow especially dangerous and bad, perhaps genetically flawed, and that the only hope for them lies in the radical renunciation of masculinity itself. An extreme outgrowth of the feminist movement, "misandry" infects many liberal seminaries, theologies, spiritual books, and pastoral care programs. Men who seek spiritual guidance in these circles need to alert themselves to its existence and to the possibility that they might receive hostility rather than help, and suspicion rather than encouragement. In turn, if Christian ministers are ever effectively to reach men just as they are, they must first recognize, confront, and subdue this brand new form of sexism. Unfortunately, many in the church deny that such misandry even exists, much less that it is an increasing problem.

The future of an effective Christian outreach to men is by no means bleak. There are many programs, rituals, and studies that could encourage the growth of a vibrant masculine spirituality; indeed, some men are developing them even now. This is not to suggest that spirituality is identical with church attendance or religious activity; nevertheless, such involvement constitutes a powerful help for most men in beginning to recover the life of the soul, and hence, to find God. One extremely important path that the church offers to men in their spiritual lives is prayerful Bible reading; the bulk of this book will explore just a few of the ways modern men might find themselves and their God through this practice.

The New Men's Movement

Concern for the souls of men is hardly a parochial matter limited to professional ministers. On the contrary, much of the energy driving the contemporary American renaissance in men's spirituality derives from a growing number of psychologists, poets, teachers, doctors, businessmen, and others who comprise what is loosely termed the New Men's Movement. Formed largely in the last decade, this movement combines diverse groups that tend to share several common interests. First, men in these groups recognize the validity of many claims advanced by feminism: that women have suffered historically under the socio-political arrangement known as patriarchy and that practically every field of human endeavor requires reform in providing women with equal opportunities, fair pay, and, above all, basic human dignity and freedom. But these men also realize that so-called patriarchal culture oppresses *men* economically, legally, politically, and spiritually. They can see all too well the devastation in their own souls and those of the men around them: workaholism, father-wounds, alienation from the family, legal discrimination, oppressive social expectations and taboos, lack of genuine male friendships, and above all, The Numbness — the inability to feel joy or meaning or sadness or *anything*.

Rather than whine and complain and stew in a state of angry victimization, these men are doing something about their quiet desperation: they are embarking together on an exciting search for the male soul. They seek to rediscover there the distinctive and unique masculine voice as it articulates its unique experiences of manhood, of life itself, and of God. Under the original inspiration and mentoring of such men as poet Robert Bly and Jungian psychologist Robert Moore, these men listen in weekly gatherings or yearly retreats to the wisdom of old fairy tales and what they have to say about the Hero's adventure. They drum together in the harmony of the primitive beat of the heart, experiencing the Wildman within. They create a space where they can tell the truth to each other: first to mourn their losses and count the wounds, then to find the resources of the heart that will carry them through. They read widely, compare notes, and probe their memories. They seek ways to relate better to their wives and lovers and children, to come to terms at long last with their fathers, and to get to know themselves.[1] For this is what spirituality is all about, after all: not the esoteric and recondite secrets of an unattainable other world, but the very real concerns that touch our deepest selves in this life — identity, valuing, and relationship with ourselves, with others, and with God.

Spirituality as Revolution

The movement of American males toward spirituality is a revolutionary development that overthrows the legacy of several centuries of culturally indoctrinated hostility to spirituality spawned by the Enlightenment, nurtured by the Industrial Revolution, and brought to term by materialistic consumerism. These cultural movements have not *enthroned* men as the critics of patriarchy would claim, but thrown men out: out of the house, out of the church, and, worst of all, out of themselves. It is no exaggeration to say that modernity has created generations of Numb Men who cannot even *feel* their own experiences, much less articulate them. Capitalism and Communism each in its own way has fabricated the Incredible Shrinking Man, a merely utilitarian robot programmed in the West to create capital, and in the East, to serve the state. Indeed, perhaps one of Mikhail Gorbachev's most telling criticisms of his own Russian people is that eighty years of Communism has almost depleted their most important human resource: spirituality.[2] Nor will they replenish it by blindly imitating their American counterpart, the Man in the Grey Flannel Suit.

As the two great forms of materialism, Capitalism and Communism, each shrink men to the emotional size and spiritual capacity of an R-2 D-2 unit, they inevitably trigger in many men a corresponding hunger for something more, a desire for the transcendentally great. This hunger is a powerful force, not always well directed. In many areas it is fuel for the worldwide phenomenon of fundamentalism, a strongly male-oriented movement that may be regarded in some ways as a kind of spiritual disease.[3] But while we may fear fundamentalism's fanaticism, loathe its authoritarianism, or disdain its simple-mindedness, we cannot easily dismiss its anguished claim that something has gone wrong with global culture — something spiritual. Whether we live in the Middle East or the Middle West, we experience a lack of faith, a diminishment in our sense of the sacred, and a strong desire for ersatz substitutes such as drugs to achieve the altered states of consciousness traditionally reached by religion. Men need the greatness of the Holy, and nothing else but the Holy will really suffice. Each man has in him a God-sized void that no one and no thing other than God can fill. Which is why, ultimately, it is not enough for liberating men *only* to drum, chant, and share experiences. They must eventually find their way to God, the Source of Being.

Feminism's Contribution to Masculine Spirituality

Men are finding the God-path. Moreover, pioneering pastoral care-givers from mainline Christian traditions are beginning to take the first steps toward ministry directed specifically to modern men.[4] One of the most important influences on the development of modern men's spirituality is feminism. For three decades, our sisters have done the hard work of beginning to liberate themselves from oppressive social roles, exploitative economic conditions, and institutional religious insensitiv-ity — almost always with stiff resistance from stultifying coalitions of Numb Men typically unable to feel compassion for what they experi-ence. The New Men's spirituality is not another roadblock on the way to women's liberation. In many ways, it is an outcome of it. For men cannot really enter into the dynamic stride of the spiritual journey if their feet are planted rigidly on women's necks.

As women have long told us, the far-reaching changes that femi-nism creates necessarily demand corresponding spiritual work by men to free themselves from their own oppressiveness, numbness, and un-consciousness. Until recently, however, this men's consciousness-raising about gender and sexuality primarily meant reading feminist literature and adopting the feminist agenda — an invaluable method of entering empathetically into women's experience and listening to their pain, but an impossible way to understand masculinity. Feminism must speak for women — it cannot speak for men. Since women can't directly experi-ence what it means to be a man, and since most men are too numb to tell them their experiences, feminist literature can't articulate much more than *women's* experience of men, which is so often the product, not of men's souls but of their numbness, of their domination, insensitivity, and even brutality. Feminist literature, as a result, sometimes concentrates on the worst side of men, and is unable or unwilling to probe beneath this cultural wreckage to find anything valuable or graced. Most contemporary conversation about the male gender, therefore, is clearly one-sided and tainted with prejudice, which is why men themselves must correct the unbalance and speak forcefully from their own experience.

Much of this strongly negative current literature and rhetoric about men is influential in academia, the media, the arts, and liberal religion, where it has achieved "politically correct" status. Moreover, there is presently little information or discussion that would give a correspondingly positive treatment about the male spirit: few men's classes in college gender studies programs, few empathetic programs about men on television,[5] and no courses on men's spirituality in any theology school of my acquaintance. One measure of the distance men have to go in articulating their unique experience is available in any serious bookstore; volumes on women's spirituality sometimes occupy entire walls while books about men (many of them strongly negative) often conveniently fit on one shelf. What is at stake here is not numerical competition or sexual debating points, but the entire public intellectual, affective, and spiritual atmosphere in which men live and young men grow up. The growing cultural inability to fathom men, however, creates an opportunity: the challenge for men to understand and speak for themselves. Men must therefore do their own intellectual work, define their own terms, set out their own agenda, confront negative projections and stereotypes, and engage in constructive self-criticism — all in the context of calm and reasonable self-affirmation.

Patriarchy and Clericalism

Despite extensive discussions about feminist spirituality in recent decades, one key barrier to the development of a genuine men's spirituality is simply the still widespread unawareness in religious as well as cultural circles that one's gender has anything to do with spiritual matters. Fortunately, a host of feminist writers have already shown convincingly how deeply relevant sexuality is to women's religiosity. Within the last decade, numerous works have appeared along a spectrum of feminist religious issues ranging from spirituality to biblical hermeneutics, and from the role of women in the church to the feminine dimension of God.[6] The ideas in these works now permeate most liberal Protestant and Catholic theology schools, creating fruitful new lines of thought and insight. Yet perhaps the most beneficial by-product of this exciting new work is the deepening of the realization that the human relationship to self, other, and God is strongly affected by gender and sexuality.

How does our maleness or femaleness affect our religiosity? The question is a fascinating and neuralgic one. At the most superficial socio-political level, there is no question that cultural forces and social expectations highly determine religious behavior based on gender alone. Feminist writers have documented well a history of oppressiveness in the Judeo-Christian tradition that has denied women a full and equal place in the public life of their faith. Patriarchy has consigned women to an inferior place in the synagogue and church, encouraged acceptance of stereotypical identities and roles, and created difficulties in relating to a deity who is usually described exclusively in masculine terms. The issue of self-worth is a real one; if a woman cannot participate fully and equally in religious celebration and decision making, what does this say about her relative worth before God?

Today this problem creates pain for everyone at what otherwise would be a joyful occasion: ordination to ministry. While their male counterparts, with whom they have often studied and shared as equals, rise and approach the altar to receive the sacrament of Holy Orders, young women theology students must remain seated in their pews quietly, except for the expected burst of enthusiastic applause that signifies the congregation's approval. Even in those churches that ordain women to the ministry, sexist prejudice still erupts sporadically among the laity as well as the hierarchy; Anglican women priests, for example, have experienced many slights and indignities at the hands of men and women alike. One can only wonder at the untold damage patriarchy has inflicted on female spirits in their quest for God over the centuries.

Yet no one thinks to ask whether men have also suffered from sexism in the same tradition; it is almost universally assumed that they "enjoy" the privileged positions that patriarchy affords them. But only the most insecure and pompous men have "enjoyed" their positions of ecclesiastical power and privilege. In my experience in the Roman Catholic tradition, the great majority of priests regard their ministry as a burden of service, undertaken with love, sometimes at great personal cost. Quite apart from scandalously low wages and, in some cultures, inferior social position, these men often suffer great loneliness under mandatory celibacy. The irony of it all, of course, is that though they must possess a male sex organ to serve as priests, they are not allowed to use it!

The clericalism that isolates and alienates clergymen also tends to demean lay men. Where "real" religious service seems to mean the abandonment of generative sexuality, it is difficult to escape the subliminal implication that men who are sexually active cannot achieve spiritual potency and are not, therefore, fully adequate religious beings.

Even in those churches where celibacy is not an issue, the professional status of the clergy is frequently a subtle barrier for lay men. Priests and ministers seem like spiritual "experts" to whom one defers as obsequiously as to a computer repairman or a brain surgeon. This attitude is appropriate with reference to the arcane details of canon law or the fine points of a theological argument, but not when the subject is one's own soul or conscience.

Platonism and Male Spirituality

Though from the most obvious sociological perspective no honest observer could deny that cultural attitudes toward gender have strongly influenced male and female religiosity, many traditionalists would claim that this effect is purely superficial. Specifically, they would deny that the male's alleged divinely ordained religious power at all implies spiritual inequality between men and women.[7] They argue that at a deeper spiritual level, men and women enjoy full freedom and equality before God regardless of their social position. This view implies that the superficial "outer" shell of sexual equipment and physiology with its attendant social roles cannot actually affect the "inner" reality of the soul before God. This Platonic notion, stressing as it does the utter distinction between the real world of the soul and the illusory world of the body actually, of course, masks patriarchal interests; purveyors of the same kind of doctrine once tried to convince blacks in pre–Civil War America that their status as slaves in no wise affected their God-given human dignity.

Yet the implications of Platonism have also worked insidiously against men in the Christian mystical tradition in a surprising and largely unrecognized way. This is of key importance in our discussion since it explains the paradoxical fact that, while the church's political structure is clearly patriarchal and male-oriented, its spirituality is both heavily directed toward females and often quite alienating to men. Since, in the Christian Platonic view, power and position belong to the outer (phenomenal) world, the *real* spiritual person is the one who concentrates on the pure inner life of the soul in prayer, silence, and retreat.[8] By this logic, while some males in the church might rise to ecclesiastical dominance, the better choice — and the road to real holiness — is to abandon the world, the flesh, and the devil entirely. In this respect, the lowly social state of women is actually assumed to provide a kind of spiritual advantage: the opportunity to develop the highest and most noble powers of the soul in an atmosphere of humility, powerlessness, and meekness.

We thus arrive at the great oddity of traditional Christian spirituality. While males clearly rule the church patriarchally, they do so with the strong implication that their very power, position, and wealth violate the essence of the spiritual life! The church seems to suffer these males as a kind of necessary evil — *someone's* got to run the institution. But the real "soul" of the church are the very poor, the lowly, the humble, and the passive: most especially, the women. In this view, if a male is to live a *genuine* spiritual life, he must retreat meekly and humbly into the monastery in order to suffer mortification, renouncing with his vows of poverty, chastity, and obedience some of the most masculine of enterprises: economic activity, sexual generativity, and autonomous independence. Bluntly, if a man is to live spiritually, he seems required to enter into the cultural role of an oppressed woman: poor, sexually abandoned, and dependent.

The kind of ascetic life described here is a genuine and noble path to God travelled by men of many religions throughout history. Moreover, it is founded solidly in the Christian tradition on precepts that originate in the teaching of Jesus (for example, the Beatitudes in Mt 5). But this way to God, like all others, is not without real perils. Besides the obvious hazard of elitism, there is an ever-present danger of what Nietzsche called *ressentiment*; that is, the pernicious hatred and jealousy of the "powerful" by those professing "meekness and humility."

To the extent that men perceive the ascetic path as the only authentic way to God (to the exclusion of other genuine Christian spiritualities) and regard this route subliminally as an unmanly one to take, we have the conditions that engender radical male alienation from spirituality. And this is indeed what seems to have happened in Western Christianity: "Real (spiritual) Men" must abandon most of the values and enterprises nearest to men's hearts — competition, fighting, sexual expressiveness, generativity, economic productivity, adventure, autonomy — in favor of a eunuch's existence.[9] The eunuch motif is even present in the premier model held up to *married* Christian men: Joseph the husband of Mary, usually presented as an old man, a sexless and frozen ideal.[10] It is little wonder that so many men get a strong unconscious message that involvement with Christian spirituality requires a kind of emasculation. It seems to them that the men best suited for Christian life are odd and asexual, nerds, or very old and "out of gas." Perhaps with some guilt and regret, most men therefore just go their own way. Still somehow attracted by the gravity of the reality of God, they remain in a kind of high orbit around what seems to be a religious Black Hole, beckoning them to annihilation. That is where we see them today: on the fringes of involvement, in the back of the church, on the edges of the faith, orbiting.

Our paradox remains: though patriarchal in its structure, Western Christianity is dominantly feminine in its heart and soul. In this mentality, men who insist on working actively in the profane world of business or politics relate to the ultimately real world of prayer and worship primarily through the grace of a saving feminine presence in their lives (usually the wife or mother) or, alternatively, through contact with a "real spiritual man" (a priest or minister) in annual retreats to the monastery or occasional visits to a church. But the bulk of their best time and energy still goes to pursuits considered "secular" or "worldly." This is the heritage of Christian Platonism: the unconscious impression that women are *naturally* religious while men, by virtue of some hormone, chemical, or gene defect, or just out of plain mean-spiritedness, are carnally interested only in the material world and all its benefits.[11]

Men do not have to accept passively this sexist assumption. It is encouraging to note that many Christian men do firmly reject it, and find a meaningful Christian spirituality in the warp and woof of their life and work. One thinks here primarily of conservative Christian men such as politician Jimmy Carter and businessman H. Ross Perot, or evangelical organizations such as the Full Men's Gospel Fellowship or the Fellowship of Christian Athletes. The Catholic and liberal Protestant churches seem to present greater problems for men in finding a spirituality that speaks to them, although one can point to exceptional refreshing examples such as Governor Mario Cuomo or actor Martin Sheen. These men, and many others both famous and obscure, have done the hard work of rejecting sexist cultural stereotypes and embarking deliberately on their own unique spiritual journeys. Their willingness to witness to their religious convictions while remaining active in the world reminds men that the spiritual dimension does not remove them from reality, but puts them in more wholesome contact with it.

Androgyny: The New Sexual Ideology

Since it has become obvious that political, economic, and cultural forces as well as gender stereotyping highly influence feminine and masculine spirituality, a new sexual ideology has developed that is touted as a solution to historic inequalities: *androgyny* (Greek: "male and female"). The androgynist agenda seeks to eliminate or downplay any *essential* human differences between men and women. Many proponents of androgyny would argue that, except for minimal genital dissimilarities, male-female distinctions are primarily culturally nurtured and socially reinforced and should, therefore, be eradicated. This idea recognizes that human beings are, in fact, a complicated mix of masculine and feminine characteristics and that purely "masculine" men or "feminine" women do not exist.[12] The androgynous ideological agenda, however, goes on to urge the suppression of dominant masculinity or femininity in individuals, and the balancing of both male and female psychological qualities. Moreover, many androgynists demand that society reflect their proposed gender equilibrium in its institutions, laws, customs, and values. In theological circles, this program finds its scriptural basis in the famous words of St. Paul, "there is no such thing as Jew and Greek, slave and free, male and female; you are all one person in Christ Jesus" (Gal 3:28).

The intention of theological androgyny is to stress the common humanity and equality of all people before God and to undermine those ecclesiastical structures and social roles that tend to oppress women and deny them full human rights. This approach promotes full ministerial equality between men and women, insisting on inclusive liturgical language, sex-neutral God-talk, and deconstruction of patriarchal hierarchical authority. As is commonly the case with ideologies, many features of this particular program are sound. In particular, its insistence that religious institutions accord full human rights and equal participation at every level of ministry and administration to both men and women would seem to be a matter of fundamental human justice. Moreover, its realization that humans are composed of a complex mixture of male and female physical, emotional, and psychic elements helps free people from simplistic notions that "men are all alike" or that "women are basically the same." Finally, it rightly insists that male and female legal rights, career interests, social and family roles, and religious sensibilities should not be regarded as a function of. genitalia.

Yet to the extent that the androgynous program is an attempt to impose a philosophical abstraction (sexual equality) on the complicated paradox of human sexuality, it can only result in new oppressiveness at least as serious as that which the ideology set out to correct. The imposition of an androgynous ideal on individuals, society, and the church would sacrifice one of the most precious human emotional and psychic gifts — sexual distinctiveness — in favor of a bland uniformity. That each male and female should be regarded abstractly and treated fairly as a generic "human" at the level of legal rights, job opportunities, wage scales, or positions in ministry is an increasingly obvious truth and one of the urgent goals of the sexual revolution. But to believe therefore, that except for superficial genitalia there does or should no longer exist between males and females any natural emotional differences or distinctive psychological qualities is to ignore evidence from scientific investigation as well as to deny the most human instincts of the human heart.[13] To ignore or repress essential sexual — and spiritual — differences between men and women not only violates common sense and experience, but sets the stage for more oppression in the name of abstraction, a hallmark of the twentieth century.

The attempt to repress or obliterate sexual differences and produce the ideal androgynous person or society, moreover, disguises a devastating attack on masculinity and males. As we shall see in the next chapter, in many ways the whole phenomenon of masculinity is founded on its separation from the feminine world and is energized by its continued contrast to femininity; to eliminate sexual distinctiveness amounts to an unconscious attempt to suppress masculinity. In practice, androgynous rhetoric is heavily invested in bringing about its ideal mainly by mitigating male "excesses" such as aggression and competitiveness in favor of values that in fact are highly "feminine" in nature, such as harmony and relationship.

One could compare the androgynous ideal to the once-fashionable mythos of the Melting Pot, which dominated American culture earlier in this century. On the surface, the Melting Pot symbol appeared to offer various ethnic groups a chance to "be American" by abandoning their native languages, ancient traditions, folk literature, traditional dress, distinctive humor, unique foods, and eventually their inherited religions. In reality, as the bland, melted-down second-generation offspring of this ethos eventually realized, the Melting Pot ideal proved to be an attempt to impose White-Anglo-Saxon-Protestant values on groups that seemed to threaten WASP culture. One of the great strengths of late twentieth-century America as it abandons the Melting Pot ideal is the rediscovery of ethnic heritage as a means of finding roots, psychological orientation, and mythic identity. The exploration and celebration of one's roots — whether African, Polish, Latino, or Irish — is a powerful experience of finding a history and a heritage that give identity, direction, and "spice" in a boring and homogenized society.

Sexuality is no less an important expression of identity than ethnic background. For most males, whose masculine energy thrives on the tension of sexual opposition and psychic distinctiveness, the ideological attempt to create androgynous equality between the sexes by eliminating all relevant gender differences portends a spirituality of the lowest common denominator, an artificial ideal that values moderation and sameness and homogenization. If there is anything true of dynamic virility, it is its aversion to such levelling; masculine spirituality is all about the heroic, the unique, the extraordinary, the odd, the wild, the unusual, and the individuated — qualities of men seldom affirmed, encouraged, or valued in Platonic Christianity.

In the developing androgyny of modern Christian spirituality, masculinity seems undesirable and even dangerous. The focus is on what men *should* be, rather than what they are, on the repentance they must undergo, rather than the gifts they have to offer. One of the tasks of a genuine masculine spirituality, by contrast, is to confront male problems in a context that values and even celebrates masculinity and the graces it gives to the human spirit. In short, a true spirituality for men will show that their sinfulness, shortcomings, and mistakes can be healed, and that they can come closer to God not by being less a man, but by becoming more of a man.

Masculinity: Nature vs. Nurture?

Masculine spirituality must found itself securely on grounds that show that male qualities are anything but totally socially or culturally condi-

tioned; otherwise, critics will always claim that such a spirituality is nothing more than a religious attempt to legitimate patriarchy. Fortunately,
a wealth of modern physiological, psychological, and anthropological
research indicates convincingly that both feminine and masculine spiritualities are the fruits of organic sexual phenomena rooted in biology and
physiology, nurtured by elemental human psychological processes, and
cultured by social forces of great antiquity. The aetiology of masculinity,
therefore, is not subject to serious debate over the question of "nature
vs. nurture," which is a false dichotomy. In the past, this discussion assumed that the old and complex social processes in every culture that
reinforce male distinctiveness are purely arbitrary inventions that can
be changed by social engineering (dress Johnny in pink, give him a doll,
and he won't turn out to be such a beast). The truth is that the social
conditioning that augments gender-roles is itself ultimately a product
of nature. Culture distinguishes between and supports masculinity and
femininity on its civilized plane precisely because nature does the same
thing on a biological level. Masculinity and femininity are clearly the
result of a synergistic combination of *both* nature *and* nurture.

So Human an Animal

Human sexual roots grow deeply in the rich soil of our natural animality. We are intelligent beasts. Though spiritual writers always knew this
truth, it tended to be a fact more lamented than celebrated. Most ancient
and even modern philosophical discussions on the nature of humanity
tend to emphasize the qualitative gap between humans and animals as
if the essence of "human" were that which is not bestial. In traditional
spirituality, too, whatever is truly human relates to the soul, while the
body trucks with all that is merely animal. This schizophrenic dualism
presents a person interested in spiritual growth with a terrible dilemma:
whether to concentrate on the soul, tragically mired as it is in mundane
matter and otherwise unable to attain its spiritual goals, or whether to
enter fully into the life of the body with all its joys, weaknesses, and
problems. Among the consequences of this disastrous bifurcation is not
only the devaluing and even demonizing of our physical qualities, but
also a corresponding error that concern for spiritual things is therefore
unerringly good. This is a dangerous assumption; some of the most evil
things people have ever done to themselves and others were inspired
by "spiritual" motives.

Happily, a way out of this false division is developing, largely through
the insights afforded us by a century of scientific research. Gradually, we
are coming to realize that the soul is intimately connected with the body;
we don't *have* bodies, we *are* bodies. Perhaps more surprising, this attitude is not a modern invention, but a very ancient concept, putting us

far closer to the spiritual world of the Old and New Testaments than we might realize. For the biblical writers assumed that our life is a thoroughly embodied one. That is the reason why the Christian teaching of the resurrection (both Christ's and our own) is so central — life without a body (earthly or raised) is not a life at all.[14]

In one of the great rediscoveries of the twentieth century, medical researchers are realizing that the human being is truly *psychosomatic*, a term uniting two Greek words — *psyche* ("soul") and *soma* ("body") — in a way that symbolizes their unity in human life. Medical researchers now know that the soul and its thoughts, emotions, and attitudes influence the workings of the body even on the molecular level; correspondingly, the most basic bodily conditions affect the status of the spirit; they are inextricably unified. Some of the most important recent discoveries in the medical field relate to psychosomatic illness, namely, the terrible and even fatal effect that sadness, depression, and despair can have on our physical health. However, this same insight is empowering some doctors to reverse the process, as the most successful doctors always have, in order to bring about physical recovery through psychic healing. These doctors are treating their patients as more than complicated conglomerations of cells susceptible only to chemotherapy or radiation. In a more holistic approach to medicine, doctors are learning to ally themselves with the patients' untapped natural spiritual powers, employing such practices as psychotherapy, visualization, art, and conversation in a context of love and personal care. These doctors regard drugs, surgery, and other medical interventions as necessary but secondary steps that allow the soul/body to heal itself more rapidly and fully than would otherwise be the case.[15]

As the psychosomatic concept grows in acceptance in the medical field as well as in popular understanding, so are the implications of the soul/body truth beginning to impact our thinking regarding the relationship between our animality and our spirituality. In ways in which we are often only dimly aware, the natural rhythms, cycles, and needs of our animal bodies, the amount of light or nourishment we receive, greatly determine the motions, moods, and desires of our souls. Until recently, popular Christian spirituality seems to have concentrated primarily on the negative aspect of the psychosomatic truth; namely, how such obvious bodily influences as sexual passion, hunger, and fatigue dull or destroy the life of the spirit. The elaborate ancient tradition of *asceticism* (the ordered discipline of these passions) developed in Christianity as well as other religions in order to bring bodily needs and desires under control and into good order. At their best, such valuable spiritual practices as fasting, yoga, night vigils, and certain penances enriched spiritual adventurers with the same kind of hearty self-discipline practiced, for example, by Olympic athletes.

In practice, however, twisted philosophies and self-hatred often infect such asceticism. In the Christian tradition, diseased mutations of Gnosticism and Platonism contaminated spiritual practices through the ages. One such recent movement known as Jansenism, though formally branded as heretical by the Catholic Church, has poisoned European and American seminaries for centuries; one still views its effects in the puritanical and repressive attitudes toward sexuality often found, for example, among older clergy. Rather than promoting a healthy bodily self-discipline, attitudes such as Jansenism twist asceticism into masochism, teaching us to treat the body with a hostility appropriate to an enemy or a lazy and disreputable employee. Remembering the psychosomatic principle (as you treat your body, you treat your soul) it is small wonder that many Jansenistic Catholics usually communicate at a subliminal level not Christian love and compassion, but a harsh and almost "kinky" sexual masochism. Worse, among those who have at tragic emotional cost beaten their bodily desires into submission, there often rage horrendous spiritual diseases such as narcissism, self-righteousness, pride, ego-inflation, and contempt for the "weak."

Genuine ascetics (Greek: *askesis* = "exercise"), by contrast, love, value, and revere the body in much the same way that great athletes appreciate the body, listen to its wisdom, and exercise it strenuously, not to punish themselves, but to develop their full human potentials. How different our spirituality would look if we came also to hold our physical nature in high regard and respectful reverence rather than ongoing suspicion and pervasive animosity. How different the Christian attitude toward sexuality would look if we regarded gendered sexuality as a friendly partner of the spirit rather than its worst enemy. The famous French biologist Andre Dubos laid the scientific foundation for such a body-positive spirituality in his beautiful essay on human physiology *So Human an Animal*, which appreciates and celebrates the natural animality of men and women.[16] His work reminds us of the proud biological heritage that shaped our evolution and still affects the most intimate details of our human lives.

Most of the spiritually valuable things we do arise out of this natural animality: feeling compassion for another's pain, sharing energy generously, experiencing our physical limits, perceiving genuine humility, and loving one another tenderly. Our animality doesn't entrap the soul in the prison of matter — it embraces our spirit in the strong arms of a humanizing humility, mercifully restraining the soul's occasional trips of unfeeling arrogance, cold self-righteousness and overweening pride. For human humility requires that we accept gracefully, even humorously, the fact that there is nothing animals have and do that we don't. We are all animals — human animals. And nowhere do we experience this fact more keenly than in the area of our sexuality and gender.

The Gift of Gender

Our humanness expresses itself spiritually most vividly through our masculinity and femininity. This is true not only through the direct effects of cultural nurturing and expectation, but because sexuality etches itself upon all our cells, courses hormonally through our veins, and erupts voluptuously in the shape of our genitals, the tenor of our voices, and the attractiveness of our faces, determining even the size, curves, and ripples of our body. Our sexual embodiment even influences the way we think and reason and value, the way we feel and sense and perceive, and the ways we relate to ourselves, to others, and to God. At every somatic and psychic level men and women typically exhibit qualities and differences both subtle and obvious.

One of the people who first investigated scientifically the qualitative differences between the typical male and female psyches was the famous Swiss psychiatrist Carl Jung, whose work lays the empirical foundation for much of this book's exploration into masculine spirituality. In one of his most fruitful insights, Jung realized that his patients' dreams often contained symbols and figures signifying much more than the particular individual issues each faced. Jung recognized in these dreams striking similarities to the classic themes, patterns, and motifs of the world's greatest art, its oldest myths and stories, and even its most profound religions.[17] Explaining these uncanny links between a given individual's dream-life and the chief themes of world mythology, Jung proposed that there exists a "collective unconscious" in each person and the whole human race. This common human memory tends spontaneously to produce richly varied motifs that may appear in the dreams of an African child or the ghost stories of a Japanese raconteur, in the sand-paintings of a Navajo shaman or the rituals of a Roman liturgy, in the mythology of Hindu religion or in the awesome primitive etchings of a Paleolithic cave.

Jung called these primary and instinctive psychic patterns the *archetypes* of the unconscious. For Jung, any given individual inherits from the ancient collective unconscious a tendency to produce as well as grasp subliminally certain common archetypes that appear according to typical, recognizable patterns in dreams, art, stories, and ritual. In the archetypes, humanity possesses a common unconscious language; while people may babble away in a cacophony of thousands of languages that are mutually unintelligible without the hard work of conscious translation, they possess at an unconscious level a primal "vocabulary" of symbols that is perfectly understandable to the heart and soul. Among the most fundamental typical expressions of the human psyche are the two sexual archetypes, the *animus* (masculine spirit) and the *anima* (feminine spirit).

Jung discovered the sexual archetypes in the context of his realization that the human psyche, like the body, is androgynous; that is, though each body-soul is typically *predominantly* masculine or feminine, each contains significant qualities of the opposite sex that can be ignored or repressed only at great cost or even danger. The feminine side of males Jung termed the *anima* (from the Latin "enliven") and the masculine side of females he called the *animus*. Jung did not consider the existence of androgyny or the *anima* and the *animus* as theories or hypotheses, but as psychological facts that could be demonstrated empirically. Several important implications follow from this discovery.

First, Jung's insight proved that our very psyche is sexually charged. In opposition to Platonic spirituality, he showed that there is no such thing as a sexless, "neuter" spirit any more than there is a sexless "neuter" body. Second, psychological androgyny means that each individual is animated by spiritual qualities typical of the opposite gender. Every male must discover, discipline, and incorporate successfully into his personality certain feminine qualities, just as every female needs to relate healthily to her masculine side. Third, Jung's work begins to suggest the true psychic cost of male misogyny and female misandry: hatred of the opposite sex is hatred of oneself; the first thing damaged by sexism is one's own spirit. Put in more positive terms, to the extent that each man and woman comes to value and love the actual women and men in their lives, he or she gains the ability to love the femininity and masculinity within; conversely, a man who embraces his own *anima* and a woman who integrates her own *animus* is empowered to love real women and men as they are encountered every day in concrete relationships.[18]

Jung's discovery of the psychological reality of androgyny by no means implies that people are or should be *equally* masculine and feminine, or that their sexual identity should in any way be altered. Moreover, Jung proposed no social-sexual program, political agenda, or spiritual goal to promote androgyny ideologically. On the contrary, he assumed that people would identify in their ego-consciousness primarily with their given gender and accept the physical, mental, social, psychological, and spiritual influence that comes with it. That is, in fact, what happens in most cases to most people, and that is the basis for discussions of both masculine and feminine archetypes, characteristics, spirituality, psychology, and religion.

The Masculine Archetypes

Jung's discovery that our sexuality entails relationship to the deep material from our individual as well as collective unconscious greatly influences the approach to masculinity taken in this book. If, in effect, we are much more spiritually than our own individual experience, if we contain at least potentially the inherited psychological sexual experience of hundreds of generations of our ancestors, then the route to the discovery of our own spirit runs through the ancient and even primitive myths and stories handed down to us. For Jung showed that we cannot understand or successfully come to terms with our own spiritual issues without relating them to the language of our own unconscious and the inherited collective unconscious of humanity as expressed in the powerful myths that pervade human storytelling.

In Part Two, our book will pay special attention to the meaning of masculinity as expressed in the language of myth and storytelling. We will explore some of the archetypes of the masculine unconscious — those typical patterns that emerge again and again in old stories about men as well as in the lives of men today. We have chosen to discuss only ten archetypes: the Pilgrim, the Patriarch, the Warrior, the Magician, the King, the Wildman, the Healer, the Prophet, the Trickster, and the Lover. We will explore them as they appear in the spiritual tradition most familiar to us, one of humanity's greatest spiritual treasures, the Bible. As we uncover the biblical wisdom regarding classic male issues and problems, we shall begin to see our own indistinct images reflected in this distant mirror. We shall learn from these stories not only the ancient warnings of danger in each archetype that we may find in ourselves, but the ways in which we may seek healing and in which we may serve — in short, how we may live heroically in our own way, and thus find God.

Chapter 2

Masculine Spirituality

What is masculine spirituality? Where does it originate and how does it develop? What are its characteristics, qualities, and attributes? What are its distinctive gifts to humanity, and why do we need them? What are the pitfalls of masculine spirituality "gone wrong"? These and other such questions are only natural when considering a new notion.

We could begin our exploration of masculine spirituality with extensive biological and anthropological evidence showing the distinctiveness of males in nature and humanity. This data, however, involves arcane and technical research that usually confirms the most basic impressions of masculinity people have developed over the ages. Our approach, instead, is a "common sense" treatment that relies on the experiences people have of masculinity in nature and society as expressed in the English language. It is immediately obvious in this approach that our views of human masculinity are strongly related to observations of males in nature.

Males in Nature and Language

One ordinarily would hear the claim "men are animals!" expressed after a particularly egregious story of male perfidy or insensitivity. But it is true: men *are* animals. Biology influences everything men do, think, and feel. Sometimes the results are unfortunate; more often, the outcome of all those hormones and chemicals coursing through the evolution-designed male body is quite wonderful: hard work, intense play, strong protectiveness, outrageous humor, ardent passion, and feats of heroism. It is no shame for a man to realize his animal kinship with a stag or a bull or a rooster; on the contrary, such an insight is instructive and almost always humorous, as *Far Side* cartoonist Gary Larson proves every day in the newspaper.

One scientific discipline that exposes the link between male behavior and our animal nature is the burgeoning science of sociobiology.[1] This scientific research proves that no matter how distinctively human, how intellectual, or how spiritual a thought we think or an act we perform, our sexual heritage and gender always comes into play, shaping our decisions, influencing our feelings, and guiding our intuitions. Yet it does not take an advanced degree in biochemistry to realize this. Common sense and millennia of human experience teach us that males — whether animals or humans — act differently from females. Even the ancients knew this; they realized full well, for example, that the removal of the male gonads causes marked behavioral changes in males, whether in a farm animal or a court eunuch. We have inherited their practical wisdom even in our everyday English language, in the phrases we use and the slang we sling.

We know, for example, that stallions (spirited, unpredictable, difficult to control or ride) behave quite differently from their castrated counterparts called geldings; in slang, "stallion" has come to mean a virile and tough young man. Bulls, likewise, are noticeably wilder than oxen (castrated bulls); in slang, "bullish" connotes enthusiastic optimism while "bull" implies eye-rolling, overblown conversation. To call someone an ox is no compliment; it means that that person is dumb or overly compliant. A cock is clearly more vigorous than a capon (his castrated colleague); in American slang, the term suggests the erect penis, ready for action. Its adjectival form "cocky" connotes a certain confident spiritedness, swagger, or even arrogance. Sometimes we combine terms: note that a "cock *and* bull story" is an exceptionally outrageous tale!

Our slang exudes other expressions that link men with male animal behavior. A "buck" is a dandy and sexually dashing fellow; the verb form means to charge, oppose, or resist, as in "bucking the system." The "stag" is an unaccompanied man, a loner, while the "stud" won't be lonely long — virile and sexually active as he is (at least until he ages somewhat, when folks might think him an old "goat"). An awkward man might be called an "odd duck" or a "silly goose." Corporations want to hire a real "tiger," someone who will watch for new customers "like a hawk" in order to get the "lion's share" of the business. And so it goes. Taken together, these common terms go a long way toward describing culture's gut-level impressions of the basic psychosomatic ingredients of the male spirit: pride, competition, comedy, aggression, courage, confidence, and independence.

If our animal counterparts exhibit male qualities in the wild, how do these bear on human psychology and spirituality? What are the basic elements of the masculine spirit, how and where do they originate, and what roles do they play? It would seem that there are four "primary colors," so to speak, of the masculine spirit that, blended together in unique combinations, compose the ingredients of masculinity: competition, vulnerability, independence, and responsibility.

1. Competition: Fighting for Life

Perhaps the most distinctive quality that males exhibit is what Walter Ong characterizes as "adversativeness," or *agonism* (Greek: *agon*, "contest").[2] The male tendency to fight seems almost universal; in the wild, one may observe stag fights over reproductive rights, prey-stalking for food, and skirmishing over territory. Civilization is scarcely different. Men fight over women, debate ideas, argue over fine points of law, strive with one another in business, battle in war, and compete with each other in myriads of games just for the pure fun of it. Nothing about men is so controversial, so loathed, so prized, and so characteristic as their combativeness. Male adversativeness is also key to the masculine spirit and originates in age-old natural behavior that serves several necessary purposes.

First, male bellicosity is essential in protecting the female and offspring of a species from predators. As a consequence of this protective role, many males are killed in combat, a loss easily compensated by the vigorous sexual activity of survivor males with the often numerically superior females. In human society as well, males traditionally shoulder the burden of defense to the death, whether on the street or on the battlefield. This role is one noteworthy contradiction to glib accusations of a historical patriarchal conspiracy against women: males are clearly the expendable gender, the first to fight, and the first to die. Protection of women and children at all costs is one of the highest of male values.

Second, and closely allied with this protective role against predators, is the male task of food gathering and territorial expansion. As the flock, herd, or family grows in population, so does its need for food, shelter, and living space. It is the aggressive behavior of males that enables the continued growth and success of a species: hunting over wider areas, acquisition of safer nesting areas, and increases in the amount of prey. In the human sphere, such male aggression can yield a new home in a safer neighborhood, heightened educational opportunities for the children, and greater comfort and enjoyment of life for the entire family.

A third function of male adversativeness is the production of superior progeny. It is a familiar axiom of evolutionary and socio-biological theory that the competition that pits aggressive males against each other for "breeding rights" results in the hereditary production of more successful offspring and, thus, even better protectors and providers for future generations. This competition usually takes the form of highly ritualized contests both in the animal and human species.[3] Aggression and violence are by no means male monopolies (no human virtues or vices are); females can fight as fiercely as males, especially when offspring are threatened by predators. What distinguishes male aggression, however, is its ritualized quality; females rarely show interest in the formal etiquette of combat or the gamesmanship of competition that males display.[4] Male conflict possesses a unique trait: it is usually governed by strict codes of honor and elaborate rules of engagement that tend to "civilize" the strife. As a result, men tend not to take conflict and disagreement too personally; after an intense debate or brutal boxing match, the combatants might typically retire to the nearest bar for a few beers — and possibly more competition (pool, cards, or Nintendo).[5]

As painful and difficult as it may feel, male "againstness," from the primordial to the most civilized level, seems designed by nature ultimately for survival, safety, success, and even a little fun. At its best, a man's spirit is characterized by this quality of struggle that Ong termed a "fighting for life." For *life* is, finally, the goal of the male struggle. Unfortunately, the male instinct to fight for it often proves a curse as well as a blessing; some men end up fighting not for life, but to inflict pain, exact revenge, and bring death.

Because the destructive potential of male agonism is so great, traditional religion once invested a great deal of time and energy in disciplining and ordering this potent force through the institution of rules, rites, stories, and myths. As civilization increasingly dispenses with a religion that relates to men and thereby fails to address their adversativeness in a convincing and helpful way, it reaps a whirlwind of devastation of unbounded male bellicosity: unfettered business competition, gang warfare, abuse of women, and homicides. It was not always so. Traditional society and religion once honored and ordered male aggressiveness by creating an entire mythos, ritual, and ethical code system around its principal spiritual archetype, the Warrior.

The Warrior, the Prophet, and the Trickster

Once it was a high honor for a man to say, "I am a Warrior." This statement meant that his society had deliberately chosen him and honored his skills. It meant that his life had clear meaning: to defend at the greatest personal cost his people, his family, his traditions. To be a Warrior meant that a man was carefully initiated into a disciplined male aggression by elders who taught him the art of battle and the technology of war, but even more importantly, the meaning of courage and the value of self-sacrifice. The Warrior bore great religious significance as well; elaborate purifying and sanctifying rituals attended his initiation as well as his preparation for every skirmish, and strict divinely given rules governed his every action on the battlefield.

The Warrior archetype survives today in most men, though usually in an unconscious state; religion now largely neglects it. Yet men may discover as they potentiate this archetype a powerful ally in their lives and spirituality. For though a man might rarely need his Warrior anymore for physical combat, he does need the Warrior's psychic strength as much as ever in everyday life: to fight for what he believes, to defend his boundaries, to struggle for success in his job, to train diligently for professional competence, and to discipline his body and mind.[6] In chapter 4, we shall discuss this archetype more thoroughly as we consider Moses.

Other masculine archetypes derive energy from the Warrior; one is the archetype of the Prophet, a spiritual figure of great antagonism who insists on battling falsehoods and telling the truth to society without regard to his own safety, success, or welfare. The Prophet is one of the most refreshing archetypes a man can have if he can reach it; it is his power to tell the truth in love and fight the spell of lies that often surrounds us. Most men love honesty and can excel at telling the blunt truth; they hate phoniness, and many seem to possess an intuitive "Bullshit Detector" when it comes to religious and spiritual matters. We shall discuss these qualities as we explore the archetype of the Prophet and the life of Jeremiah in chapter 10.

Another archetype of male adversativeness is the Trickster figure, that impish little devil who capsulizes in myths and stories all the delightful irreverence of the masculine spirit. One sign of modern religion's masculine poverty is its utter bankruptcy in the humor account. The Trickster is that archetype in men that pokes the pomposity and mocks the haughtiness of self-righteous and arrogant religiosity, wreaking havoc with stale symbols and clearing the ground for fresh growth. In chapter 11, we shall play with this archetype as it appears in the biblical satire of Jonah.

2. Male Independence and Autonomy

The second strong masculine trait is the drive for personal freedom. Men treasure their individual liberty. Men do not like to be captured, told what to do, interfered with, bound, gagged, domesticated, tamed, or otherwise bridled by anybody. Seeking the source of this characteristic, one thinks of male animals and their solo stalking expeditions — "going stag," so to speak. Yet the dynamic of human psychology undoubtedly plays an even more relevant role in creating the fierce independence of most men.

It is universally true that women exercise primary influence over the most intimate areas of a man's life during his earliest years — most obviously in the first nine months of his life, when the child in the womb depends on his mother for oxygen, water, and nutrition. The boy-child also remains primarily dependant upon his mother's nurturing for years after his birth. Physically and emotionally, men first experience human life in a dominantly feminine environment; whatever its loving intent and its nurturing ambience, this home-world is as totalitarian a "matriarchy" as one can imagine. Wrapped in the warm arms of his mother's care, suckled at her bosom, rocked, stroked, diapered, and coddled, the boy lives for years in an extended Womb.

At the heart of masculinity is its resistance to this matriarchal world, life-giving, nurturing and comfortable as it is. In the most basic sense, the masculine is defined by its opposition to, separation from, and contrast with the feminine.[7] The feminine is primary, the masculine secondary; from the first stages of his fetal development to the earliest years of his life, the male differentiates himself from the feminine environment and reacts to his maternal world in a distinctive process of individuation. It is a hazardous enterprise. Too little differentiation, and the male develops a weak masculine ego-identity (*animus*) with poor boundaries and an undeveloped sense of self; a character like the pitiful Tom in Tennessee Williams's *The Glass Menagerie* illustrates this poverty. But the opposite extreme is worse and more dangerous; too much reactive energy creates the alienated and violent loner, unable to establish himself in committed relationships. We hear about this type of man mainly after he cracks up and hangs himself — or wipes out a schoolyard recess with an AK-47 semiautomatic rifle.

The achievement of masculine independence is a perilous and painful process even for the great majority of men who fall between these extremes. The male urge toward a differentiating individuation creates in normal men psychic stress, anxiety, and guilt — a perpetual love/hate relationship with intimacy — as they feel compelled to protect their ego boundaries from maternal influence.[8] Ancient societies eased the separation burden enormously for their men with vivid initiation rites and their accompanying myths; culture once communicated to its boys that they *must* separate (the gods willed it), while simultaneously providing for the initiates the attachment of a new kind of relationship: men's societies. Most of this crucial process is today left to the vagaries of fortune: perhaps a boy's parents will encourage his individuation — but perhaps they won't; and perhaps the boy himself will succeed in intuitively groping his way to a successful male initiation — but perhaps he won't.

Miraculously, most men muddle through. They develop a spirit of independence and autonomy that allows them the power to think for themselves, to march to their own drummer, and to "follow their bliss." Their spirituality vastly enriches the world. Whenever we speak of a love of freedom, a willingness to take risks, or a desire for adventure, we talk in a masculine tone of voice. These values, of course, are not absolute; we need also to hear and develop the feminine "different voice" that bespeaks relationship, interdependence, and mutuality.[9]

The Wildman and the Pilgrim

Two archetypes symbolize the male drive for freedom. The first is perhaps the most ancient male paradigm, the Wildman. He is a figure representing man's primordial connections with nature; in the myths, he dwells in the wilderness in swamps, caves, or lonely desert tracts. Totally liberated from the trappings of modern civilization, he still possesses almost magical powers over the forces of nature and his animal brethren; he can conjure up storms or find hidden waters, befriend beasts or sense distant trouble. In the psyche, he represents male earthiness, that grubby and gritty manly energy radically free from the effete effects of deodorized and cosmetic modern male narcissism. Poet Robert Bly likes to retell the old fairy tale about hairy old "Iron John," the mythical swamp Wildman whose encounter with an innocent little boy leads the child to "make the break" with his mother and follow John into the forest for exciting adventures.[10] That's the Wildman — that dangerous and attractive fellow beckoning us out of our ruts and into the wilderness. We shall discuss him in his biblical *persona* as Elijah in chapter 8.

The second archetype of male freedom is the classic figure of the Pilgrim. Every major ancient religion featured the practice of pilgrimage, the deliberate journey to a specific holy place in quest of special blessings. In acting out this sacred ritual over many days and across numerous miles, the Pilgrim sacramentally recreated the essentials of his own hero journey. He has become the image in the psyche for all the leavings we must do in life, all the detaching and separation we must undergo in order to find our way again to new life, new challenges, and higher danger. We shall discuss Abraham as the biblical prototype of the Pilgrim in chapter 5.

3. Agonia and Male Vulnerability

The third — and most paradoxical — ingredient in the male spirit is one men prefer to avoid and tend to deny: vulnerability — even fragility. At first glance, these qualities seem strange in a list of basic masculine characteristics. Aren't vulnerability and fragility feminine traits? Aren't real men tough, sturdy, thick-skinned, and rugged? But precisely the male attributes of adversativeness and independence create their own distinctive kind of male fragility. Masculinity is stressful: to break free, to struggle, to compete, and to take risks is also to make oneself terribly vulnerable. This is not the shrinking-violet kind of weakness, the effete delicacy of a Milquetoast. It is the weakness of a Warrior and the vulnerability of a Pilgrim.

Surely the most important myth in this regard is the story of Achilles, the great Greek warrior at Troy who displayed in his armature only one weak point: his heel. The mythical significance of the heel is that an injury there brings down the whole body, no matter how well it is armored or developed. The Bible tells the same myth in Daniel's account of Nebuchadnezzar's dream of a great statue of gold, silver, bronze, and iron, which collapses and shatters because its feet are made of clay (Dan 2:31–35).

Every male has an "Achilles heel" or "clay feet," which threatens to bring him down and destroy everything he has accomplished. His particular point of weakness isn't necessarily pedestrian in nature, but may originate in the heart, seat of values; in the stomach, center of emotion; or in the genitals, source of passion. Whatever their locus, all males — especially the most successful ones — have major weaknesses. A man who doesn't know this is a fool. And as if a man's self-destructive potential were not great enough, we also live in a culture that punishes powerful and successful men, and that pounds away at their vulnerabilities, probing for weaknesses and attacking them when found — just ask Gary Hart, Jimmy Swaggart, Donald Trump, or Bruce Ritter.

Even men who wisely finesse major disasters must struggle on, sometimes in great pain and with gaping wounds. The spectators in the stands might guzzle beer and gorge themselves on hotdogs, but the real contestants have to learn to "play with pain." The Greeks coined an apt term for this virtue; rooted in the word *agon* ("contest"), *agonia* is the intense pain of combat, even unto death. Unless a male chooses just to be a spectator, unless he decides simply to observe life from a rocking-chair, gossiping on a porch and sipping lemonade with his maiden aunts, he must learn to live with agony.

It is difficult for a man to face his own agony. The Numb Man is hardly even aware of it — at least, until his stomach lining gives out or his heart valves close up. The Wounded Man feels his pain every day all right, but he doesn't know what to do about it; cultural taboos forbid complaint: pain is bad, and admission of it unmanly. So he suffers, alone and unredeemed. But pain has something to teach, and agony something to say; they present opportunities for growth. The old Easter Vigil liturgy once celebrated Adam's Fall as a *felix culpa* (Latin: "happy fault") because it merited so great a Redeemer in Jesus. Male vulnerability is like that. God spare us from the man who doesn't know his own pain (or anyone else's); God protect us from the man who thinks he's invulnerable.

The Shaman-Healer

The deepest, most manly, and most human men are those familiar with suffering, men who have faced agony and allowed it to affect their lives. Frequently, some disaster or some pain triggered their *metanoia* (Greek: "change of heart"): a divorce, a disease, or a financial failure. Crises like that can cause men to grow worse, to sink into the quicksand of anger and bitterness. But the disaster may also contain a *felix culpa* in disguise, an opportunity to find inner spiritual resources that permit great healing, both physically and psychically. Many men who have encountered the Twelve-Step program as recovering alcoholics or drug addicts have experienced this.[11] A similar phenomenon is also occurring in the gay community as many men with AIDS find in the midst of tragedy unexpected sources of hope and healing for their lives.[12]

The archetype that guides this spiritual transformation is the Healer; anthropologists know him in his cultural incarnation as the Shaman. The true Healer is always one who is wounded himself, who has struggled himself with the demons of disease and despair. Out of his intensely personal spiritual combat come alliances with good spirits powerful enough to master evil; a Healer is a Master of the Spirits. If a man can enter into this spiritual archetype within, he can transform his personal disaster into a kind of personal healing ministry; alcoholics and drug addicts are best helped by recovering alcoholics and addicts themselves. The Bible tells us about many Healers, but we shall explore only the story of Elisha in chapter 9.

4. Masculine Responsibility and Accountability

The most distinctively human of masculine traits is the particular way in which males express care for others. In nature, the direct care of a male for its offspring and for others is tenuous; the same is probably true of the early human community.[13] Overcoming their animal tendency to roam, men learned through long and painstaking experience to commit themselves to their families and societies as nurturers and care-givers in a uniquely masculine fashion. Mature manly care for others is characteristically firm, guided by rules and principles, consistent, dependable, and fair. In social roles such as father, tribal elder, judge, priest, and king, males have guided society for millennia, creating law and order, empires and institutions.

This phenomenon is now called patriarchy. Its modern critics rightly point to its historic and present abuses such as rigidity, domination, misogyny, and violence. Yet the storm of abuse presently raining on patriarchy is also in many ways uncritical; it is unfair, unscholarly, and unwise only to characterize a system by its abuses. One rarely hears a genuinely critical account of patriarchy that also takes into account its vast contributions to human history; the word is used invariably in a highly polemical and political fashion.

As healthy masculinity deteriorates in our culture, the first qualities to disappear are the historically latest to develop: responsibility and accountability. Society began to abandon masculine psychological nurturing centuries ago with the disappearance of male adult initiation rites; fathering and husbanding began to deteriorate as the Industrial Revolution took males out of the home and away from continual contact with wives and children. Today male responsibility in the form of social leadership is under attack in both the church and politics. The symptoms of these widespread and long-term patterns include: higher divorce rates, an enormous increase in mother-dominant families, "wilding" sprees and gang warfare among adolescent boys, a dive in male seminarian enrollment, and the beginnings of male estrangement and detachment from political involvement. Male irresponsibility and lack of accountability are in part at the root of these problems, but the way to solve them does not lie in male-bashing. The answer lies in heightened male consciousness and pride and the restoration of masculine responsibility.

The Patriarch and the King

Two of the most important male archetypes of responsibility are the Patriarch and the King. Each encapsulates and represents a specifically male kind of caring. The Patriarch embodies the unique male energy that a man can give a family: emotional stability, sturdiness, firm correction, world-wisdom, constructive criticism, moral principles, and a sense of fun. Without doubt, the role of father is severely wounded in our culture, but the archetype is not. It is available to men willing to discover it and who wish to be responsible for wife and children, workers, students, and parishioners. Such fathering and mentoring are desperately needed today, virtually everywhere. In chapter 5, we shall explore the archetype of Father/Patriarch, with all its blessings and curses, as lived in the story of Abraham.

The King is not just a Father writ large. He is the archetype of masculine greatness and spiritual largesse, of self-possession and dignity. The King makes the hard decisions and takes us to places we must, but do not wish, to go; he is the classic male image of a leader. He is magnanimous and noble, generative, creative, and bears criticism and defeat with equanimity. His measured spirit knows when to stop and how far to go. His is an archetype that every male who leads needs to develop. We shall explore in chapter 7 the benefits and pitfalls of the King as exemplified by Solomon.

Other Male Traits

Our identification of the key male characteristics of adversativeness, independence, vulnerability, and responsibility — along with their major archetypes — by no means exhausts the list of male qualities or depletes the field of masculine archetypes. Among the latter that we shall not specifically treat, but that play important roles in masculine psychology and spirituality are the Poet, the Wiseman, the Priest, and others.[14] Regarding other masculine spiritual traits, several bear mentioning.

It is well known that males possess a penchant for abstract reasoning.[15] Men tend to be thinkers rather than feelers, prefer logic over intuition, the ideal over the concrete, and analysis over synthesis. These tendencies — and they are only that — bear important consequences in the ways males typically reason morally and value spiritually.

Males tend to cherish an intellectual approach to human moral decision making that operates according to an abstract system of universal principles.[16] For men, following time-honored and carefully reasoned rules permits true justice and prevents emotional whims from determining important moral decisions. This approach gives male morality a sense of rational groundedness, consistency, and universality — but also a feeling of coldness and a tenor of legalism.

The male preference for abstraction also means that men typically judge the world according to what it *should* be, rather than what it is. It is not surprising that such idealism usually results in a distinctive kind of male cynicism (all cynics being former idealists). Every institution is subject to male idealism and cynicism, but none more so than religion. Arguably the most frequent reason men give for their estrangement from organized religion is its hypocrisy; expecting perfection, they see sin and contradiction. In the main, religion is thus for men a moral or ethical enterprise more than a spiritual or metaphysical one.

A final masculine spiritual trait we will mention here relates to male territoriality and distancing.[17] On an interpersonal level, males prefer a certain distance and "elbow room"; males tend to think in terms of exterior space, geography, and maps. Translated into spiritual terms, in contrast to feminine spirituality, which is inward and interior and rooted in Mother Earth, male spirituality is outwardly oriented and spatial.[18] Masculine spirituality is almost geographical in nature, whether that is expressed in the concept of a Holy Land, the physical journey of pilgrimage to a distant shrine, or the zealous missionary behavior that seeks to spread the faith to new lands.

Sky and Earth Gods

Male spatiality expresses itself most strikingly in the classic masculine feature of sky religion. Unlike the feminine religion of *Gaia* (Mother Earth), masculine spirituality is primarily concerned with sky gods (Apollo, Mars, Hermes) and, ultimately, the great Sky Father or Grandfather (Zeus, Jupiter, Allah, Yahweh, Wakan Tanka), who dwells in the heavens. Masculine spirituality tends to regard God as One who dwells above and judges all from an immeasurable distance, One who is not

soiled by earth-affairs, an eternal deity of unspeakable holiness. Male religiosity is consequently relatively harsh and stark, awesome, humbling,
grand, and sublime. Its premier sacrament is the sky. It is no accident
that men tend to feel most religious when they are out under the heavens, particularly on mountain tops or in desert regions where the day
sky overwhelms with its sublimity, and the night sky coldly demands
awestruck silence.

Not all male deities were celestial. There once existed in a minor key
to the music of sky religion a masculine earth spirituality. Its deities were
fertility gods (Baal, El Shaddai) who roam over the earth, or chthonic
deities who dwell under the earth in caves or other mysterious places
(Pluto, Freyr, Hades, Osiris, and Tammuz). Not surprisingly, these gods
tended to represent men's "shadow side," those qualities both good and
bad that cultural forces tend to repress in the male psyche: earthiness,
sexual wildness, sensuality, and any behavior regarded as "dirty." One
unfortunate effect of male sky religion is the demonization of these
deities (and male earthiness) in the popular imagination: in Christian
myth, God expelled Satan from his angelic existence in the heavens and
set him over the monstrous little demons that live under the earth in Hell.
The Satanizing of chthonic deities produces a largely unrecognized effect on men in Western Christianity: the personal face of evil is male.
Among those demanding inclusive language and feminine images for
God in the Christian church, there does not seem to exist a movement
for a corresponding feminization of the images of evil. Liberal Christianity seems perfectly content with a religious language that invariably
refers to the enemy of human nature and the embodiment of evil as "he."

The Myth of the Hero

If masculine spirituality is composed of ingredients such as againstness,
independence, *agonia*, responsibility, abstraction, and territoriality in the
form of various psychic archetypes, what activates these qualities and
archetypes successfully in the spiritual life of a man? What agent keeps
these traits from "going wrong," as all of them indeed can? What is the
decisive factor that catapults a merely biological human *male* into a *man*
in the best sense of that word?

The catalyst for dormant masculine potentiality is none other than
the "mega-myth" or "super-archetype" of the Hero. The Hero, and the
mythology, storytelling, and ritual that accompanies him, galvanizes
latent masculine capabilities, charging and enlivening them with a spiritual energy that sets them in healthy psychic motion. Without the energy
of the Hero myth, male characteristics either atrophy like paralyzed
muscles or run wild in both self- and other-destructive excesses. The
activation of the Hero archetype is the single most important factor in

the creation of a man's masculine identity. How the Hero energizes the *animus* is a complex and intertwined process involving myth, ritual, and, most important, concrete action.

The Hero myth is a worldwide psychic and literary phenomenon that relates how a given character makes a salutary contribution to society through an extraordinary deed. The eminent mythologist Joseph Campbell identified a classic pattern to this universal "monomyth" as perceived in the concrete Hero stories of thousands of world cultures across time.[19] The Hero myth involves three stages of activity. The first, *separation* or *departure*, relates how an ordinary person feels called by a voice, an inner need, a "chance" blunder, or a crucial event to leave his familiar environment in order to embark on an adventure that will win a new destiny and a better future. In biblical mythology, this is the call to leave "Egypt," a land of bondage, for a Promised Land of freedom. Psychologically, this stage involves the painful male issue of separation from the comfortable prison of the undifferentiated feminine world as a first step toward masculine individuation.

In the next stage, *ordeal* or *initiation*, the Hero encounters a range of obstacles to his goal; if he is on a journey, he must cross a blazing desert, forbidding mountains, or a wild sea. If he seeks a treasure or elixir, he might have to battle dragons, mean knights, or cruel magicians. Subtler impediments lie in wait; but though strange enchantments or forbidden seductions make him forget for a time his original call, the real Hero struggles on toward his goal. He changes. He transcends the passivity of boyhood and finds hidden inner strength as well as outer guides and helpers as he achieves his purpose. Biblically, this is Israel in the Sinai, that place of wilderness trials that makes it a people worthy of covenant with God. Psychologically, the initiatory ordeal involves every interior struggle and outer battle a male must undergo and win on the path of individuation: fear, guilt, and self-doubt, as well as parents, bosses, and authorities of all kinds. Male individuation is not a gentle, organic process; it is an ordeal and it hurts.

The third and final heroic stage is that of *return* and *reintegration* with society. Having won his boon of a treasure, a life-giving Grail or a salvific Truth, the Hero returns with his contribution to the people. They may cheer him and make him king — or they may kill him. Whether society is ready for his gift or not, whether it appreciates his heroism or fears it, the Hero has done his great deed and accomplished his task: he has given it all over for the people. In the Bible, Israel finds the Promised Land, flowing with milk and honey, where it can live a free national life under God's gift of Torah. In psychological terms, the return stage represents the male need to give a contribution and provide a boon for the world. To do this, he must reintegrate himself with the ordinary, especially and including the feminine world, but now in terms not of passivity or dependence, but of generativity and confidence.

Male Initiation Rites

If he is fortunate, a modern boy learns the mythical patterns of success-ful, heroic manhood from his family, religion, and culture through the examples they set, the stories they tell, and the rites they celebrate. But many contemporary youths' family situations are so dysfunctional, and their culture so bankrupt, that they are never properly educated and nur-tured into adult masculinity. At one time, primal societies ensured that this crucial achievement occurred; it was unthinkable that such an im-portant event in the life of a man and his people could be left to chance, or that a boy could be left with the unimaginable task of having to ini-tiate *himself* into manhood. As recently as several centuries ago, most societies celebrated some version of the ancient male initiation rite.[20]

Cultures varied widely in their particular rites of initiation,[21] but a classic motif emerges in them that matches the pattern of the Hero myth itself. A typical initiation rite in a primal society might have occurred something like this. On a prearranged but secret day, masked village male elders appeared at the homes of young boys, aged about ten or twelve years, and seized them. Feigning surprise, their mothers put up a symbolic fight, only to lose the child to the male elders, who spirited them away to a secret location accessible only to men. The stage of *departure* was a vivid and decisive one; the tribal ceremony told the boys with shocking and unmistakable clarity that they could neither remain children for the rest of their lives, nor could they live in the feminine, domestic world of mother any longer. They had to leave. They had to become men. By contrast, modern culture gives mixed and confusing messages to its young boys, telling them in many ways that they never need to grow up and that becoming a man is not a very good thing in any case. Now it typically takes modern men years of struggle with guilt and self-confidence, alone and in psychotherapy, to negotiate a stage that once occurred in a few days or weeks.[22]

The next stage, the *ordeal of initiation* itself, always occurred in a sacred place for men only. Males need holy space at a distance from the feminine world, and they require rituals there to reenact and reinforce their masculinity, which needs constantly to be reexperienced and won anew. During the adult initiation rites, the elders forced the boys to undergo painful but carefully controlled trials that inevitably involved humiliation and mutilation. The humiliation expressed disdain for the world of boyhood and mother that the children were to leave so that they would never pine for Oedipal return. The mutilations — circumcision, scarring, small amputations — expressed a terrible truth in the most vivid way possible: becoming a man is a painful, wounding, but proud experience. Lest we regard these rites as barbaric, we should consider that, in their absence, modern males are left to initiate themselves — usually unsuccessfully and unconvincingly — in gang rites, drinking bouts, punk mutilations, and the like, without any supervision or adult help.

The initiatory ordeal often lasted for days. Typically, the elders recited the tribe's great Hero stories, imbuing the young men ritually with the crucial link between their own individual adult initiation and the ultimate welfare of the tribe: they were now called to be great, too — like the heroes of old. The gods demanded it; indeed, their whole world expected it. At the end, blessedly, the elders finally did for their young men something that virtually never happens today: they officially and ritually accepted them *as men*. They were children no longer; by virtue of their brave initiation, they had become heroes.

The final stage of the male initiation rite was *return* and *reintegration* into society. The village would mark the reappearance of their new men with a great celebration or feast; clothed or named anew, the young men won new respect. They were important now, they mattered. Now they were expected to join the hunt, to learn how to defend the village, to rule the tribe, to pray on behalf of the people, and to heal the sick — to live lives of concrete and everyday heroism.

The Grail-Quest and the Hero in Everyday Life

Modern society struggles, incoherently at times and always in fits and starts, to initiate its boys into heroic manhood. Its men are restless and unhappy until they find it, and find it again. Somehow, many men do find their inner Hero. Perhaps they have wise fathers, brothers, or uncles who model him; perhaps they see a movie or read a book or have a dream that pictures him and feel his beck; perhaps they encounter that rare teacher or tough coach, that sports or political figure who embodies the heroic and makes it irresistibly attractive; somehow, the Hero wins out and emerges once again in the life of a boy who won't let him go.

Jungian psychologist Robert Johnson describes this psychic force exquisitely in his brilliant study of male psychology entitled *He!*[23] Johnson understands masculinity according to the famous myth of the Holy Grail. In this medieval story, Parsifal left his mother and joined King Arthur's circle of knights; his quest led him on a dangerous mission in search of the Grail, Christ's saving cup of the Last Supper. For Johnson, every male potentially is a Parsifal on a journey; every young man on the way to spiritual growth experiences almost overpowering restlessness for the great Grail: his own individuation and the gifts that will flow from it for others.

The Grail looks different to each man. It seems to some like a stetho-scope or a gavel, a wrench or a saw; to others, it appears as a chalice, a pen, a book, a badge, a hardhat, or a big desk. Whatever its mani-festation, the Grail is the "bliss" that leads men on to whatever they feel for them is Great. Thank God so many follow. Day in and day out, these are the men who build our houses and guard our streets, treat our diseases and write our books and make our movies, point to God and heal our memories, lead our nation, grow our food, deal us justice, sing our songs, craft our furniture, cut our hair, wire our houses, teach our classes, and fix our computers. These are the men who have found the way to heroism by following, as did Parsifal, their own secret archetypal Wildmen, Warriors, and Kings.

Most of these men will never be known to us, though they have built the world. Their Hero is mostly quiet, hidden, and very ordinary . . . at least until a baby Jessica falls down a well. Then he springs to life, and men old and young labor fifty-eight hours around the clock, digging shafts and shoring them up, donating $50,000 drill bits anonymously, hoping and cheering each other on, and finally succeeding. Or until I-880 collapses in an earthquake, and the feared black men of West Oak-land emerge from their housing projects to work long days and sleepless nights in twisted beams and shattered concrete amid dangerous after-shocks, probing, pulling, and hoping for survivors. And if you ask them, "Why did you do it?" they will disown their own heroism and answer with a shrug, "Because it had to be done."

The Grail and the Christ Archetype

The Grail myth is also about something even more important than a successful career of contribution to society. For Parsifal seeks, not just a beautiful chalice or a dazzling treasure, but the object closest to Christ, the cup of suffering that Christ himself had to drink (Mt 20:22). Ulti-mately, the Grail is a symbol of the last and greatest of all archetypes, the Christ: that human quality of such self-surrender and magnanimity that it partakes in the very life of God. It is the Christ that Parsifal — and every man — seeks; for in every man gapes a "God-sized void" that hungers for God and thirsts for the Christ. Nothing else will fill it. In chapter 13, we shall discuss the Christ archetype as lived out by Jesus of Nazareth.

The Encounter with the *Anima*

The Grail myth also teaches important truths regarding a man's *anima*, or feminine psychic aspect. Parsifal learns after rescuing a fair damsel in distress that he must ally himself with her in a relationship of purity and respect. For Johnson, this event symbolizes a man's need to come to terms with the feminine, both his own inner femininity and that of the flesh-and-blood women in his life. Proper relationship to the feminine is of crucial importance in the development of healthy masculinity. But the task is not an easy one.

Every man carries a woman inside himself.[24] Unfortunately, it is very difficult for men to encounter this inner *anima* both because she is subtle, and because incomplete masculinity is threatened by the feminine rather than complemented by it. Young men especially feel threatened by their inner woman: she is all too often emotionally similar to the mother from which they very much need to separate. Two things tend to happen to this denied and repressed *anima*. Neglected, ignored, and even abused, she may become a Witch, attracting attention and exacting terrible revenge for her abandonment by afflicting her man with dark moods and depressions — what the Jungians call an "*anima* possession."[25] Men also tend to "project" their repressed inner femininity onto the real women they encounter. A positive projection results in the well-known state of infatuation, that experience of seeing much more in another person than is really there.[26] Many men are completely unaware that the "ideal woman" — soft, gentle, and mysterious — that they can never find, or sweeps them off their feet when they do, is within themselves. The only kind of women "out there" in the real world are real, flesh-and-blood women.

A negative *anima* projection is dangerous. Men can propel their own hated or feared inner feminine image onto the nearest convenient woman; the tendency results in "misogyny," the emotional and physical abuse of women. It is not uncommon for a man, falling out of infatuation with the woman onto which he had projected his "ideal," next to project onto her his inner Witch without ever having really experienced the real person; this is surely the psychological dynamic in the biblical story of Amnon's rape of Tamar (2 Sam 13). Another variation of denial and projection is the phenomenon known as "homophobia," the irrational fear and hatred of gay people. In some cases, homophobia indicates repressed homosexuality; but in others, the punishment of men who are perceived to possess femininity in themselves represents hatred and fear of the *anima*.

Encountering the feminine is an art. Males who accomplish it are gifted with the ability to relate successfully with fully half of the human race, as well as their own souls. This project is aided spiritually by the Lover, the archetype by which a male, secure in his masculine identity, risks the adventure of reintegrating himself once again with the world of woman, both in relationship to his beloved and to his own *anima*. The Bible celebrates the Lover archetype in the erotic poetry attributed to Solomon (see chapter 12).

Masculine and Feminine: The Cycle of Growth

Spiritual growth for men is a life-long process demanding patience, a variety of skills, and the ability to change and seize opportunities. It involves different seasons and moments; there is no objective program — including this book — that a man can follow in a predetermined fashion. Each man is unique. Though there are many guides, groups, and communities that can help, and books, tapes, and workshops that can assist, much of the work has to be done alone and according to trial and error. Yet it helps to have a roadmap for a journey. The following pattern describes something of the cyclic process of masculine individuation in a conceptual way; it may also help in understanding the process both for individuals and for culture as a whole.[27]

There exist four "moments" in the male spiritual journey; each is either prominently masculine or feminine, static or dynamic. Each moment is valuable, and each has its archetypes; we tend to progress through the stages by fulfilling them and accomplishing their tasks, before moving on to the next stage. One sign of the need to move on is whether one experiences his present stage primarily in its negative aspect and in its destructive archetypes. The process described below could represent a life-long project, or repeat itself in cycles over the years.

The first stage, the *static feminine*, represents the elemental feminine environment of the womb, the home, and the tomb. This is the place from which all men come and to which all men go; it is Mother Earth. It is ceaselessly creative and devouring, nurturing and ensnaring, life-giving and indifferent to the individual. It is a place of security and domesticity; all needs are met and all troubles comforted. In its positive aspect, it is the Womb, ruled by the archetype of the Great Mother (*Gaia*), the purely natural feminine spiritual source of life and fertility. In Christian terms, it is Holy Mother Church, ever nurturing and ever forgiving; it is the Blessed Virgin Mary and such manifestations of her as Our Lady of Guadalupe.

In its negative aspect, the static feminine is symbolized by the Tomb and ruled by the archetype of Kali, the terrible Hindu goddess who traps her children and smiles as she devours them, or the terrible and vengeful apocalyptic Virgin, seething with threats, who is described in numerous private visions never officially accepted by the Catholic Church. That which creates also destroys; all beings that give life also survive by devouring life. Men experience this aspect of the static feminine as the Witch featured so prominently in fairy tales.

The second stage, the *dynamic masculine*, employs the qualities of adversativeness and independence — the masculine energy that separates and differentiates — to move beyond the confines of the static feminine. This is the first thrust of masculinity, marked in the male by abruptness, initiation, and leaving the womb and the home. In its positive aspect, this stage is guided by the myth of the Hero as it informs the archetypes of Warrior, Wildman, Pilgrim, and Prophet. It is the energy to "hitch your wagon to a star." It is a spirituality of initiative and action, courage and adventure. In Christian terms it is the "Pilgrim Church" described by Vatican II — ever on the move, always learning and changing, heading toward new places.

Without the guiding wisdom of the Hero myth, however, this stage easily turns negative. Instead of a Warrior, there develops the Crusader, who attacks all that is strange or different (fundamentalism); in place of the Wildman evolves the Recluse, who runs from the world in fear (millennialism); rather than the Pilgrim, a Wanderer appears who strays from one spiritual fad to another (New Age religion); and in lieu of the Prophet, there grows the cynical Crank: carping, whining, and complaining (some forms of atheism). Many men live in this realm as radically alienated and hostile individualists and cynics.

The next stage, the *static masculine*, capitalizes on the achievements of heroic masculine dynamism by establishing its gains permanently. It involves the urge to settle down, consolidate, and create institutions — and maintain them against the vicissitudes of time (conservatism). This stage is ruled by the archetypes of Patriarch, King, and Magician — masculine figures of great power and generativity who create government, science, and law as bulwarks against the natural tendency toward chaos. This is the stage of the apotheosis of the highest Christian spiritual metaphor, God the Father, who creates order out of chaos, hands down law as a guide to his people, and rules the universe with justice and reason. The negative shadow of this stage is what feminists call "patriarchy." The static masculine easily degenerates into sheer legalism, rigidity, defensiveness, and authoritarian behavior backed by violence. This stage is ruled by the figure of the Tyrant, an intolerant despot afraid of change and willing to go to any lengths to prevent it. Middle-aged and older men often find themselves in this stage, angry that all their life's contributions to society and family seem devalued and threatened.

The final stage, the *dynamic feminine*, represents the undirected movement away from the reasoned order of the static masculine toward spontaneous experience, novelty, vitality, and playfulness. Its positive archetype is the Muse, source of "music" and all inspiration, or Sophia, the origin of experiential wisdom. In Christian terms, this is the privileged moment when the Holy Spirit blows breaths of fresh air into the church or into a man's life. Many men experience in this stage an invitation to take up a creative craft or an artistic hobby, to learn to play the piano or to pray spontaneously in yoga or the charismatic renewal movement. This movement is often a function of the "midlife" crisis that has exposed the inadequacies of static masculine life.

The negative aspect of this stage is the impulsive, destructive, and irrational behavior symbolized in the figure of Cassandra, who sows wanton hysteria, intoxication, and moodiness wherever she goes. Some men come under her spell after years of paralysis in the static masculine and do foolish things: impulsively quit jobs, have affairs, or take drugs. Cassandra is also the archetype guiding extreme feminists who, in reaction to patriarchy, attack the Christian community.

The accomplishments of the dynamic feminine are solidified in the movement back to the first stage, the static feminine, and a cycle of "eternal return" is completed. We could chart these sexual movements in the following fashion, remembering of course that they are only symbolic and suggestive:

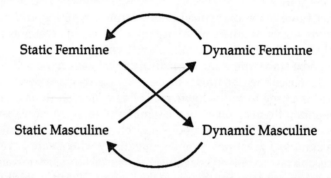

This diagram indicates the need for healthy movement and balance between the *animus* and the *anima*, a truth expressed millennia ago in the symbol of the Taoist religion, which shows the circular movement from the Yin (feminine) to the Yang (masculine) and back. Chinese medicine still conceptualizes physical health in this way as a balance between the masculine and feminine forces in the body — surely an apt metaphor for spiritual health and religious sanity as well.

Gay Men and Masculine Spirituality

The discussion of masculine and feminine characteristics within men inevitably raises questions about homosexuality; hackles rise, and the questions fly. "Will getting in touch with my *anima* make me gay?" Or, "Doesn't all this 'masculinity' stuff just mean more oppression for gays?" The subject is a painful and sensitive one both for straight and gay men and an indication of how tragically estranged gay and straight men have become from each other.

The underlying assumption to these tensions is the supposition that gay men are more feminine than their straight counterparts; the popular images of the drag queen, the "campy" hairdresser, or the gentle restaurant waiter are instrumental in this belief. As with many popular notions, there is an element of truth to the supposition that many gay men evidence more femininity and androgyny than their straight brothers. It may even be true that some gay men develop a primarily "feminine" ego-identity and display a rather tense love-hate attitude toward masculinity and other men. Yet it does not follow that such people are completely alienated from masculine spirituality. They may just play it in a minor key and experience its archetypes less vividly and frequently than most straight men.

The popular imagination is quite wrong, however, in supposing that all — or even most — gay men are psychically built in a dominantly feminine mode; the reverse is true. Centuries of homophobia have driven most gay men to live as inauspiciously as possible "in the closet" and away from public examination. Most gay men are no less masculine than straight men, and they do not conform to society's prejudiced stereotypes of the "homosexual." They are politicians, lawyers, doctors, soldiers, priests, athletes, carpenters, and policemen. They fix plumbing, teach children, audit taxes, deliver mail, and program computers. They compete in sports and the marketplace, run businesses, read books, plan vacations, and volunteer for community projects. Some become heroes, as we have seen recently in response to the AIDS plague.

Masculinity is not about whom you sleep with; it is about who you are and who you wish to become. For gay men as well as straight, it is about becoming your own man and following your bliss. It is about experiencing the Wildman or Warrior inside, about finding the inner King in order to live with dignity. It is unfortunate that some gays feel alienated from their own powerful inner archetypal allies, and sad that some straights reject their gay brothers. But whether gay or straight, they are men and they share most of the same joys and suffer most of the same ordeals together. They can teach and help each other.

The Spiritual Climate for All Men

In the broadest cultural terms, as viewed from our masculine/feminine cycle, the Christian church along with much of Western culture is presently experiencing a transition from centuries of static masculinity (patriarchy) to dynamic femininity (feminism); this movement is as inevitable as the tides and it cannot be stopped: the feminine is ascendent, the masculine in decline. This, too, shall pass. But in the meanwhile, men must live, work, and grow in this difficult new climate; for along with the beneficial and spontaneous action of the dynamic feminine Spirit, Cassandra is also at large. Masculinity itself is under attack — and not only its negative shadow, but its most positive qualities, too. We live in an age witnessing the decline in masculine values and the emergence of "misandry," which increasingly affects every major human institution in the West. Men must be very clear about this and recognize what is happening around them. More than ever, men must do their spiritual work.

What is at stake is whether men in our time can live happily and productively according to their nature — or whether they will merely exist, schizophrenically estranged from the elemental physical and psychic forces that pulse within them. But also at stake are the primal spiritual gifts that men have to offer to their world. For masculine spirituality contributes distinctive and irreplaceable graces to human culture, such as fighting for what you believe in, loving freedom, and taking responsibility for others. Masculinity means standing out from the crowd and offering a different vision of things. It means coming to the rescue when people get in trouble, and thirsting for justice and fairness. It means thinking logically and upholding the law, and being accountable for your promises. It means reverencing God as Totally Other, holy beyond all words.

Masculinity must not be taken for granted; it is also amazingly fragile and subject to failure and ridicule. It is surprisingly ephemeral, and ever in need of renewal and reassertion. It is an endangered resource. For all its blessings and curses, masculinity is no better — and no worse — than femininity; it is one-half of what it means to be human. So if we do not treasure masculinity, we cannot truly be said to love humanity. And if we do not know the masculine voice and tone, its values and qualities, its metaphors and archetypes, we cannot begin to understand God.

Chapter 3

Misandry: The Hatred of Men

Western culture and the Christian church are becoming more feminine and less masculine; the great transformation has been underway for well over a century. Every major institution in the West, from the military to the academy and from politics to religion, is experiencing the change from static masculine (patriarchal) values to dynamic feminine ones. Symbolically, the dynamic feminine Age of Aquarius has begun, and nothing can or should be done to stop it. This is an exciting time to be a woman; the future holds the promise of increased power, equal political rights and economic opportunity, and a fuller share in responsibility for the fate of the earth.

This is also a difficult and even depressing time for many men: masculinity is in eclipse. Patriarchy is undermined, its values collapsing. Society is withdrawing its exclusively male privileges, positions, powers, freedoms, honors, and joys. The electorate is replacing men with women candidates, the church inserting female ministers into the pulpit, and academia preferring women teachers in the classroom. The time is coming when men will no longer pray in thanksgiving, as in the Jewish tradition, that they were not born women.

Yet much of this loss for men represents possible gain, and liberation rather than failure. For with patriarchy, men carried most of the burden of civilization, law and order, government, and culture throughout history. The weight of this load on men is heavy, and its damage clear: shortened lives, high stress, and strong susceptibility to disease, suicide, and alienation. It is time for women to bear more of this cultural burden; in so doing, they will share in the glory and partake in the privileges. But they will also have to assume the responsibility, take the heat, and accept the blame for civilization as men have done for millennia. It is an open historical question whether they will "do better" than men — the jury is still out. But feminists will no longer be able to blame all that is wrong with the globe on men, on masculinity, and on patriarchy.

Every man needs to get clear about this great cultural transition taking place around him and adjust to it accordingly. As hopeful, promising, and positive as many of these transformations are, every man also needs to grow conscious of the shadow side to the Feminine Transition, the undertow to the new cultural tide. For as male dominance falters, so declines men's immunity; the loss of power and privilege is accompanied by the loss of protection. As a consequence of this vulnerability, a new cultural disease is developing, an opportunistic infection so recent that most people neither know its name nor even recognize its existence. The term for this societal disease is only now materializing in a few English dictionaries: "misandry" (Greek: "man-hatred"), the mirror opposite of "misogyny," which is the hatred of women.[1] Every man needs to include this word in his private glossary of important terms:

> **Mis•an•dry** (mis'-an'-drē) *n.* hatred of men. **1:** the attribution of neg-
> ative qualities to the entire male gender. **2:** the claim that masculinity
> is the source of human vices such as domination, violence, oppression,
> and racism. **3:** a sexist assumption that (a) male genes, hormones, and
> physiology, or (b) male cultural nurturing produces war, rape, and phys-
> ical abuse. **4:** the assignment of blame solely to men for humanity's
> historic evils without including women's responsibility or giving men
> credit for civilization's achievements. **5:** the assumption that any male
> person is probably dominating, oppressive, violent, sexually abusive, and
> spiritually immature.

Misandry is an ideological spinoff of extreme feminism. Its practice is by no means limited to women; many men, full of self-hatred and guilt, also purvey it. It is often present alongside feminist influence in such major institutions as academia, the church, the arts, business, and law. Misandry is not yet as pervasive or as harmful as misogyny has been, but it is on the way. Where it prevails, whether in a school, in a parish, or on the job, it presents a bizarre and Kafkaesque form of moral algebra to the males who live under it. Their very masculinity attaches to them a negative value; no matter how hard they try, no matter what they do to prove themselves, the best they can do is remove the "minus" male sign and work themselves up to an even zero: inoffensive, harmless, and acceptable.

"Men Are All Alike!"

Though "misandry" is a neologism, hatred of men, of course, is not new. A function of the eternal Gender Wars, it has simmered quietly since history began. Until recently, however, it had bubbled away on the backburners of resentful women like a Poison Stew — no doubt in response to many very real injuries suffered. Who among us as children did not hear the exclamation, "men are all alike," or something like it, chorused in unison around a kitchen-table coffee-klatsch after yet another tale of male perfidy? Yet in recent decades, as women increasingly exit the kitchen and enter public life, male-bashing has left its domestic *Sitz im Leben* and begun to appear prominently on the popular menu of evils that society is forced to digest. Many forms of feminism serve up misandry in spiced-up form as an ideological side dish, if not the main course, of their offerings. Men are ingesting these misandrist toxins, usually unknowingly, and feeling unwell.

Many male-bashers are unaware of what they are dishing out. As women take their rightful places in important positions in business, politics, academia, and the media, they must confront the fact that their once relatively innocuous domestic misandry takes on weightier consequences in direct proportion to the increase in public power that they now wield. Yet many women are unprepared for such an awareness, and seem to dwell in a state of denial about (a) their own misandry, (b) the growing power they are achieving, and (c) the fact that their hostilities might in any way threaten men under their power. It is no less painful for women to face these realities than it has been for men to confront men's historical oppression of women as well as their own individual forms of misogyny.

In broaching the topic of misandry in print and in conversation, I have been met with stares of incredulity, sarcastic scoffs of dismissal, and expressions of outright anger. One controversial article of mine mentioning male-bashing, for example, was excoriated as "hogwash" and deemed worthy of an April Fool's paper by a few readers, though not the hundreds of men who responded with letters and comments acknowledging the reality of the misandry they have experienced.[2] They know the phenomenon very well.

Misandry in Everyday Life

Men have related to me reports of misandrist prejudice and sexual harassment that they have experienced from superiors on their jobs. An interesting explanation for the tyranny of female bosses, incidentally, is given by some feminists; while admitting that many women in authority are becoming just as ruthless as their male counterparts, they claim that this is only because the women have been coopted by "patriarchal" values. In this explanation, men are still to blame, even for female actions.[3] Still other men report being warned in threatening terms in sexual harassment seminars at the workplace that, as potential woman-abusers and rapists, any sexual comments and innuendoes made to women could become grounds for dismissal. This relates to the frequent feminist charge that rape is a "normal" thing for a man to do and that men therefore require special suspicion because of this proclivity.[4] Does this prejudice create an unreal paranoia? Perhaps, but in the present climate, a mere unsubstantiated accusation of sexual harassment can wreak great havoc. A recent "Dear Abby" column, for example, contains a remorseful letter from a woman who had an innocent boyfriend imprisoned on a false rape charge because she once grew angry with him; the boy still sits in jail. Similar false-rape charges are reported increasingly in the press.[5]

The legal system of our country also conveys prejudice against men in many ways. Men are sometimes required to pay huge alimony payments to working wives who initiated the divorce solely on the grounds of incompatibility; child custody is awarded to the mother in over 90 percent of the cases.[6] Male felons are not only given much longer sentences for the same crimes that women commit, but are forced to live in more degrading prison environments than women.[7] And though women benefit from the personal freedoms and economic opportunities that America affords, only males are required to register for the draft, and only males are permitted by federal law to engage in military combat.

Arts, entertainment, and the popular media sometimes provide dramatic outlets for hateful attacks on men. One thinks of recent films such as *The Color Purple*, *The Women of Brewster Place*, *Terms of Endearment*, or *Thelma and Louise*, in which every male portrayed was in some way loathsome, violent, cowardly, selfish, or insensitive.[8] Television frequently pictures men (especially fathers) as ineffectual boors, bumbling idiots, and one-dimensional fools; extraterrestrial life picking up TV signals would think that practically every American man was accompanied by a laugh-track. Tuning into Oprah, Phil, or Geraldo during the afternoon hate hour can also prove an ugly experience, with programs like "Male Child Molesters and the Women Who Love Them" produced before jeering audiences. Readers of the *Kansas City Star* were recently treated to an especially hateful piece by Susan Dundon entitled "Why Men Are Jerks";[9] imagine a major American newspaper publishing an article with the sweeping claim that Jews or blacks are "jerks." Popular media psychology is no less unkind; Dr. Joyce Brothers, for example, recently explained the phenomenon that males tend to laugh and joke more than females as evidence that males are less intelligent.[10] Further out on the feminist fringes of the creative world, the hatred gets raunchier. Karen Finley, whom *Time* described as a "talented toiletmouth," spews out in her solo dramatic act abusive and scatological attacks on men (whose taxes, by the way, help fund her government grants from the National Endowment for the Arts).[11]

Misandry at School

In public education and higher academia, where all young men are formed in their thinking, cultural sensibilities, and self-identity, the prejudice directed against males is less scatological but probably far more harmful. In the first place, it is increasingly difficult for many men to find jobs as teachers in higher education; many schools exclude highly qualified males from hiring because of affirmative action sexual quotas.[12] To add insult to this injury, one of the reasons often adduced as justification for this discrimination against men is that they are not "nurturing" and "sympathetic" to students as are women. These people never met my fourth grade teacher.

The growing presence of extreme men and women feminists on many faculties means that textbooks, lectures, and classroom conversations are sometimes charged with highly derogatory comments and innuendoes against men that male students are in a poor position to challenge.[13] Moreover, college gender studies programs are inevitably heavily stacked in favor of the feminist agenda; courses on men's studies are in a distinct minority.[14] The effect on students of misandrist indoctrination was illustrated dramatically recently in the hysterical uproar that followed the decision (later rescinded) by all-women Mills College in Oakland to admit males. Demonstrating, crying, and screaming, the girls called a campus strike, some likening the decision to rape; they had been convinced by certain extreme feminist professors that the presence of males on their campus would victimize them because men students intimidate women colleagues and interfere with their learning process.[15] In none of the media accounts of the Mills decision I witnessed, by the way, was this charge ever questioned.

Misandry in Religion

While the increase in male-bashing in areas of liberal feminist influence is cause for concern, the spread of misandry in religion is cause for definite alarm; spirituality is an area where men are probably most vulnerable and where misandrists, in turn, seem to make the most far-reaching and malicious claims. The most virulent sources of this hatred are found in post-Christian feminist religious writings, especially in the burgeoning field of Goddess religion. Here one glimpses sometimes unrestrained sexist hatred and witnesses the full-blown symptoms of misandry.

A minority of women feminists, offended by the historical patriarchy of the church, have split away from traditional Christian life, worship, and theology and formed religious groups that they feel will be more conducive to the feminine spirit. For the most part, these groups are resurrecting forms of ancient matriarchal religion featuring worship of the Goddess (also known as Mother Earth or *Gaia*), including an Old European form of religion known as Wicca (the old English word for "witch"). Feminist "witch" spirituality is not to be confused with satanic cults that employ the same motif (although many men might feel "hexed" by either form). To explain and provide an ideological basis for Goddess religion, scores of women (whom we might call "Gaialogians") are publishing serious works of scholarship that investigate the archaeological, anthropological, and sociological implications of ancient Goddess religion.[16] These studies are fascinating and contain valuable insights and information; they are often also infected with some of the most vicious misandry in print.

God was not always viewed as a man or described in masculine metaphors. There is little question that many ancient societies, from the Neolithic through the Bronze Ages (8000–1200 B.C.E.), worshipped an astonishing variety of female deities. The chief divinity in this ancient pantheon was the Goddess, whom we commonly today call Mother Earth or Mother Nature, the fertile source of all life.[17] Gaia's manifestations are as numerous and various as life itself; thousands of etchings, bas-reliefs, and statues have been unearthed showing her varying forms, whether as voluptuous fertility goddess, or Sophia, the serene guide of all culture, or Cosmic Mother, the divine matriarch whose womb gives birth to all creation and whose breasts nurture her children in growth. I have myself excavated tiny figurines of the Middle Eastern goddess Asherah in ruined houses from Iron Age Palestine, testifying to her popularity during the biblical era. Indeed, Gaia's veneration perdures even today in the Roman Catholic Church (that supposed reliquary of patriarchy!) in devotion to Mary, in Hinduism as worship to deities like Mariamman, or in Chinese religion in reverence to Quan Yin.

Sometime during the Bronze Age, it is apparent that most cultures began to shift from Goddess worship (the static feminine) to the adoration of predominantly male sky deities (the dynamic masculine). This great transformation precursed the establishment of patriarchal (static masculine) religion, which has remained in force around the globe for many millennia. No one really knows why these great spiritual transitions occurred; for one thing, they took place before widespread writing, and at profound unconscious psychological depths beyond the scope of contemporary observers.

The lack of data does not stop the Gaialogians, however. They theorize that warlike men simply obliterated the idyllic feminine religion and culture ("men are all alike") and enshrined their male gods over the new pantheon of deities as a guarantee of masculine social dominance. This misandric theory attributes the most profound spiritual shift in human history simply to military force and social exigency, without ever inquiring into the possibility that Goddess religion was in any way inadequate or that ancient cultures found their spiritual needs met more effectively by masculine deities.[18]

The Evil Male God

The paradigm of a masculine Fall from a feminine State of Grace amounts to a warmed-over version of an ancient myth that easily lends itself to hate ideologies. Gnosticism is a type of religiosity that has appeared in various permutations for at least two millennia, including certain Christian forms such as Marcionism. This early heresy held that Jesus revealed a good God who had finally emerged in order to overthrow the sway of the previous evil deity revealed in the Hebrew Scriptures, the god Yahweh. Gnostics usually claim to possess secret "knowledge" (*gnosis*) of the way to truth that is unavailable to unenlightened and uninitiated people who remain locked in the ignorant thrall of their evil gods. Typical gnostic "revelations" inform us that an idyllic Golden Age in the distant past has now been supplanted temporarily by the present Evil Age, where dark and satanic powers rule over the ignorant masses, persecuting the bearers of the Spark of Knowledge. But to select initiates granted *gnosis* in esoteric cultic rituals, knowledge of the true God of Light grants salvation in the present evil era until the arrival of a utopian New Age when the powers of darkness will disappear.

The Christian church wisely condemned many forms of Gnosticism as heretical, yet types of this tendency have continued to emerge over the centuries in areas as disparate as Islam (the Shiite Muslim movement in Iran), twentieth-century Germany (Nazi mythology), modern America (both the Black Muslim movement of Elijah Muhammad and its opposite, the Aryan Nations ideology), and probably certain contemporary forms of fundamentalism. The myth of Gnosticism often justifies and encourages hate in several ways. First, it identifies members of the oppressive "out" group (the ignorant) as fundamentally and even biologically inferior and evil. Hitler's intellectuals created the false myth of the supremacy of the white Aryans over all the dark and inferior peoples, while Black Muslim apologists reversed this racial angle and made *white* people into "blue-eyed devils." Second, by identifying its own esoteric group as oppressed and victimized by evil oppressors, Gnostics attempt to legitimize the punishment of the evil ignorant through a range of measures ranging from genocide (Nazis) to expulsion of people from the nation (Aryan Nations) to denial of certain human rights (Shiite fundamentalism).

Elements of this hate ideology are clearly visible in the feminist Gnosticism that drives the Goddess movement. In its most extreme form it is apparent in a rash of books such as *The Great Cosmic Mother*, where authors Sjoo and Mor "prove" the biological inferiority of males with "scientific evidence" reminiscent of Hitler's racist apologists; in *Beyond God the Father*, Mary Daly claims that, biologically, males are simply misbegotten females.[19] Most feminist extremists do not make this biological inferiority claim overtly; however, it often lies just beneath the surface as an unspoken explanation for their frequent assumption that males are culturally and spiritually inferior to females, predatory subhuman types (like the "money-hungry" Jew or the "white-woman-raping" black man).

In a hatefully advanced ideological version of the old rhyme that little boys are made of "snails and puppy-dog tails," the claim is made that males "on the neuron level are . . . wired for oppression."[20] In a statement reminiscent of the anti-Semitic charges of Jewish thirst for the blood of Christian babies, Daly speaks of "the insatiable lust of males for female blood."[21] John Rowan begins his Goddess book *The Horned God* with a confession: "I am a man," an admission he feels is analogous to saying, " 'Yes, I dropped the bomb on Hiroshima.' Except that it goes further, into the tiny details of everyday life. It is like adding, — 'And I'm putting a little arsenic into my wife's tea every day.' "[22]

On a historical plane, according to the Gaialogians, this male biological and spiritual inferiority has played itself out across time in suppression of women through "patriarchy," that catch-all term that has come to encompass a full range of misandrist notions as well as legitimate analyses. The term is frequently charged with Manichean gnostic elements, the masculine equalling all that is bloodthirsty and dark, while the feminine connotes the life-giving and innocent. This typical motif is pervasive in a work such as Riane Eisler's popular *The Chalice and the Blade* (chalice = nurturing feminine culture, blade = the masculine culture of death).[23] Reisler imagines an idyllic Neolithic era ruled by the Goddess, imbuing culture with peaceful feminine values without in any way being "matriarchal." To create this past Golden Age, Reisler severely overinterprets the extremely limited Neolithic archaeological data, freighting it with a host of sociological assumptions that this meager evidence simply will not bear.[24] Reisler's gnostic Neolithic Nostalgia conjures up primitive societies characterized by *gylany*, her neologism meaning shared power, partnership, and equality between the sexes.[25] For the Gaialogians, this was the real period of human cultural advancement; it was women who created culture and originated human speech.[26] Reisler wants us to believe that Stone Age people lived under the Goddess's benign gaze in idyllic pastoral societies without domination, war or violence, their lives filled with music, art, and dancing; if this existence sounds like the Garden of Eden, that is simply because, for Reisler, this myth is nothing other than an allegorical description of pre-patriarchal "gylanic" society.[27]

What brought the Golden Age to an end? Men (and their male gods) ruined the Garden of Eden.[28] Waves of barbaric and bloodthirsty males swept into the civilized world and destroyed it, wiping out Goddess worship and its attendant pacifism, erecting in its place brutal patriarchal societies under a war-religion that "literally worshipped" the sword.[29] The ensuing patriarchy produced millennia of domination, violence, war, strife, oppression — all with the blessing of the male deities. For Reisler and the Gaialogians, not the least horrific of patriarchy's products is the religion of the Bible. Such Bible-bashing often carries strong anti-Semitic overtones not dissimilar in its sweeping condemnation of Jewish faith to gnostic Marcionism or Nazism.[30] The real cause of historic evil and current strife in the world is patriarchy and maleness, which has produced warfare, domination, political oppression, deadly technology, and environmental pollution; the world is endangered, as Carl Sagan has repeatedly stated, by "testosterone poisoning."

In Christian theological language, the ideology of Goddess religion amounts to a massive imputation of original sin to males only and a virtual assumption that not just the Virgin Mary, but every woman, is graced with an Immaculate Conception.[31] There exists hardly a hint in Gaialogy that women have cooperated in the historic evils that plague our planet, that they have shared in injustice, encouraged exploitation, benefited from oppression, profited from slavery, or participated in violence. Nor is there the least suggestion that more than a few extraordinary men (like Jesus) have also opposed these evils. Moreover, one would not know from reading Gaiologist history that, in addition to the admitted male involvement in the products of war and economic exploitation, males were also overwhelmingly active in the creation of such gifts to civilization as philosophy, science, medical technology, spirituality, circuses, university education, painting, sports, jazz, cinema, novels, poetry, rock'n roll, slapstick comedy, nonviolent resistance, French cuisine, astronomy, cartoons, weather satellites, tap-dancing, architecture, mathematics, clowning, classical music, chess, electricity, democracy, legal codes, women's fashions, vaccines, mass communications, and so on. No indeed; in fact, as a result of extreme feminism, for men even to acknowledge pridefully their heritage of male contribution to civilization is to fall vulnerable to the charge of a porcine "male chauvinism."

What, then, do the feminist Gaialogians propose in bringing about the end of patriarchy? The recommendations are usually vague; Reisler's work is uncharacteristically moderate on this point, suggesting that feminist values can transform society through a peaceful evolution. In order to disarm patriarchy, however, some feminists have suggested a more drastic solution: mass castration; after careful consideration of this option, Rowan finally concluded (generously, I thought) that this solution was "too threatening."[32] Mary Daly, on the other hand, proposes castrating only the patriarchal system and its language (one is perhaps bemused

by the appearance of this kind of metaphor in a movement so intent
on presenting itself as a nonviolent alternative to historical cruelties).[33]
Extremely vague in their concrete proposals to rectify patriarchy, the
Gaialogians seem to ask our trust that, as an enlightened and gnostic in-
telligentsia, they will simply "know" the right things to do in castrating
the system and bringing about a return to the Garden.

Misandry in Christian Feminism

Compared to their Goddess religion counterparts, the literary advocates
of Christian feminism have been relatively moderate and measured in
their analysis of patriarchy, in the main restricting the word in scholarly
publications to a reasonable description of male-dominated political arrangements in the Christian tradition. Undoubtedly the most influential
Christian feminist work, Elisabeth Schüssler Fiorenza's *In Memory of
Her*, for example, while containing many debatable analyses along with
many penetrating insights, is free of the kind of misandry favored by the
Gaialogians.[34] While some male-bashing does occur in the theological
writings of Christian feminism, other feminists have begun to notice it
and offer criticisms of the tendency.[35]

Unfortunately, sometimes virulent misandry tends to break out in
less scholarly feminist circles and in popular publications in the Christian
press. The influential *National Catholic Reporter* is increasingly allowing
itself to become a conduit for this toxic waste-product of *ressentiment*.
Columnist Demetria Martinez, for example, recently invented the novel
charge that abortion is predominantly the fault of *males*, that women
are merely the *victims* of abortion.[36] Martinez's rhetoric performs the
neat trick both of blaming the male politicians whose policies ostensibly
create the conditions in which victimized women seek abortions, *and*
blaming the male priests for their ineffectual measures in stemming the
abortion tide; this way, males are scapegoats whether "pro-choice" or
"pro-life." Martinez goes on to trot out the stock-in-trade feminist charge
that men kill "in the name of abstractions and ideologies," adding the
nasty implication that this is all to obtain "shiny medals" (illustrating
a frequent misandrist motif that portrays males as little boys or idiots
dazzled by medals or toys). In an even uglier vein, *NCR* published a
vicious hate-poem by Ntozake Shange in which the author, on seeing
three random men on the subway and in a restaurant, wonders to herself
which particular crime each habitually commits: child molestation, wife-
beating, sodomy, rape, torture, dismemberment, or murder?[37]

Usually instances of misandry in liberal Catholic publishing are more
subtle. Joan Chittister, for example, casually referred to the murderous
policies of pharaonic Egypt of Moses' time as simply a case of a society
"where 'men were men,'" parroting the extreme feminist assumption

that destruction and oppression are natural expressions of masculinity.[38] Subtler still, "Mary's Pence," a relief agency created entirely for women and directed solely by women, recently ran an advertisement seeking financial support for "elderly women; women with AIDS; battered women; women in recovery; women in detention centers," etc.[39] Only on reflection does one realize the emergence here of a unique Christian idea: gender-specific charity. And what of elderly *men, men* with AIDS, battered *men, men* in recovery, and *men* in prisons? Does ignoring them here in some unconscious way "serve them right" for being men?

The subtlety of literary Christian feminist misandry does not mean that the vice is mild on the popular, day-to-day level of conversation and praxis. On the contrary; just as one rarely finds instances of overt scholarly or media racism directed at African-Americans but encounters it constantly in popular jokes, practices, and unconscious comments, so Christian feminist misandry largely expresses itself in its liberal environment in operating assumptions, casual conversations, and undocumented claims in sermons, classes, and even spiritual direction. In the liberal Christian circles in which I have lived and worked, it is "politically correct" to claim that maleness is inherently dominating and patriarchal, that masculinity is the source of violence, that males are not naturally religious, and that men are really only interested in money and power. Whether they have noticed them or given them credence, any men who travel in these circles will have heard assertions like these repeatedly in the last decade; our brief survey of Goddess-religion feminism begins to indicate some of the probable intellectual origins of these claims.

The encounter on an everyday basis with this widespread and largely unchallenged Christian misandry is potentially far more harmful to males in the search for spirituality than any esoteric ax-grinding tome marketed in a New Age bookstore. Let us imagine what a modern young man who has begun a serious quest for a spiritual life might experience, remembering that he has already been exposed to widespread misandry in the arts, media, and education. Let us suppose that at college he decides to get involved more seriously with religious activity; in that case, he might go to the campus ministry office to sign up as a lector or volunteer for a social justice activity. However, it is possible that he might find, as did a friend of mine in the Midwest recently, the campus ministry office festooned with radical feminist slogans and posters screaming out at him: "If Men Could Have Babies, Abortion Would Be a Sacrament," "To Succeed, A Woman Has to Work Twice As Hard As a Man — Fortunately, That Isn't Difficult," or "A Woman without a Man Is Like a Fish without a Bicycle." At this point, he is likely to feel like a black man signing up with the Ku Klux Klan.

Perhaps our young man will begin to attend church and listen attentively to sermons for spiritual guidance. Unfortunately, he might encounter a preacher trained in the orthodox feminism of a seminary such as the Episcopal Divinity School in Boston, which means he might be regaled with accounts of the patriarchal church's long history of racism, misogyny, homophobia, colonialism, and probably environmental irresponsibility. Our young man might feel, as he looks around the congregation and finds only a few scattered males (almost always men much older than himself), a bit like a fish out of water; in time he is likely just to feel like a fish without a bicycle.

Should our young man desire to enter the priesthood or the ministry in a liberal church seminary, he is likely to find frequent experiences of prejudice against his gender and virtually no support for or understanding of himself as a male. He may be taught a biblical studies course centering on the claim that the Bible oppresses women, while he is introduced to the "hermeneutics of suspicion" (which teaches students to regard any given text from a socio-political angle as a justification for patriarchy). He might find, in an ethics, history, or systematics course, a professor primarily interested in pushing the feminist agenda. And of course, if he has a conversion experience and renounces his masculinity, he can choose from a menu of "Women and . . . " courses, filling in the blank with "spirituality," "ethics," "politics," etc. His mandatory field education experience is likely to be politically correct as well. Recently a Catholic seminarian in the Graduate Theological Union in Berkeley flunked his oral examination because the feminist director of the program made him choose in a hypothetical test case between an orthodox feminist position and one consistent with Roman Catholic tradition. He mistakenly opted for the traditional solution, which revealed "rigidity" and "insensitivity." In this climate, incidentally, there is sometimes a vague undercurrent of feeling that resistance to feminism is indicative of psycho-sexual problems, which can, in turn, raise questions regarding possible ordination.

Our young man might face some rather intense questions and crises at this point. He will almost certainly be challenged informally, as was I by a Catholic feminist who teaches in a seminary, to forego ordination or resign from the ministry if he has any sympathy at all for his excluded sisters.[40] In view of this environment, it is hardly surprising that males are now a diminishing minority in most liberal seminaries. When the president of one seminary consortium was questioned by a journalist *why* the number of males was declining, the official replied (yes), that *white* males were now primarily interested in making money and not serving the church.[41] As you may have heard in your kitchen long ago, those men are all alike.

What to Do about Misandry

Whether a man is a young college student in a course, a member of a parish council, or an employee of a large firm, he is increasingly likely, as time goes by, to encounter misandry in some form. What should he do about it? The first and most important thing is to become conscious of it. One of the most dangerous qualities of misandry is its ability to creep into conversations on little cat's feet or get dropped into policy-making decisions like a cyanide pill in a martini. Males need to know when someone is poisoning their wells, whether in the media, at school, or at work. At the very least, their internal "Bullshit Detector" should go off when they hear a sweeping indictment against males, or when an innuendo against them personally as a man hangs in the air.

It may also be appropriate to confront misandry through an immediate verbal objection or a later memo or letter. Even if the protest is ignored or ridiculed (part of the game is to call men "cry babies" if they oppose male-bashing), at least the practice will establish an internal attitude in the man that, though perhaps not "mad as hell," he is at least determined not to "take it anymore." If, however, the misandry involves something more serious than a verbal cheap shot — e.g., job discrimination, a child- or sex-abuse accusation, or a sexist policy decision — a man must take calm and measured action immediately in the proper legal arena. The same laws and policies created to protect women from misogyny also can protect men from misandry, and they must be used.

The day must come when a male-bashing comment marks the speaker, not as "politically correct," but as bigoted. The day must come when the automatic elimination of a male from a job search is seen, not as an instance of affirmative action, but as a case of sexist job discrimination. The day must come when a misandrist policy is regarded as atavistic, as out of place in modern society as Jim Crow laws, anti-Semitism, Know-Nothing rhetoric, and misogyny. And the day must come when church ministers look on men with empathy rather than antagonism.

Chapter 4

The Crisis of Men and the Church

The care of souls (*cura animarum*) is one the most vital tasks of the Christian church. As modern men gradually lose access to healthy masculine archetypes, suffer disorientation, and experience a loss of the male energy they need to prosper individually as well as contribute to society, they need this soul-care more than ever before. Men need spiritual healing. And society desperately needs its men to be healed, for wounded masculinity in some way contributes to every major social problem our culture faces: drug addiction, gang warfare, militarism, crime, poverty, and so on. The question is, how can the church help heal men?

The Symptoms

The first thing a doctor does for a patient is to diagnose the illness; the church, too, should recognize the signs that indicate the severity of the problems that affect men in our culture. If the church is to help men, spiritual care-givers must recognize the symptoms of wounded masculinity as they appear in individuals as well as society. Statistics only begin to suggest the dimensions of the problem: in relation to women, American men have eight years' less life expectancy, commit suicide three times as often, show higher rates of alcohol and drug abuse, and suffer disproportionately from fatal illnesses such as AIDS, cancer, and heart disease. Men are most likely to be both the victims and the perpetrators of most crimes; males are the most frequent victims of assault and murder and outnumber women in prisons by nine to one. Nowhere are the problems of wounded masculinity more obvious than in the black community, where drug addiction, unemployment, crime, and poverty have made black men virtually an endangered species.[1]

A sensitive eye can also observe what statistics fail to detect. Even among many apparently successful middle-aged and older men (the "patriarchs"), one often notices a palpable sense of emptiness, a lack of greater purpose, and a tone of what Thoreau called "quiet desperation."[2] These men play well such limited social roles as the financially lucrative "boss" at work and the generous "provider" at home, but, in turn, they often feel valued for little more than the business deals they garner or the bacon they bring home. Moreover, their very success is a source of enormous cultural resentment. For these are the Great White Males, the villains and victimizers of liberal rhetoric, the reputed sources of all that is wrong with Western culture; no matter that their enterprises may have provided thousands of jobs, their activities raised standards of living, their high taxes funded social welfare programs. For all the hype and hostility that surrounds them like a cloud, can anyone see through the fog and find the real persons underneath? Can they themselves?

At the other end of the socio-economic scale are the men society wants to forget: the poor and the homeless. Whole sections of large American cities are littered with the wreckage of male lives gone wrong; eastern downtown Los Angeles, for example, resembles a scene from *Night of the Living Dead*. As one drifts through block after block of soup-kitchen lines, labor pools, and hordes warming themselves from trash-can fires, the realization dawns: the overwhelming majority of these people are men. The outrage of social commentators at the growing number of homeless women and children among us only underscores by contrast the relative tolerance and equanimity that our culture displays toward the devastation of its males. What broke these men, and what happened to them? Who will reach out to them as persons?

Between the extremes of the lifestyles of the rich and famous and the devastation of the homeless, the vast majority of men in our culture suffer unrecognized spiritual ailments almost invisibly. Among these problems is the "father-wound," the aching alienation from physically distant or spiritually noninvolved fathers portrayed so vividly in films such as *Death of a Salesman* or *I Never Sang for My Father*. Since the Industrial Revolution, economic forces have driven men out of the home and away from their children. As a result, relatively few men now living ever received the firm, intimate guidance into what Robert Bly calls the "masculine mode of feeling," the everyday proximity to the father once provided to boys as if by osmosis. Nor do many men know how to relate with each other or their wives intimately as friends; still less can many men feel, much less articulate, the resulting isolation and alienation. The church, however, possesses the resources to help heal this father-wounding with, for example, the ancient biblical stories and teachings that encourage the family-involved father.[3]

Undoubtedly the males most vulnerable to such wounds of masculinity are young men and boys. Far and away the most serious problem in this regard is that our society is failing to initiate its male youths into manly adulthood, thus shifting the entire burden of achieving maturity onto the isolated individual boy. Many boys somehow achieve this task, but most do not; it is clearly too great a weight for most young men to carry. Increasingly we see the phenomenon of the male who extends his adolescence well into middle age, becoming the classic *Puer Aeternus* ("eternal boy"), the Peter Pan who never wants to grow up, make commitments, or invest energy in anything but his own narcissism. Equally common is the sun-tanned and blow-dried Nice Man: cool, coiffed, and detached. Cut off from his reservoir of masculine archetypes, he can achieve, at best, only the nonthreatening status that makes him acceptable to so many women. A survivor, he takes good care of himself. Just don't expect him to help you out if you get in trouble: he's clear that this sort of thing is Co-Dependent Behavior.

The alternative to uninitiated male life is even more tragic. Feeling the desire to become men but lacking the wise guidance of elders, many young boys haplessly attempt to initiate *themselves* into adulthood according to the brutal rituals of gang pressure. Such unsupervised initiation takes place every day in our cities, whether in drive-by slayings in San Francisco or "wilding" sprees in New York. Hungering for genuine masculine models but not finding them, other alienated boys seize on the cheapest and most exploitative fantasies of Hollywood: Conan, Rambo, and Dirty Harry. Lacking flesh-and-blood male involvement, the image of manliness our young men receive is nothing more than a gross caricature, a cartoon, an exaggerated comic-strip machismo.

In the last few centuries, Western religion has utterly abandoned its ancient role of initiating young men into manhood. Today, only one institution in our society still ritually initiates large numbers of boys into masculine adulthood with any effectiveness: the military. Generations of American men have learned manly pride, resourcefulness, and responsibility for their country under the stylized liturgies of boot camp, and a trip to the army remains one of the most available options for straightening out a screwed-up kid. But this initiation is directed only at the development of one archetype — the Warrior. Is it any wonder that American masculine spirituality is so impoverished when our society invests the time, resources, and energy to initiate boys formally into only one masculine archetype?

The Crisis of Men and the Church

To paraphrase a line from the film *Young Frankenstein*, "a crisis is a terrible thing — and it's about time we had one!" For if we say that the church and modern men face a crisis, we are merely claiming that some key decisions and changes need to be made about the relation of religion to men in our society; a *crisis*, after all (Greek: *krisein* = "to choose"), is a condition that calls for new choices. Painful and frightening as those choices may be, a crisis can prove a good thing; certainly no human growth can take place without one. In any case, the larger crisis of men in our culture is already well underway; millions of men are making the kinds of choices that lead to new growth, doing hard and even painful spiritual work, abandoning outmoded roles and superficial identities, adjusting to the liberation of women, and exploring their human potentials. The spiritual growth of men is an inevitable wave into the foreseeable future. The question is, will the church wake up to this tide and plunge into it to help men stay afloat? Or will it draw up its skirts and flee to the shore, convincing itself that all of this uproar is yet another Modern Bad Thing?

Church people who would dive into the men's crisis must remember something, however. The church can play only a limited part in the rediscovery of masculine spirituality for men; it is a latecomer to the movement. Most of the energy that drives the men's movement comes from the "secular" world of fairy tales and mythology, Jungian psychotherapy, anthropology, and New Age spirituality. The church can prove a valuable healing partner with people trained in these disciplines if it acts as a concerned team member, open enough to learn from the insights and wisdom of the men who have long been laboring in the field, and willing, in turn, to contribute its own collected wisdom to the endeavor in a truly collegial manner. Still, men's groups are already eagerly calling on the church for its expertise and its wisdom in helping men find their way.[4]

Two important phenomena also need to be well understood when considering the relation of men to the Christian church; they are discussed in some detail below. The first is the largely unacknowledged reality of the historical tilt in Christian spirituality toward feminine values; as a result, many men today have a difficult time relating to the language and values that they encounter in church. The widespread alienation of men from Western Christianity inevitably led both men and church people to write one another off. The second unrecognized truth about males is that they are not, despite our Western prejudice about them, basically indifferent to religion or uninterested in faith. The intense attraction of men to God in religions such as Islam and Hinduism proves that males possess a strong, natural longing for religious meaning. The question is whether a religion knows how to identify this desire and speak to it.

Holy Mother Church

One of the greatest obstacles to men's identification with Christianity is the highly feminine nature of the worship and spirituality of the church. This problem is not universal, however; both Protestant Evangelicals and the Greek Orthodox, for example, retain a spiritual flavor attractive

to men. But many males in the Catholic and liberal Protestant traditions have a difficult time relating to the liturgical, devotional, and social
life of their churches. This claim may surprise and irritate women who
are so painfully well aware of the patriarchal nature of most Christian
churches; yet a strong distinction exists between the male-dominated
polity of the church, and the highly feminized *soul-life* of that same
church, particularly in the West.

The first indication that the spirituality of many Christian churches
seems to appeal primarily to women is easily obtained: one can simply
"count heads" at a local worship service. It is not at all unusual to find
a female-to-male ratio of 2:1 or even 3:1. I have seen ratios in parish
churches as high as 7:1. Among the males who do attend these services,
one frequently finds either very young boys in the company of their parents or quite elderly gentlemen. Some liberal Presbyterian or Methodist
congregations are practically bereft of middle-aged men; the few who
do attend are inevitably accompanied by the family.

A further sign of male alienation from American religion is that many
pastors experience a difficult time involving ordinary men in the everyday life of the church: committees, lectoring, volunteer ministerial work,
teaching, and so forth. Men, in turn, often reply that they do not feel qualified to serve in such directly spiritual ways. Typically, they are willing to
work only on practical church matters such as financial boards or building projects where they can bring their economic or pragmatic expertise
to bear; others might feel comfortable serving as ushers. But most of the
men who attend most Christian churches usually don't feel they have
anything especially religious or spiritual to offer anyone else.

How did this sense of alienation between men and Christianity develop? How did "real" masculinity come to imply hostility to Christian
piety, to "goody-two-shoes" morality, and to "churchy" activities? When
did men come to fear that their religiosity might subject them to the epi-
thet "holy Joe," so that they could feel peer permission to pray earnestly
only in foxholes as bullets whizzed by overhead? A brief historical
overview of the phenomenon might prove helpful.

Men and Christianity

The notion that spirituality or religion is inimical to males is totally absent
from the Christian Bible, both in the Old and the New Testament. On
the contrary, as we shall see in Parts Two and Three of this book, the
Bible is a treasury of male spirituality. Jesus was himself a very manly
figure, and the biblical metaphors for God in the ancient Judeo-Christian
traditions are charged with masculine archetypal energy. Nevertheless,
even in the New Testament one can begin to detect the first hints of the
feminine Christian spirituality that would develop centuries later.

The early Christian church featured a markedly positive attitude toward women and femininity in contrast to the Jewish patriarchy out of which it developed.[5] As a largely urban and Greek phenomenon of the first century, Christianity offered a balanced and gentle alternative to the harsh religions and philosophies with which it competed and an advance beyond the static, patriarchal masculinity of the Pharisaic tradition. In many ways the new faith blew with the fresh breath of dynamic femininity; the Christians were people of the Spirit (*ruach*), that spontaneous and creative feminine quality of God. The great preacher St. Paul (an extremely masculine figure himself) characterized the gifts of this Spirit as "love, peace, patience, kindness, goodness, fidelity, gentleness, and self-control" (Gal 5:22–23). To this day the adjective "Christian" applied to a person connotes in the popular mind one who is nice, kind, and gentle.

Christianity was and is distinctive among Western religions in its high valuation of feminine religious qualities. Its worship centers around the domestic motif of the eucharistic meal, and its morality encourages meekness, humility, and even a certain passivity. The irony in all this is that, though the early Christians focussed on the newness of the feminine gifts, they displayed thoroughly masculine qualities in promoting their new doctrine! Masculinity is *assumed* in early Christianity and shoots through the whole New Testament like an electric charge: Jesus' bold confrontations with the Pharisees, Peter's courageous leadership of the new sect, Paul's aggressive missionary strategy, and so on. Most of the first generation was martyred for its beliefs — hardly a mark of the meek and mild! And though one is hard put to find a New Testament text urging Christians to the masculine values of aggressiveness, independence, bravery, or resistance to injustice, these are precisely the qualities these people displayed in the face of Jewish and Roman oppressiveness.

A few centuries after its birth, Christianity began to institutionalize itself within the safe confines of the former Roman Empire. There its political structure soon began to exhibit the classic signs of static masculinity: patriarchal authority, canon law, dogma, ecclesiastical penalties, and so on. But Christian spirituality also shifted during this period from the dynamic femininity of Spirit-filled religion to the static femininity of Holy Mother Church, that protective spiritual womb where all questions are answered and all spiritual needs fulfilled. No need now to search for God on one's own or even seek the personal experience of faith: Mother Church provided all. Puzzling problems of theology could be brushed off with the dictum, "it's a mystery"; no need to question or worry. It is worth noting that in time, the ecclesiastical authorities discouraged and even forbade the reading of the Bible, with its powerful stories of masculine spirituality. It was enough for the faithful to take part passively in the attractions of a beautiful liturgy.

In the grand scheme of things, the femininity of Christian spirituality over the centuries surely provided a needed balance and a refreshing alternative both to the stark masculinity of church politics as well as the aggressive nature of European imperialistic culture. Nevertheless, a disparity emerged between the masculine spiritual values of the Scriptures and the feminine *élan* of traditional Catholic practices. The Protestant Reformation of the sixteenth century reacted to that gap and sought a return to masculine, biblical values and principles. Among its many complicated theological, political, and economic causes, we might view the impulse that propelled Protestantism as an outbreak in a static feminine spiritual world of dynamic masculinity featuring energetic protest, separation, strong personal conviction, and highly individuated faith. Protestantism's masculine spirit is captured strikingly in the gruffness of the testy Martin Luther, the German preacher who broke so dramatically with Mother Church. In scathing denouncements and passionate treatises, Luther challenged his followers to an intense and directly personal faith in God based on biblical teachings. To this day, the many strains of biblically based conservative and evangelical Protestantism retain a strong masculine flavor and attract spiritually hungry modern men with striking success.

As the Protestant churches began to break with Rome, an equally energetic outbreak of dynamic masculinity occurred within Catholicism. A handicapped ex-soldier named Ignatius of Loyola and his small band of Jesuits, wisely dissuaded from setting off for Palestine in order to convert the Muslims, decided to channel their passionate energies into the Catholic Counter-Reformation. Jesuit spirituality vibrated with military images, Warrior and King archetypes, and courtly mythology; it quickly attracted thousands of men to its cause. Within a century the Jesuits had trekked to China and penetrated the court at Peking, founded churches in Japan, established missions in Africa, started hundreds of colleges in Europe, and constructed among the Indians of the Americas the Reductions so beautifully portrayed in the film *The Mission*. With great struggle and no little opposition from Holy Mother Church, the Jesuits created a spirituality that broke out from the domesticity of convent and monastery walls and took Christian faith into the streets, theaters, marketplaces, and city halls of their time. To this day the order retains its reputation for innovation, intelligence, experimentation, and independence — as well as arrogance. No one, however, accuses it of being boring.

The dynamic masculine outbursts of the Protestant Reformation and the Catholic Counter-Reformation eventually solidified, predictably, into the rigid institutionalism that usually marks the second and third generations of formerly energetic religious movements. The legacy of strict Protestant Scholasticism and uncompromising Catholic Tridentine orthodoxy lasted well into the twentieth century, steeping generations of Christians in a staunch and stern Christianity: dour, legalistic, anti-sexual, and dogmatic. But within Catholicism, important feminine spiritual devotions throughout this period offered emotional relief from strict ecclesiastical clericalism. One such devotion, to the Sacred Heart of Jesus, offered a compassionate and understanding Lord who forgave and loved sinners. The iconography of the devotion, however, eventually developed the well-known androgynous picture of an effeminate Jesus who appeared to be wearing rouge and lipstick. Such florid artistic presentations of Christ as appeared in the last century exemplify a spirituality that tended to feminize "gentle Jesus, meek and mild." One can only wonder how many men, their skin crawling at such saccharine mawkishness, turned away from a prayerful spiritual encounter with Christ.

By far the most significant development in popular Catholic spirituality in recent centuries is the resurgence of devotion to the Blessed Virgin Mary. Marian spirituality centers around a series of apparitions reported in such places as Guadalupe, Knock, Lourdes, Fatima, and, most recently, Medjugorje; the message of these appearances always includes an exhortation to prayer and moral conversion and an invitation to greater closeness with God. They always occur among "little people" — children and the poor — in an atmosphere of great gentleness, compassion, and even humor. Mariology reached its zenith in the promulgation of the doctrine of the Assumption, which proclaims the bodily assumption of Mary into heaven. While most Protestants winced at this teaching (and at much of Marian spirituality), psychologist Jung rejoiced, claiming that the Catholic Church had at last formally included the feminine in its theology and worship.

The heavy presence of the feminine in Catholic life is, by itself, no barrier to masculine spirituality. On the contrary; the phenomenon surely encourages an encounter with the *anima* for many males. The problem is that, for many generations, the church has provided only occasional devotions and spirituality of a masculine character, and most of these disappeared during the sweeping changes that occurred after the Second Vatican Council. As Western culture increasingly tilts toward the feminine, the need for masculine-affirming religiosity grows steadily.

The Religiosity of Men

The alienation of many men from the femininity of Christian spirituality has created grounds for an enormous misunderstanding about men and religion that every pastoral care-giver must recognize and confront. The absence of so many men from so many churches, their lack of involvement, their diffidence and even hostility to Christian piety, has created a mostly unconscious assumption in our culture that *men are not naturally religious*. It is widely assumed that prayer and spirituality are basically

female enterprises, and that all but a few unusual men can relate to
religion only in a peripheral way.

A trip outside the bounds of American Christian culture, a journey
into the temples, monasteries, and shrines of the world's religions, would
quickly shatter such a misandrist illusion. In an imaginary tour, we could
circle the globe and find an astonishing variety of men fiercely plunging
into the heart and center of their religions. Flying to Japan, we observe
the strange sight of a Zen *roshi* striking his errant disciple for missing
the meaning of a mysterious *koan;* the way to truth is harsh — and
sloppiness will never do. Continuing on to Thailand, we find a field
of saffron-cloaked men reverently sitting before the Buddha; the discipline needed on the path to liberation is great. And in India, we are swept
along in an ocean of men making pilgrimage to Benares; Hindu men take
their religion utterly seriously and brook no distractions. Monks in Tibet
shake their temple with the deep-throated *Oam* as their nearby Chinese
countrymen clap their hands and light incense in honor of the ancestors. But nothing can prepare us for the sheer masculine intensity of a
mosque in Jordan or Syria as thousands of Muslim men gather for Friday prayer; here, the concept of male alienation from worship of God is
unthinkable. And if we watch the Hasidim *daven* in prayer at the Western Wall in Jerusalem, we begin to glimpse the potential forcefulness
of masculine prayer; no less bracing is the purifying ordeal of a South
Dakota *initipi* ("sweat lodge") as Lakota shamans cleanse the body and
spirit in honor of Wakan Tanka. Whether one prays among Mexican
penitentes, dances to the drum-songs of Zulu animists, or chants ves-
pers with French Trappists, one joins in the worldwide symphony of a
billion male voices praising God, repenting of sins, crying for visions,
and seeking help along life's painful road. It has been going on for ten
thousand years.

Our religion-alienated American men represent neither a wave of
the future nor a rational advance over centuries of superstition. They
are an anomaly, a quirk, an oddity in the community of all the men
who ever lived, who ever wondered at the Unspeakable Mystery, sought
alignment with the Eternal Tao, burned with affection for the Great Holy,
or trembled before the Totally Other. And all of this ancient affinity
for God — every bit of it — still lies buried deep in their unconscious,
waiting to be called forth into a spiritual life that will make them a little
less mad and a little more human. It waits there, this penchant for the
Holy, drowned out by Muzak and numbed by the dreariness of shopping
malls, paralyzed by stress and enervated by neglect, until something
wakes it. Who will call religiosity fully to life in men, invigorate it, and
nurture it in the face of the death-dealing boredom of modern secularity?
That is the task of the church in its care of souls.

Seven Suggestions for Reaching Men

How can the Christian churches assist men in finding expression for their natural religiosity? How can pastors reach them? And how can modern men find their own way back to God again? Most of the remainder of this book (Part Two) is concerned with just one of many approaches, namely, biblical myth and story. By reading and reflecting upon the Christian Scriptures in an imaginative way, modern men can find themselves in ancient narratives about ancestors whose stories vibrate with the energy of the same archetypes that still lie so deeply within us today. These myths have much wisdom to teach; the task is learning how to get access to it. But there are many other ways the church can reach out to men to wake up, to evangelize, and to heal. What follows are seven brief points indicating problem areas for men, and with each, suggestions for strengthening the church's faltering outreach to men, overcoming male religious alienation, and speaking to men convincingly in a spiritual language they can understand.

1. Male Initiation Rites

Commentators on men's issues are in widespread agreement that the greatest need among young men of the next generation is a convincing experience of initiation into male adulthood. This concern is directly related to the church and its role in society. The most important service the church could perform in this regard is to take seriously once again its ancient role of ritually initiating young males into responsible adulthood. Unfortunately, this is a much easier step to propose on paper than to carry out in reality; with the loss of supportive culture, much of the value of these archaic rites is certainly lost forever, and moderns cannot artificially reconstruct them. Nevertheless, the church can make positive, though limited, contributions toward marking the initiation of boys into manhood, beginning at the local parish and diocesan levels.

A parish church might regularly send a half dozen or so of its adolescent boys on weekend retreats in the country with an equal number of knowledgeable and interested adult males. The experience could commence with a ceremony establishing the sacred time and space in which the youths are about to enter; then, a rite could mark the death of the child's *puer,* including a physical action such as a haircut or a tattoo, indicating that the boy is leaving something palpable behind. The rite could continue with an account of what is expected of a Christian adult man. This experience could offer the older men a chance to tell their stories and offer their wisdom to the youths (as well as each other). A final ceremony — a eucharistic meal, for example — could offer prayers for the young men in their adult responsibilities; they could at that time take new names of patron saints as was the custom until recently at confirmation ceremonies.[6] After these rituals, the church as well as the family ought then actually to treat the youths in a new and adult fashion; the young men could take a more visible part in church decisions and ceremonies and enjoy new rights and duties at home. The handing over of car keys to the boy, for example, would be a very meaningful expression of this trust to everyone.

One shining example of what the larger church can do for young men was created in the 1970s by Father Ken Leoni of the archdiocese of Denver: the Christian Outdoor Leadership School. Based on the Outward Bound program, this training challenged high school youths to three weeks of intensive physical, social, and spiritual training at a base camp 10,000 feet high in the Rocky Mountains. The first week consisted in the basics: physical conditioning that included obstacle courses and rock-climbing, culminating in a ten-mile run; fundamental instruction in mountaineering, map-reading, and wilderness survival; and simple talks and discussions focussed on the basic truths of the Christian religion, including prayer and liturgical services. During the second week, the students moved to a higher camp and experienced the sublime and hostile Alpine climate. This time was climaxed by a three-day trial in which the students negotiated a lengthy hike across the Continental Divide entirely on their own (though unknowingly supervised by their instructors). The final week offered a grueling and rare opportunity: each adolescent retreated into the mountains for a twenty-four-hour prayer-fast, equipped with only basic survival equipment and a Bible. This experience culminated with a healing break-fast and sweat-bath and a moving ceremony marking their graduation from the program. Many personal breakthroughs occurred in these short weeks; young people responded to the challenges with striking courage and maturity. Unfortunately, the vast majority of young people are never so challenged, nor do they ever experience much interest in their growth and development from the church as a community.

2. Missions

Another valuable experience of adult masculinity that the church is well positioned to provide is the challenge of *mission* — being sent to serve other people evangelically. The Church of Latter-day Saints has taken the lead in this regard; Mormon young men serve long and valued stints together in preaching and passing out information about their church — and they love it. In a similar vein, the Jesuit Volunteer Corps offers Catholic college graduates the opportunity to spend a year or two contributing their services to the poor in inner cities or to native peoples in Alaska, Central America, Micronesia, or the United States. Among the opportunities for mission service that Christian churches could provide: teaching in inner-city grade schools, building houses for the poor (e.g., the Habitat for Humanity program), serving in paramedical training in Christian hospitals, or reaching out to the homeless or drug addicts in street shelters and downtown parishes.

Though not without danger, these kinds of placements could give young men a chance to *give back to society* for a change, experience some adventure, pick up some street smarts, and, often enough, meet like-minded young women who share decent human values. But above all, the church in its missioning could concretely confront young men with a vision of heroic life-service, in sharp contrast to the now-dominant ethos of American culture in which most are steeped from childhood: greed. To be an adult male in our culture does not have to mean narcissistically exploiting the capitalistic system to maximize profit opportunities; it can mean having a big heart and learning teamwork with others striving to correct injustices, binding up wounds, and teaching wisdom. Not all young men would accept this alternative view of manhood; the shame is that so few are ever confronted with such a vision and such an opportunity in the first place.

3. *Pilgrimage*

The Christian practice of pilgrimage once offered men a powerful experience in humility, trust in God, and prayer, acted out over days and weeks and extended over many miles. The devotion was strenuous and even dangerous, and the more meaningful for all that; as the hours and miles slipped by and the body grew weary, the pilgrim really felt the cost of his commitment and paid the price of his search. It is an axiom of human nature that we most value the things that we really have to pay for; perhaps one reason prayer is so widely ignored is that it doesn't seem to cost us much personally. Pilgrimage today is just a pale ghost of its former self or worse — a parody; one religious magazine, for example, offers "golf pilgrimages to Ireland" (single price, double occupancy, airfare included).

The first ingredient of classical Christian pilgrimage is a burning need, an insoluble problem, or an aching desire of life-altering dimensions that everyday prayer and ordinary devotion can't solve. Great problems (vocational choices, life-threatening diseases, chronic faith-doubts) require great solutions. Every pilgrim is, in effect, saying clearly to himself and to everyone else that he needs help; pilgrimage is never for the complacent. The second component of the practice is the pilgrim's outlandish faith that an extravagant gesture of faith will yield overflowing grace — everything ventured, everything gained. Pilgrimage is not for the cautious, but is a bold and spiritually risky business that requires a bit of the gambler in a man. The third element in pilgrimage is a clear and concrete goal such as a famous shrine or holy place where prayers are answered and grace given — a Mecca or Lourdes or Benares. Some people think certain geographical places on earth offer focussed spiritual energy that wakens the human heart and soul; whatever the cause of this phenomenon (and millions have felt it), true pilgrims know intuitively the feeling of clarity and excitement that attends their reaching the goal, the spiritual electricity around Jerusalem or the gentle love that suffuses the shrine of Guadalupe. Pilgrimage is not an act of the rational mind; it is a belief that God imbues certain places with a Deep Magic that heals and answers prayer.

Pilgrimage is an act of high faith and is not to be taken lightly. The true pilgrim experiences vulnerability at every turn and feels often the need for food, safety, rest, and companionship. He places all in God's hands. For this reason, pilgrimage is a sacrament of the hero journey, and one of the oldest religious metaphors for life. The experience tells a man that his whole life is a pilgrimage demanding heroism, goals, and an abiding knowledge that, through it all, God helps.

Young men struggling with life choices or middle-aged men wrestling with demons might consult a pastor or spiritual director about making a pilgrimage. Together, the two can discern an appropriate experience; each pilgrimage is completely unique and the individual free to tailor every detail to his own needs. The results can be life-changing.

One day in 1969, a wise Jesuit novice master called one of his young charges unexpectedly into the office. The novice, then about twenty years old, was an exceedingly generous and adventurous young man who did not seem able in those turbulent years to make a fundamental choice about continuing in religious life. The son of a good suburban Catholic family, he had not yet "found himself " or discovered his greatest dreams; he remained confused about his deepest desires. As he sat across from his novice master in stunned silence, he heard his orders: to hitchhike on a pilgrimage to the Shrine of Our Lady of Guadalupe in Mexico City to seek and find God's will definitively in his life. Weeks later, on a warm June morning, he set out, and he did not return until he had accomplished his task two months later. The experience of "acting out" his previously nominal trust in God on a daily basis and, above all, joining thousands of poor Mexican pilgrims humbly at prayer dramatically transformed his life. Today he is a Jesuit priest laboring heroically amid poverty and military oppression in Central America, preaching faith and promoting justice.

4. Liturgy and Preaching

If pilgrimage provides a rare but deeply meaningful faith experience for a few men, the weekly public worship of God in the liturgy and the proclamation of the Word in preaching are the most widely available contacts with religion for most men. For this reason, priests and ministers concerned with men's spirituality ought to take extra care in organizing liturgical celebrations and planning homilies if they wish to invite men to prayer rather than repel them from it. They have not always done so in the recent past.

For many years liturgists felt that highly formalized worship services bored people and turned them off; "creative" liturgies were proposed as a solution. Unfortunately, the resulting Butterfly, Banner, and Balloon Extravaganzas severely alienated many men. The most saccharine outbreaks of forced liturgical excitement featured fluttering dancers floating down church aisles like wood-nymphs, goofy pseudo-rites forced on the congregation with almost fascist authoritarianism, and a host of silly *schticks* usually accompanied by inane music. It was exciting all right; many men felt excited enough to rise from their pews and walk right out the door. What was their problem? It seems that most men are instantly turned off by surprise spontaneity in ritual circumstances; moreover, ceremonies that are entirely nice, sweet, and happy usually strike men as phony and completely unconnected with the harsh world they experience every day.

What attracts men to public prayer, then? Men need a certain regularity and consistency in their worship; spontaneity has its appeal for men, but not in the midst of ritual. The highly popular masculine traditions of Judaism and Islam, for example, encourage set times, places, and formulae for daily prayer and worship, and men respond to these demands very well. Ritually, men like to know exactly what is expected of them and what the rules are; religion helps men when it challenges them to clear, reasonable, and achievable goals, whether liturgically or devotionally. Men like to be able to succeed at *something*; their lives usually are filled with enough failure, real and imagined, as it is.

Even more central to masculine worship is the notion of the Transcendent. In deemphasizing in recent generations a concern with absolutes and ultimates, heaven and hell, and eternity and infinity, modern Christianity has taken a decisive turn toward feminine religion, which is typically interested in the immanent and the incarnational, in finding God in the small things, the everyday, and the mundane. These are genuine Christian qualities and mark the beautiful spirituality of a Thérèse of Lisieux or a Mother Teresa of Calcutta; without doubt, men also need such grounding emphases. These traits are not, however, essentially masculine in nature. As liberal religion stresses increasingly the immanent and "horizontal" dimension of faith to the exclusion of the transcendent and "vertical" reality, it inadvertently ignores the voracious appetite of men for the Great, the Wholly Other, and the Eternal.

A liturgy or a sermon that truly speaks to men will tend to "pitch" men outside themselves, confront them with the Absolute, and offer them an eschatological viewpoint on life. Admittedly, this is hard to do in the Mass or eucharistic liturgy, which is structured around the domestic motif of the dining table. Yet a service that simply emphasizes the sacredness and eternity of the eucharistic actions, the infinite value of the ceremony, and the worldwide solidarity of the prayer is already on the way to capturing the male imagination.

If we are to ask males to take worship seriously, we ought to provide rites that themselves are serious. A liturgy that appeals to men possesses a quality the Hebrews called *kabod* ("glory") and the Romans *gravitas* ("gravity"); both words at root mean "weightiness" and connote a sense of dignified importance and seriousness. Ceremonies that are trivial or flighty don't command male respect. This does *not* mean liturgies have to be grim or long; one friend of mine has a saying, "Too much church makes you sick," and most men would heartily agree. Sermons, too, can be both short and effective if they get to the point and say something important about God or faith rather than rambling around with vague niceties that only sound pretty.

A final comment on one particular kind of liturgy is in order here. One of the most alienating worship services that most men ever encounter is their own wedding ceremony. The blunt truth is that Christian nuptials are rarely celebrated anymore as a rite truly sensitive to the spiritual needs of both husband and wife. On the contrary, the typical wedding is often a once-in-a-lifetime chance for the bride and her mother to fulfill their childhood fantasies. No expense is too high or detail too frivolous. While some men endure the numerous niceties and high expenses of their weddings generously, others visibly grind their teeth and roll their eyes at all the gushing over and fluttering about. Does anyone really ask men what kind of wedding rite they would prefer and give them choices any more meaningful than which Karen Carpenter song will be sung? Real liturgical reform is in order here; men, too, have a right to find their wedding ceremony a meaningful and appropriate experience.

One final note on preaching: it is surprising how very few sermons today use masculine language and metaphor or employ examples drawn from the everyday life of men. Yet Jesus did not feel embarrassed coining parables from the business world, nor did Paul shrink from using marathon imagery to describe the Christian life. Why then are so many homilists today loathe to use a sports metaphor or a business image? And why are the connotations of the oft-preached Christian exhortation to "love" almost always feminine: e.g., sensitivity, gentleness, passivity? One might never guess from today's sermons that "love" is also a masculine virtue and that real love can also be tough, firm, and aggressive.

5. *Prayer and Devotions*

The Catholic Church once provided its people a wide range of prayer experiences called "devotions" (Novenas, Stations of the Cross, Benediction, etc.) After the Second Vatican Council, many pastors ended these practices in their churches with the argument that the Eucharist ought to serve as the central focus of worship. It should. In retrospect, however, it appears that the devotional purge eliminated many prayerful experiences that men found deeply meaningful without replacing them with viable substitutes. One example was the reenactment of Christ's sacrifice at Calvary called the Stations of the Cross.

In many cultures, masculine prayer is amazingly severe. In extreme cases such as the Lakota "sun dance" or Mexican penitential rites, men endure intense physical pain as an integral part of the prayer experience. In these cultures the practice of physically painful penance is regarded highly as a heroic gift of atonement on behalf of the whole people, a vicarious act that focuses on one man the suffering of the whole people. Spiritually, such prayer evokes in the psyche the Christ archetype (see chapter 13), the redemptive *persona* of substitutional suffering. The Catholic Stations of the Cross served this function as well. In praying serially at the fourteen symbols of Christ's suffering and death, men could relate their own pain and suffering to Christ and feel encouraged and ennobled to suffer as he did: with grace, dignity, and love.

The joymongers decided that this was all too morbid; we should focus on the Resurrection, they said, not on the Cross. Soon, the Stations came down from church walls, the devotion fell into disuse, and many men lost a beautiful rite that spoke deeply to them, that admitted and even celebrated the fact that life is a crucifixion in which spiritual greatness can be found. At issue here is the fact that a key element in classical masculine spirituality — suffering in atonement — was radically misconstrued simply as masochism and summarily dismissed.

Pastors ought once again to encourage prayerful devotions that relate to men's experiences. Older prayer forms such as the Stations still offer spiritual power and strength, and new forms are also possible. Moreover, men urgently need encouragement to develop personal prayer lives. Many fine books exist that offer valuable help in establishing the regular patterns and habits of prayer that men need to remain spiritually centered. One excellent example is De Mello's *Sadhana: A Way to God*.[7] Silly books that perpetuate cloying triviality also exist; lest they grow nauseated, men ought to be steered away from "magical mystical bears" that go "whee we wee all the way home."

6. Men's Discussion and Support Groups

The church is in an excellent position to help men understand themselves as they negotiate a host of challenges: midlife crises, career changes, growing children, failing physical capabilities, liberating wives, and so on. Parish buildings offer convenient meeting sites, while many on staff are highly trained in group dynamics, psychology, and social issues. At present, however, parish men's groups usually consist of little more than a raucous Monday Night Football contingent or a faithful cadre whose main purpose is to organize the annual spring grounds clean-up.

This picture is beginning to change. A few pastors are beginning to take tentative steps to identify male issues and find ways to form discussion and consciousness-raising groups of men ready and willing to explore such topics as male bonding, feminism at home and in the workplace, relationships with children, and so on.[8] Until recently, the danger existed that such discussion groups would eventually degenerate into little more than gripe sessions about feminism, women, and modern life in general. The growing literature of the men's movement, however, now has the capability of challenging men more profoundly, raising deeper questions, and pushing the discussion into much more fruitful spiritual territory. A growing library of books, cassettes, and videotapes by, for example, Robert Bly, Richard Rohr, or Robert Moore, can now launch provocative conversations on the topic of the masculine archetypes, the father-wound, the "naive male," the masculine mode of feeling, and so on. Church sponsorship of such groups would not only serve parish men in a valuable way, but provide an eye-opening and consciousness-raising experience for any pastors who might attend.

7. Church Reforms

All the measures discussed above relate to steps that individuals or local churches can take to enhance Christian masculine spirituality. In addition to these grassroots proposals, there are reforms and measures that only the larger church can initiate. The agenda of men's concerns for the Christian church might include the following proposals.

A. Church leaders ought officially to address men's issues with studies and analyses comparable to those that have been addressed to women's concerns. The U.S. Catholic bishops, for example, conducted extensive hearings and discussions in the preparation of a Pastoral Letter on women in the church entitled "One in Christ." A similar effort might alert the church leadership and membership as well to the equally urgent problems confronting men.

B. The problem of clericalism as it affects men's spirituality needs to be addressed. This problem is mentioned repeatedly in analyses of problems with both lay spirituality and women's issues in the church; it is a significant barrier to fully adult participation in the church both by women and men. In particular, the Catholic Church needs to confront the difficulties that a policy of mandatory celibacy presents not only to its priests, but to its laymen as well. The forced renunciation of sexual expressiveness as a condition for church ministry is both a scandal to Christian laymen and a frequent cause of scandal within the clergy itself. The presence of married clergy would not represent some trendy innovation of the twentieth century, but a return to the most ancient practice of the church, a convention still practiced in Greek Orthodox and Oriental Catholic rites.

C. The church needs to institute men's programs and courses in masculine spirituality in seminaries, theology schools, and other centers for the study of pastoral ministry; virtually nothing of this kind presently exists. Moreover, in the hundreds of programs and courses in feminist spirituality in these schools, church leaders need carefully to monitor the development of misandrist attitudes and policies that affect so negatively the dwindling number of male seminarians and ministerial students. Misandry must become as inappropriate in ecclesiastical settings as racism, misogyny, or anti-Semitism.

Concluding Comments

Most of this chapter relates to measures that the official church can take to develop an effective outreach to modern men. It would be unfortunate if the impression were given that men should therefore act passively in all this, that is, wait for the church to reach out to them. The opposite is true; realistically, men must reach out to the church first. To do that, they must take responsibility for their own spiritual lives. Men must become as aggressive and responsible in finding an appropriate church community as they would be in locating a well-built house or buying a dependable truck. Men must do their own spiritual work, and do it well. Part Two of this book offers just one method among many for unlocking the secrets of spirituality for men.

PART TWO

Masculine Archetypes
and the Bible

THE BIBLE IS MANY THINGS TO MANY PEOPLE: God's eternal law, the church's source of revelation, Israel's history book, a tome of spiritual reading and prayer. The second part of this present work, however, will treat the Bible in a new way: as a source-book of masculine spirituality. For the biblical myths and stories teach us wisely and eloquently about manhood: how it looks when it succeeds, and how it sometimes goes wrong. The difficulty, however, is helping modern men get access to this teaching.

The greatest obstacle to Bible reading for an educated and intelligent man of the late twentieth century is a yawning credibility gap: most of the biblical stories seem so filled with fabulous occurrences, fantastic miracles, and obvious myths that they can't be taken literally. So we won't take the stories literally. Instead, we shall read the Bible stories mythically, that is, as artistic expressions that tell truths about God and the human soul. Those readers acquainted with Joseph Campbell's compelling works on the relation of worldwide myth to the dynamics of the human psyche will find themselves on familiar ground here; they know that a genuine myth is not a falsehood about the world told by primitives, but a true story about the workings of God in the human soul told by geniuses. We shall read the Bible mythically, seeking its spiritual truths — not literally, in search of scientific or historical facts.

Several centuries of historical research, archaeological investigation, and literary criticism have demonstrated to anyone who is intellectually honest that the Bible is not a literal account of historical or scientific reality; attempts to force it into this role are artificial and strain credibility. The notion that the Bible must be historical or scientific to be true is a peculiarly Western concept with truly unfortunate results. On the one hand, some fundamentalists are so insistent upon proving the historicity of isolated biblical verses that they ignore the deeper meaning of the entire story that contains them; moreover, their attempts to explain biblical miracles scientifically are usually more difficult to believe than the original miracle stories themselves. On the other hand, many humanists commit an error very similar to the fundamentalists; scoffing at a miraculous narrative, they reject its deeper mythological meaning and cut themselves off from its psychological and spiritual wisdom.

Rejecting the literalist mistake, we shall read the Bible stories in a way very close to that employed by the early Church Fathers: allegorically and spiritually. With a sophistication that might surprise us moderns, the patristic exegetes in the first centuries of the Christian church knew that they could not read some biblical passages factually, but rather had to search beneath the literal text for the deeper, spiritual meaning it contained. Such a cultured method alerted the Fathers to the presence of "types" and "archetypes" in the narratives; for example, these early Christian theologians became adept at finding the spiritual archetype of Christ in Old Testament passages where he was not literally present.*

Similarly, our reading of Scripture will listen for the presence of the classic masculine archetypes in the old biblical stories and myths. If we free ourselves from the persistent literalist tendency to wonder whether a given event actually happened or a certain person historically existed, we shall free up our imagination to find in a story the Wildman, the Warrior, or the King. We shall then sense what that story is teaching us about the archetype, what it is telling us about ourselves as men, and, ultimately, how it is guiding us toward God.

---

* For a modern, Jungian treatment of the nature of archetypes, see Anthony Stevens, *Archetypes: A Natural History of the Self* (New York: Quill, 1983).

Chapter 5

Abraham: Patriarch and Pilgrim

Around the fifth century B.C.E., the Priestly editors of the Book of Genesis wove together three old literary sources that related differing versions of Israel's foundational myths and stories. Each of these documents — the Yahwist, the Elohist, and the Priestly sources — represented distinctive literary and theological interpretations of Israel's origins.[1] Despite their differences, however, each source shared a concern to preserve carefully the old stories about Abraham, the great mythical patriarch of the people of Israel. The resulting editorial blend, which we can read today in Genesis 12–25 (the "Abraham Cycle"), presents a wonderful narrative about a pilgrim's faith and a patriarch's love.

The biblical character named Abraham may never actually have lived; not a shred of independent literary or archaeological evidence exists that would place him in a known historical context. The name *Avraham* (which means "great father" or "patriarch" in Hebrew) suggests that the stories about him derive from the realm of myth and folktale. These Abraham stories probably originated among ancient Hebrew raconteurs who regaled their fellow tribesmen with campfire stories about their primordial ancestor — where he hailed from and how it was that he came to Canaan. At one level, the Abraham narratives thus informed the Hebrews about their wandering origins and how they came to dwell in a land called "promised." In another way, these old accounts taught values such as hospitality and virtues such as fidelity to God, even as they provided enjoyable entertainment. But at the deepest level, the Abraham stories created a mythos for the people of Israel that guided them through a brutal history right through to this day. For "Abraham" is a symbol of every Jew, and each Christian and Muslim offspring from his seed. His character is rich with archetypes of masculine spirituality, but we shall here contemplate only two. Abraham embodies the faith of the Pilgrim and the love of the Patriarch.

Abraham the Pilgrim

The Yahwist begins the story of Abraham with God's startling, bolt-out-of-the-blue command to the seventy-five-year-old man: "Leave your country, your family, and your father's house and go to the land that I will show you" (Gen 12:1).* No explanations here, and no apologies; Yahweh gives only a promise: "I will make of you a great nation, I will bless you and make your name a great blessing." Abraham obeyed Yahweh, and immediately left the sunny land of his golden retirement years to set off with his wife, Sarah, and nephew, Lot, in search of a promised land.

It is easy to dismiss Abraham's total obedience to God in the tale as the one-dimensional act of a cardboard biblical character. But let's enter into the story imaginatively a little and wonder: how could the old fellow leave the only place he had ever known, abandon the land for which he had labored his life long, and give up his Aramean retirement benefits just because a Voice claiming to be God told him to do so? Sheer obedience, after all, isn't quite enough when it comes to hearing voices; you've got to have something else working for you, too. What Abraham had going for him, despite his advanced age and great wealth, was a very active Pilgrim archetype.

Abraham possessed an unusual quality for a Middle Eastern patriarch: dynamic masculinity, which is the energy that feeds the Pilgrim. As we know, patriarchy in any culture easily becomes dreary and rigid: knowing all the angles and answering all the questions, laying down the law and punishing the wayward, brooking no opposition, refusing to be surprised, steadfastly avoiding anything new, and intending down to its last breath to force its ways on everyone else (for their own good, of course). We've all seen the rigid patriarch and the paralysis he creates in all those vulnerable to his rule: the desperate sigh of Willie Loman in *Death of a Salesman*, the frozen gaze of the Ayatollah Khomeini, or the cruel visage of Deng Xiou Peng, Butcher of Beijing. Part of the tragedy is that each of these men lived great and even heroic earlier lives before they ever took some secret personal decision to build the fences, lock the doors, and close the windows.

Somehow, Abraham overcame this shadow side of patriarchy; perhaps just watching his flocks and crops and the whole of nature all around taught him the fundamental truth discovered by the Greek philosopher Heraclitus: *panta rei!* ("everything is changing"). The sick Patriarch hates change; it threatens his self-identity and power. But everything, indeed, changes, and all the tanks, decrees, threats, oaths, and blandishments in the world can't stop it. The Pilgrim is the archetype of change, the figure who emerges in the psyche when it is time to move on, go with the flow, and seek a newer world.

---

* All biblical translations are my own.

When Yahweh's voice called, Abraham's inner Pilgrim flared into life; no grumbling resentment or knee-knocking timidity here, for the Pilgrim is the archetype that transforms a negative experience of loss into a positive opportunity for change. But it takes the most gracious of human virtues — humility — to do it. Every pilgrim tacitly admits, as he moves on to any "promised land," that he never really did have it all together in Egypt. Every time the Pilgrim is evoked in the psyche of a man, he acknowledges that the answers are yet to be given and that he is open to change. This humility is the endearing human quality the Second Vatican Council had in mind when it called Catholicism a "Pilgrim Church," a community still seeking God and humbly open to change.[2]

When a man gets access to his interior Pilgrim, he thereby conjures up in himself the virtue of hope. Hope is not to be confused here with optimism, nor is it wishful thinking. Hope is that complex of courage, trust, and risk-taking that creates its own promising new future in self-fulfilling prophecy; hope, as Péguy tells us, is "that which is not yet, but *will* be." Abraham left Haran in that kind of hope, ready for newness, open to opportunity, and certain of God's blessing. Yahweh could not refuse the old man's vote of confidence; bless him he did.

That Pilgrim Soul in You

Perhaps the attitude most endemic to middle-aged and older men today is malaise, that quiet despair that's seen it all and expects no change for the better, that grows grimly comfortable in its ruts, and that confuses naiveté with hope. Something there is that wants to keep such men safely and quietly desperate; though locked in mental and emotional prisons, their paychecks keep coming, their taxes get paid, and dinner gets brought home. Pervasive economic and familial pressures are at work here to keep the Old Workhorse in his traces, and as long as he's happy with a little golf and NFL, who's to care that he's secretly brain-dead and soul-starved?

As a stimulus to growth out of this malaise, one might try the exercise of imagining one's own inner Pilgrim, talk to him, and ask if he can still remember his deepest desires and childhood dreams.[3] One might ask, what does he really want, what is he looking for, and where does he need to go? What changes does he seek? Does he simply want to learn to play the piano or take up tap-dancing? Or are deeper needs at work here, long suppressed desires to work in a more creative job or to live a rich spiritual life again? The Pilgrim knows the answers and the way out. And when the old voices say, "You can't get there from here," old Abraham might have something to share: "Life," he says, "just *begins* at seventy-five!"

Whether old or young, we ignore our inner Pilgrim only at great risk to our souls. For the Pilgrim is the archetype of spiritual movement without which we stagnate, ossify, and die. The Pilgrim is the archetype of journey, that part of us that possesses a spiritual road map unavailable to the conscious mind. So it is that the Pilgrim often starts us out in one direction, only to lead us later to something entirely unexpected. Kevin Costner's character in *Field of Dreams* obeyed this Pilgrim voice ("if you build it, he will come"), thinking to get a baseball diamond and finding his father as well; Ignatius of Loyola set out for adventure in Jerusalem, and founded the Jesuit order;[4] Saul set out for lost asses, and found a kingdom instead (1 Sam 9–10).

Abraham the Patriarch

We mustn't, of course, make Abraham out to be a Mesopotamian Walter Mitty or an Aramean flibbertigibbet: he was a *patriarch* after all. That means that he had to carry a tremendous burden of responsibility in caring for his extended family. Today this isn't as difficult, but for a patriarch of the socially outcast Hebrew people thousands of years ago, it was a lonely task. There was little other authority or social support to lean on, no real government, no church, no schools, no courts, no therapists, and no police. Abraham as the father of the clan had to do it all: educate the children, judge disputes, offer worship, give spiritual comfort, and defend the family — plus take the "heat" for his decisions all by himself.

Today the idea of being a Patriarch is extremely unpopular since the word connotes only *rigid* patriarchy and male dominance. That is unfortunate, because this archetype in a man can be a very generous and gracious one. A man potentiates this archetype in himself whenever he takes responsibility for a group of people as if he were the biological, caring father of each person. One of the great tragedies of our society is that fewer and fewer men are able to get access to this archetype, and our whole culture is the poorer for it.

Not everyone has a father. And not everyone who does have a father has a good one; a person in our culture who enjoys the constant interest, care, and blessing of his father is a truly rare and very fortunate individual. So the Patriarch is the archetype in the masculine psyche that offers to father those who are not so fortunate, who are orphaned or lost or helpless or who need guidance and wise direction. It seems that this archetypal *persona* compensates psychically for humanity's tragic losses of the biological father through death, illness, and moral failure.

Fathering did not come very easily or naturally to men. Primitive males may have paid little attention to the practice, so that the fatherly skills that did develop in culture took many millennia and much painstaking spiritual effort to evolve; in many ways, the Bible is highly responsible for inculcating these values.[5] Even today, the fathering skill is tenuous; it almost always disappears in men ravaged by psychological or social problems, much to the devastation of their children. The ensuing consequences to society are incalculable: single-parent families, juvenile delinquency, and a host of psychological problems in the youth. Yet some men are blessed with an abundance of love and fatherly care; they are able to take paternal interest not only in their own children but in other people as well. When they tap into their Patriarch, they might experience concern for fatherless or needy youths; the Big Brother program, the Boy Scouts, or the Save the Children foundation are outgrowths of this care. One friend of mine spends his Saturdays at a home for HIV-positive babies, playing, hugging, and generally giving them the "manhandling" they need to stay well. Some men express their patriarchal love as coaches, others as teachers, still others as mentors. Priests and ministers often display this archetype; in the Catholic Church, the title "Father" recognizes the personal spiritual care and interest that the people hope to find in their priest.

A few men have even extended their fatherly care to humanity as a whole. One such man was Giuseppe Roncalli, better known as Pope John XXIII. His autobiography, entitled *The Journal of a Soul*, reveals him to be a deeply traditional, even staunch conservative, and a pious priest in the Italian Catholic mold. Educated during the Modernist reaction to new theological ideas, he nevertheless retained an open mind to the trends that swirled around him. The cardinals who elected him pope in 1958 expected the aged and rotund pontiff to serve as a benign care-taker until a suitable successor should appear. But John had found ways to leave his windows open, and completely unexpectedly the Spirit blew in. He heard an inner Voice that told him, in effect, "Get up, and move the church to a land I will show you!" Shocking his curial advisors, he convened the Second Vatican Council, which refreshed the Catholic Church and sent it on a new and exciting path of change. But John also lived and breathed patriarchal openness in his personal life as pope. He resolutely reached out with a warm heart and smiling face to those who were different: to Communists, to prisoners and prostitutes, to Protestants, and to Jews. As he lay dying in early 1963, the whole world looked to his sickbed with love and compassion: they had found in "Good Pope John" one who knew what it meant to father, though he had no biological children of his own.

Patriarchal Resolve and Magnanimity

The true patriarch expresses his love for the people in his care with two special qualities: resolve and magnanimity. The first virtue is that rare trait of clarity and decisiveness; Abraham repeatedly showed this feature in his resolute obedience to the voice of his God. For despite all the damage that rigid patriarchs do in running roughshod over people, the *refusal to lead*, to decide, and to take responsibility probably causes as much harm. To lead a family, a church, or a company is a difficult task, usually filled with mistakes; not to lead is a much worse mistake. Who among us has not suffered under leaders who dither when they should decide, who "pass the buck," who refer us to another agency or pass our case on to a committee for further study? Not the Patriarch; he decides what is best for those under his care, and takes the heat. So, too, Abraham displayed the qualities of decisiveness, resolve, and responsibility for his tribe; small wonder Yahweh chose him to bless Israel, to model faith, and to serve as the biblical model of the wise Patriarch.

The stories of Abraham, written early in Israel's youth in the halcyon days of national confidence, also exemplify what Israel most admired in a man and what it most wanted to be as a nation: great of spirit, generous, and a blessing of peace for everyone.[6] So it is that, except for a brief dust-up with some nasty kings who kidnapped Lot (Gen 14), Abraham continually exhibited generosity and reconciliation to all his new neighbors in Canaan.

We call such a virtue "magnanimity," which literally means to have a "great *animus*," and it is a particularly admirable quality in a healthy man. We all know small-minded and threatened individuals; unfortunately, we continually run into these people and their petty kingdoms at work, in the church, and at city hall. We have to jump through their hoops and play their games until they've exacted their pound of flesh, humiliated us, and gotten to feel temporarily powerful. A truly "great spirit," however, doesn't act that way. He doesn't have to advertise his greatness — he's already got it, in the form of a big heart. This is the kind of man known in the Jewish tradition as a *mensch* (Yiddish: "man"), a word that means a truly human man of great generosity and wisdom.[7] So it was with Abraham; on arrival in Canaan he promptly offered his nephew, Lot (who is really like the son Abraham didn't yet have), his choice of pasture lands (Gen 13). Lot chose the Jordan plain, and Yahweh, not to be outdone in generosity, immediately promised Abraham and his descendants the whole remaining land of Canaan.

Abraham's magnanimity also shows up as classic Near Eastern hospitality when he entertained three mysterious visitors (Gen 18). Now, it is a risky thing to welcome strangers; how many of us would bring home a street person or pick up a hitchhiker? But by feeding vulnerable travellers and shielding them from the midday sun, Abraham temporarily adopts the foreigners as sons, an attribute we call *kindness*, which literally means to treat others as one's own *kinder* (German: "children"). How different from our modern niggardly narrowness, which stiffs the homeless and blames the down-and-out! The surprise, of course, is that the strange visitors are angels of God! Yahweh is not unmoved by this act of kindness to his messengers. Abraham's patriarchal largesse, his willingness to treat the homeless as sons, wins a most outrageously unexpected promise from the Lord: at long last, a son!

Perhaps the most magnanimous thing Abraham ever did, however, involved a heated argument with God. Yahweh had decided to destroy Sodom and Gomorrah, cities of infamous cruelty to strangers. But when Abraham got wind of this, he immediately began to remonstrate with Yahweh on behalf of the few righteous who might live in the city (Gen 18). In a monumental Oriental bargaining session, Abraham audaciously bartered with the Lord: for fifty righteous men, would Yahweh spare the city? For forty-five? Surely forty? Cunningly, Abraham haggled and dickered his way down to God's bottom line: for ten just men — last offer — Yahweh would pardon Sodom.

Why would Abraham risk his relationship with Yahweh — look a gift horse in the mouth — so quickly after he'd just won the promise of a longed-for son? Because no matter his own needs, a man in touch with the genuine archetype of Patriarch feels accountable for everyone. Genuine patriarchal responsibility is a kind of *noblesse oblige*, that now old-fashioned and quaint notion that from those to whom much is given, much is expected. This magnanimity is disappearing rapidly among American patriarchs. Only a generation ago, high-born clans such as the Roosevelts, the Kennedys, and the Rockefellers led the way not only in financial gifts to charity, but in concrete political and social actions on behalf of racial justice and economic welfare. What is even more endearing, however, is not rich men who are generous, but poor and humble men like Abraham who give to others. In such men, *noblesse oblige* derives, not from their bank accounts or high social status, but from a great soul.

I met old Father Horace McKenna, S.J., on a hot Washington evening in the summer of 1972. As we sat in his tiny and cluttered room, he proved a captivating conversationalist, though a frustrating one. Every so often, in the middle of a great story, a poor or homeless person would show up at the door looking for a handout. Horace would rise, greet the person warmly, and get him something to eat. Horace wasn't able to sleep much for this reason; the poor would come even in the middle of the night. By day, he could be seen careering around D.C. in his battered car in order to accompany someone to an intimidating agency, or to buttonhole a Congressman on behalf of a housing project (one of which bears his name in the city today). When anyone — whether that was a local drug pusher, a city councilman, or the archbishop of Washington — bullied one of his kindred, Horace fought him. As a result of this courage, but especially because of the look of warm kindness in his eyes, the small and the great alike respectfully called him "Father," and a father indeed he was. Horace has been gone many years now, but people in Washington still remember, with kindness, their "patriarch of the poor." Abraham would have liked him, too.

Abraham's Mistake: Ishmael

One of the best things about Old Testament stories is that they were written before the days of phony religious piety and public relations "spin-control." The biblical stories, fortunately, are primitive enough to include a look at the shadow of each important character. That is a big help to modern people; it gives us a chance to look at the whole person, learn from his mistakes, and perhaps admit our own a little more easily. There is something humbly comforting in knowing that people every bit as human as ourselves "made the Bible." Abraham is no exception.

Very late in his life, God presented the patriarch with two sons, Ishmael and Isaac. Now, if we truly believe in God's providence, we know that God does not bless us — or test us — until we are ready. It was now time for Abraham, the man never too old to change, to learn how to father his *own* sons. The experience would bring him both failure and success, pain and joy. For it turns out that not every "Great Father" is a good father! The shadow side of the good Patriarch, it seems, is that in treating so many so kindly, he gives his own kin short shrift. The Sky Father, so concerned with the world at large, sometimes can't come down to earth to help his own sons.[8]

The story of Abraham's firstborn, Ishmael, is a poignant, even bitter example of this problem. Sarah, in her barren old-age despair, asked Abraham to father a child by her slave-girl Hagar, and the old man agreed. That was one mistake; the resulting pregnancy predictably caused explosive jealousy and resentment between the two women (Gen 16). Abraham nevertheless raised his son, feeling that God had heard his desire for a child (*yishmael* = "God heard"). Yet one senses here the beginnings of a dark disruptiveness in the family, what modern psychologists call a dysfunction. In retrospect (how easy it is for *us* to realize this sort of thing so clearly), we see that Ishmael was conceived not out of love, but out of the combined manipulations of Sarah, machinations of Hagar, and desperation of Abraham. Most of us come into the world in the midst of messes such as these, but that doesn't lessen the pain as we watch the upbringing of wounded little Ishmael.

Even in the womb, a child can sense turmoil and disorder in his mother; his later childhood experiences of family strife then undermine any sense of security and well-being, and at a deep unconscious level the child will begin to feel, "I'm a mistake, I'm not really wanted, I'm all wrong." And eventually, some event will confirm his worst suspicions and reveal the family's festering dysfunction for all to see. The inevitable blow-up occurred in the Abraham family when Ishmael was fourteen, after Sarah miraculously bore her own son, Isaac. The birth touched off a family power struggle: now each woman had a child, and only one could inherit the patrimony. The jealous Sarah insisted that Abraham drive off Hagar and her son Ishmael; tragically, the old man weakly caved into her cruel demand. Strangers he welcomes, sinners he tries to save — but what of his own son? Providing Hagar and Ishmael with some bread and water, Abraham abandoned them in the desert of Beersheba.

God the Father heard Ishmael's cries and saved the boy and his mother. The story tells us that Ishmael went on to make his home in the desert and became an expert bowman and father of a great nation — the Arabs. But though young Ishmael survived and prospered, he became a wild-ass of a man, set against everyone, and carrying with him forever a "father-wound" that mythically lives to this day in the animosity between Arab and Jew. A father's mistakes last a very long time, indeed.

Few of us grow up without a father-wound of some kind, and the type inflicted on Ishmael — father neglect — is extremely common today. Every boy needs to relate to a father who will give him a permanent sense of security, a psychic safe-place of sureness and strength that tells him that he belongs, that he is wanted, and that he will make it with a little work. Every boy needs to know that his father is on his side, pulling for him, giving him paternal energy so that whatever he does, he knows he can succeed. If the boy does not receive such assurance from his father, he cannot recreate a firm psychic center within himself, and he is left with a terrible lack of self-esteem and confidence. This may cause him to become passive and weak or to overcompensate by becoming hyper-macho and wild, which is what happened to Ishmael.

Though Abraham wanted a son, he didn't take his fatherhood of the child seriously enough. As the jealousy between his wives developed, Abraham made the mistake of failing to be patriarchal enough! That is, he absconded from his duties and became a typical Sky Father, the role in which a man attends only to the great affairs of the world and the family, but leaves the direct parenting of the children to the woman — an arrangement that can work if the wife doesn't happen to be neurotic. Many men do this; feeling inadequate or afraid in the parenting role and afraid to make a mistake, they absent themselves emotionally and physically from their children — and make a much greater mistake.

And so Ishmael became a brawler and a raider (Gen 16:12), taking out Abraham's abandonment of him on everyone else as he ranged across the desert of Paran stalking prey. Abandon a child, and he will always make someone else pay for it. Our society is spawning such desperados like crazy, from the inner city to the suburbs. Many of these young men are literally abandoned by fathers who, for a variety of reasons, can't cope and won't father. Other youths are psychically deserted; though their father may reside in the house and pay the bills on time, he is not spiritually present. Their wild little Ishmaels, desperate to receive authentic father energy, get instead the ersatz masculinity of Dirty Harry, Conan, or Rambo on the cheap; where psychic holes develop, demons rush in. Unfathered and uninitiated, they go "wilding" in Central Park, slam-dancing in Punkville, and gay-bashing in the Castro. Wounded, they wound back.

The Sacrifice of Isaac

If the tale of Ishmael reveals one kind of father-wound, the story of Isaac relates an even more extraordinary account about another kind of wound. Abraham really wanted Isaac; his very name (*yitzchak:* "he laughed") suggests the old man's joy on hearing the miraculous news of his son's birth. Or at least Abraham *consciously thought* he wanted Isaac. But a terrible truth would emerge from an incident in Isaac's childhood that bespoke the dark side of this father's love, a side many young men experience but cannot face consciously.

That is why we have myths. Some truths can't be told directly; they are too awful and too mysterious. So they are related covertly in stories that seem to be about people who lived long ago in faraway lands; actually, they are about us. Such is the case with the myth of the sacrifice of Isaac (Gen 22), one of the most puzzling and awesome stories in the Bible.[9] The account opens with God ordering Abraham to take his dearly beloved son Isaac and sacrifice him as a holocaust (burnt offering) on the holy mountain Moriah. Without visible emotion or objection, Abraham dutifully takes the boy on the journey and prepares to carry out the deed. Only at the last minute does an angel of Yahweh intervene and stop the dreadful act, saving Isaac and blessing Abraham for his obedience.

This myth reveals a truth so painful that most men would deny it out of hand: there exists in many fathers a murderous unconscious hostility toward their sons. The Greeks expressed this primordial psychic reality in the myth of Uranus, which relates how the first sky god began to kill his own offspring. His son Cronus escaped but, in turn, swallowed each of *his* children except Zeus, who later overcame Cronus and became high god over the whole sky. This theme appears elsewhere repeatedly, whether in ancient times in the story of Laius, who left his bound son Odysseus to die of exposure in the mountains, or in the modern *Star Wars* trilogy, where Darth Vader murderously pursues his son Luke Skywalker.

What is coming to mythical expression here? Psychologically speaking, it appears that children, especially sons, can present a tremendous unconscious threat to a father, whether as competitors for the attention of the wife, as new limitations on his freedom, or as an appalling drain on his paycheck. A son may also represent the threat of future competition to a father or a reminder of his own forgotten dreams and hopes.[10] The father, in turn, can come to resent secretly his consciously "beloved" son; this paternal hostility usually erupts as physical child abuse. Ironically, the shocking experience of physical abuse contains an element of redemption; so clearly pathological and wrong is the practice that the father (sometimes at the behest of civil authorities) can be forced to confront his feelings consciously in psychological treatment.

More often, however, father-son tensions lie festering in the psyche, wreaking hidden damage. The father's hostility then gets justified as corporal "discipline" for the boy, or he is unaccountably tough on the son, verbally criticizing him at every opportunity. Psychologists and counselors tell us that many American men bear these father-wounds all through their lives, never understanding them much less finding healing with their fathers. The story of Abraham and Isaac is about such a relationship. We can only guess at the source of Abraham's inner hostility to his son; can it be that he unwittingly and unfairly resented Isaac for supplanting Ishmael? Could his latent murderous animosity toward Isaac even represent a way of evening the score with Sarah for her manipulations? The heart in its darkness reasons in such ways. Whatever its source, Abraham's subliminal antagonism toward Isaac surfaced in an extremely dangerous form, the most iron-clad justification for cruelty and violence ever devised: religion. "God" told him to kill the boy!

No human enterprise possesses more potential for disguising and justifying the dark impulses of the human heart than religion.[11] The so-called voice of God has been used as a divinely sanctioned rationale for the worst outrages of the human experience; who is to question its commands? Who is to question this Holy War or that Inquisition, this crackdown or that Crusade, when it is soaked in holy water and beclouded by incense? And not just institutions use God's name to cover their atrocities; individuals do, too.

So it was that Abraham, dazed and in a mental fog, obeys the demonic "voice" of his own unconscious hostility as if it were God's; with chilling dispatch he prepares Isaac for the grisly holocaust. Who will stop him? He's a patriarch, after all. Only another Voice can, this one carrying a message from Abraham's deepest Self and from the heart of the universe: "Do not lift your hand against the boy," the angel said. Ah, but which voice is the demon and which the angel? That is a great problem for a discernment of spirits even today. Perhaps Abraham's greatness lies in perceiving, even then in those primordial days loud with inner voices, the true message that God was yet to reveal to Israel: "I desire love, not sacrifice" (Hos 6:6). Nothing on earth could justify murder. And so Abraham obeyed the angel; Isaac was spared.

Modern men might rightly shake their heads at the crazy things people do in the name of God. That is partly because few of us take God — or religion — very seriously anymore; not as seriously as Abraham, in any case. But before we criticize Abraham too quickly, we might ask ourselves a pungent question: for what modern deities do *we* sacrifice our sons? Do not modern fathers simply update the ancient practice of child sacrifice with an absolute holocaust to a new and more terrible god named Career? Modern men can garb this deity in clothes as sacrosanct as ever cloaked a primitive idol and offer unto it acts of abject obeisance that would make Jehovah blanch: long days without Sabbath-rest, total dedication, unquestioned obedience, and limitless service. A "voice" says, of course, that all this work is for the family and the children, after all; besides, there is always "quality time" with the son. But however much a father might believe such Yuppie claptrap, his spiritually abandoned son won't buy it. In the painful honesty of youth, the boy will know full well that he has been sacrificed by his father at the High Altar of American Business.

At least Abraham let the angel wake him from his trance, his knife wielded threateningly over his lovely Isaac, in time to see precisely what he was about to do. As if chastened by this close encounter with demons and angels, Abraham never again acts so precipitously; enough for him to purchase a tomb and to secure his son a wife — an act of true patriarchal care in that age. As for Isaac, who can know how deeply wounded he was by his father's latent hostility and the near brush with death on Moriah? We can only suggest this: just as one wounded child may go wild, like Ishmael, so another may live passively and weakly, too damaged to accomplish much. Isaac was like that. About all the Bible tells us about Isaac is that Abraham married him off to the remarkable and redoubtable Rebekah and that she helped trick him into blessing the wrong son: Jacob, who would become Israel.

Chapter 6

Moses: Warrior and Magician

The greatest figure of the Old Testament is Moses, liberator of the Hebrews and giver of Law to Israel. The long story of Moses (Exodus–Deuteronomy) relates many heroic moments in the life of this key biblical character; of special interest to us here is the story of the confrontation with Pharaoh that triggered the escape of the Hebrews from Egypt. The description of Moses in the Exodus story involves two very important masculine archetypes: the Warrior and the Magician.

The Moses of History and Legend

There is good reason to think that the biblical character named Moshe actually existed, however heavily invested in myth, legend, and folktale that the narratives about him may be. One hint of his historical existence is that biblical literature is stamped with his presence; each Pentateuchal source relates his story, and the prophets, historical books, and even wisdom literature often refer to him. Two events associated with Moses — Exodus and the desert wandering — are theologically central to the whole Jewish tradition and are celebrated every spring in the joyous Passover Seder.[1] Moreover, these biblical events are also historically plausible; we know, for example, that in the Late Bronze Age Egyptian forces campaigned regularly into their Canaanite colonies, where they would capture bands of prisoners and bring them back to Egypt to work as slaves on state building projects.[2] It is entirely possible that the historical Moses led gangs of these captives in a slave revolt in Egypt, whence they escaped into the Sinai desert and eventually made their way back to their Hebrew villages high in the Canaanite hill country. It is also likely that Moses brought back to the Hebrews in Canaan the cult of the war god Yahweh, a deity worshipped in the Sinai and Midian desert in this era.

Moses may have converted to the warlike Yahweh-religion amid fellow captives in Egyptian labor camps or in transit to Canaan through the Sinai wilderness. His introduction of Yahwism to Canaan proved a revolutionary development both politically and theologically. The previous deity of the Hebrews was the sky god Elohim, a wonderful, patriarchal old god who mythically ruled the world from his throne on the cosmic mountain.[3] The problem with Elohim, like many sky gods, was that he had become otiose, that is, he was so busy running the universe (mythically speaking) that he didn't seem to have time to get involved in the everyday life of the Hebrews. This is a common religious phenomenon, even today; many people assume that God is much too busy for them. In this theological climate, people also think that God does not really care about their concrete economic and political problems. God is too "above it all."

Not Yahweh! In the earliest myths, Yahweh roars out of Sinai as a war deity, a storm god who blew gusts from his flaring nostrils, sharpened his lightning shafts, flexed his outstretched right arm, and let his enemies have it right between the eyes; "Yahweh is a Warrior!" Exodus 15:4 joyously exclaims. Moreover, Yahweh cared about the little people, especially folks like the Hebrews whom everyone else rejected. Yahweh fought for the poor, raised up the lowly, and protected widows, orphans, and strangers. He wanted just two things in return from his people. First, he jealously insisted on being their *only* God (Ex 20:2); Yahweh was not about to go into war only to be jilted later for some passing deity! Second, Yahweh demanded justice among the people. That meant that Israelites were themselves to give special care for the weak and vulnerable in their society: the widows, the orphans, and the poor (Ex 22:20–27). It meant also an attempt to live with one another in a society radically different from that of Egypt or any of the empires that came and went in that region: no kings (1 Sam 8:5–9), no capitalism (Deut 23:20), no exploitation of the poor (Ex 22:24), no killing, coveting, or stealing (Ex 20:13–17). Yahweh wanted his people to share their goods with one another and to live in equality and justice together. Most surprising of all, especially being a war god and all, Yahweh wanted his people to rely on *his* military abilities — not their own. His people would have to let Yahweh do their fighting for them (Deut 7:17–24).

This is the God whom Moses came to worship and under whose worship he banded his fellow slaves together as they escaped from Egypt, and this is the religion his followers spread among the Hebrews in the Canaanite hill country. The Yahweh preachers proclaimed there a kind of Late Bronze Age "good news" to the poor and oppressed Hebrews: Yahweh *is* Elohim! The great God of the universe is actually one and the same with Yahweh, who freed us from bondage in Egypt! He will fight for us! He will be our God, and we will be his people![4]

Victims in Bondage

It is not surprising that the founder of a war religion should himself be a warrior. The old stories tell us that Moses' faith was forged in the crucible of Egypt, a place Hebrew legend remembered as a rich land of opportunity — unless you happened to be a Hebrew.[5] If you didn't belong to the master race of Egypt, you didn't have any more rights than a farm animal. And that's how the Egyptian overlords treated their migrant workers, cruelly beating them and exploiting their labor. Now the amazing thing about racist oppressors is that, though they seem to hold all the cards legally, economically, and militarily, they are often quite terrified of their slaves (Ex 1:8–14). So Pharaoh ordered the Hebrews to work harder in order to break their spirit. As they play tennis and golf at the Big House, Pharaohs like to complain how lazy the poor are.

It is no surprise that the Hebrews only grew stronger, more resistant, and more numerous the more Pharaoh oppressed them. The poor have a marvelous ability to endure and to prevail the best ways they know how, one of which is having lots of children. So Pharaoh ordered the death of all the male Hebrew babies (Ex 1:16). That's a noteworthy detail in the Exodus story: oppressors are always interested in undermining the masculinity of the oppressed. Nothing suits a pharaoh more than slaves who can't get access to manliness, who can't find the Warrior energy. Better to rule Victims who complain loudly, whine convincingly, and win everyone's pity, but then shuffle off to work obediently every morning to the brick factories.

And how the Hebrews complained! They groaned and cried out for help from the depths of slavery in voices that reached the throne of God, who remembered his promise to Abraham (Ex 2:23–25). In their despair, the Israelites were ideal candidates for the rhetoric of *ressentiment*. They could rightly blame just about everyone else for their problems, justly accuse the socio-economic system of inequity, and never have to do anything about it. As Victims, they could not only claim innocence, but moral superiority over their oppressors. That is the payoff: in exchange for their slave labors, Victims get to be wronged but righteous — *"we* would never hurt anyone or oppress somebody else, not *us"* — the perfect passive-aggressive strategy. But instead of righteously "pissing and moaning," the Hebrews decided to cry out for help. Otherwise, the Hebrews would still be in Egypt slaving away today, locked in oppression but commanding the moral high ground. Fortunately, Yahweh broke through all the righteous self-pity and answered their prayer: he sent them a Warrior.

The Warrior and His Shadow

The Warrior is one of the most important archetypes in masculine spirituality and a central male role in virtually every society since Paleolithic times, when the paradigm originated as an outgrowth of the hunter's role. Eventual development of warrior culture, complete with its own mythology, rituals, ethics, art, and religion, indicates the dominance of this male task throughout subsequent human history. This centrality has proved both a blessing and a curse. The perversion of the Warrior archetype is surely the greatest single affliction to plague our planet throughout history right to this moment while, ironically, the most effective antidote to this sickness has proved to be none other than the healthy development of the same Warrior archetype.

Yet warring is not only an occupation of great armies set off against one another across the trenches. It has become the masculine psychological paradigm for opposition to every evil: we battle disease, attack problems, combat drugs, struggle with ignorance, fight fires, and make war on poverty. Over the millennia, the Warrior has become in the collective unconscious the archetype of resistance to evil in its myriad forms; lauded by poems, songs, and stories, celebrated and sanctified by rituals, and blessed by the gods, the Warrior has come to epitomize the noblest qualities of masculinity: bravery, self-sacrifice, stamina, skill, and heroic detachment.

Today, no male archetype is under greater attack than the Warrior; in some intellectual circles the type is viewed solely as a dangerous and destructive quality of males.[6] There is an element of truth to this sentiment. The tremendous masculine psychic force of the Warrior archetype is an almost irresistible magnet for emotionally wounded men unsure of their own importance, value, and maleness. This is so at one extreme for society's losers, uninitiated youths who can find self-respect only by wearing the insignia of the Bloods or the uniform of the Crips. Though they justify shootings of rival gang members as righteous retaliation or protection of the neighborhood, in reality the Urban Warrior is getting cheap and quick access to the heaviest masculine symbol available: the sword; I kill, therefore I am.

This same phenomenon also holds for some of the most powerful men in our country. Association with the sheer psychic weight of the Warrior archetype is a well-known route to power and prestige for vacuous political hacks who can't otherwise do anything constructive. These are the armchair generals who rattle their sabers, always demand the military option, propose surgical strikes, and generally counsel us to "get tough" — by sending *other* people off to war. The fact that many of these politicians (Ronald Reagan, Pat Robertson, Dan Quayle) very successfully avoided actual combat when the opportunity arose in their own lives gives rise to the bitter description of them as "war wimps."

Whether exploited by desperate kids or slick politicians, the Warrior archetype has proved itself a goldmine of psychic power and symbolism. And as long as most of us are so easily enchanted by the false lore of the Warrior, we are also susceptible to its manipulation and exploitation by every tinhorn dictator, sleazy politician, and ne'er-do-well street thug that comes down the pike. Herein lies the great paradox. As long as weak, sick, and evil men cloak themselves in the aura of the Warrior archetype for their own selfish purposes, good men must become warriors to stop them; there is no alternative. Bad men succeed only when good men do nothing.

That is one reason the disavowal of the Warrior is so dangerous. There is no other psychic choice for a man moved to oppose injustice and evil than to find access to his interior Warrior; even the greatest exponents of nonviolent resistance — Mohandas Gandhi and Martin Luther King, Jr. — operated under this paradigm. In the face of evil, the psychic alternative to the Warrior is not the Peacemaker (who himself is a kind of Warrior, though without violence), but the passive Victim, an increasingly common and unhealthy archetype in our culture. As modern society eschews the Warrior, it begins to enshrine its opposite, the Victim personality type full of indignant resentment and brimming with righteous outrage. The rhetoric of victimization fills the air; in liberal circles, political discourse is becoming a contest over who has suffered more, who is the most disadvantaged, and who is the most to be pitied. It almost seems that the disappearance of the Warrior archetype from the psyche causes a physiological change in the nasal passages and larynx called whining. That is increasingly the sound that political liberals make; only a generation or two ago, leftist social reform movements readily accessed the Warrior's energy. Being a liberal once meant struggling for labor unions, championing civil rights, attacking class injustices, fighting for the little man — and *enjoying* it.[7] Today most liberals don't bellow at injustice like a Warrior, they whine at how unfair it all is. Small wonder fewer and fewer American men identify themselves as such anymore.

The Warrior in a Man

The Warrior archetype also has profound importance in individual men's lives. Its psychic importance extends to at least three levels. The first is the most obvious: it is the Warrior who materializes in those rare moments when our life and safety — or that of those around us — falls into imminent jeopardy. The academic who ridicules Warrior Men in his books still dials the police warriors at 911 when a burglar stalks his house. There are times when we need immediate access to that *persona* that knows how to defend himself physically and isn't too afraid or too guilty to do it.

At another level, the Warrior plays an important role in our psychic lives. Every day we encounter people who invade our space, violate our rights, infringe on our privacy, and nose into our business. As Robert Bly suggests, our interior Warrior is the protector of our psychic boundaries; without him we are constantly victimized and suffer indignities great and small. Hardly a day goes by that we don't need to draw the Warrior's sword and flash it in the face of this busybody or that boor, this rude waiter or that prying relative. Note with Bly that the sword rarely has to be *used* in these kinds of circumstances; it is usually sufficient just to *show* it in order to indicate where our boundaries are.

At the deepest spiritual level, the Warrior is the archetype that marshals our psychic and physical energies to do the tasks that must be done. It is the paradigm of emotional resolve and mental stamina, technical skill and vocational competence. All of us experience competing claims for our best time and energy, and all of us get tired. But the Warrior in us battles on toward the goal, mobilizing our resources to accomplish the task at hand. Therapist Robert Moore suggests that behind every creative artist, competent author, or successful student there is an active Warrior at work who recognizes transcendent value and relativizes temporary needs or immediate demands.[8]

There are many hazards in this archetype. Anyone who has ever come off the sidelines to fight a battle knows that warrioring is dangerous not only because of the damage the enemy can do to the Warrior, but the harm the Warrior can do to himself. If this archetype possesses an individual, we have the compulsive workaholic who can't play, the isolated loner who can't relate, or the burnt-out Crusader who can't choose his battles. Clearly each person who takes part in the archetype needs to learn its problems and limitations as well as its strengths. That is why we have stories — to introduce us to the holy warriors of our spiritual tradition in order to learn *what* to fight, *whom* to fight, and *how* to fight. We can find many such Warriors in the Bible; none is greater than Moses.

Moses the Warrior

The story of baby Moses' survival is a wonderful tale of a compassionate conspiracy between the Hebrew and Egyptian women to save the boy (Ex 2:1–10); the best laid plans of pharaohs great and small are often sidetracked by the machinations of such underlings who still have souls. Though the boy was raised as an Egyptian, the story tells us nothing of his upbringing. When at last he appears as a grown man, however, it is immediately obvious that though Moses feels compassion like a slave, he still acts like a pharaoh, not a true Warrior. We must remember that to this point in the story of Israel, the Hebrews had practically no experience as fighters and knew virtually nothing of warrioring.[9] It will take Moses awhile to learn, and Yahweh himself will have to teach him.

Observing a foreman strike a Hebrew slave, Moses grew angry and stealthily killed the man (Ex 2:11–15). It was the first and last time he would ever directly kill an Egyptian. When his deed was discovered, the coward Moses fled to the desert, to the land of Midian.

Those who would be Warriors are charged with certain sacred obligations, recognized in almost every culture. The first is never to act violently out of blind anger or revenge; a genuine Warrior acts deliberately and with a strategy. The Japanese relate a story about a samurai who broke off his battle with a rival warlord because the man spit in his face; the samurai could not honorably kill the man with anger in his own heart. The second obligation is to take full responsibility for one's actions, up to and including death. Moses' sneak attack on the Egyptian simply mirrored the injustice and cowardice of his enemy, something a thug or terrorist would do — not a Warrior. Ethical considerations of this kind were once fostered in educated and initiated warriors, creating the knight's code of personal honor, noble restraint, magnanimity to defeated rivals, and individual humility for one's deeds.

Yahweh Goes to War

All seemed lost to Moses as he hooked up in the desert with the family of Jethro, a priest of Midian. We can only guess what went through Moses' mind as he wandered the wadis, tending his measly sheep. Perhaps the noonday desert devils stoked his isolation into a resentful determination never to get involved again: "It only gets you in trouble." Perhaps the demons harped on a sense of failure: "You coward, safe here while your people groan in slavery!" We can only guess at the depth of Moses' alienation, but one hint of it is that he called his new son Gershom (*ger* = "alien, stranger") because "I am a stranger in a strange land" (Ex 2:22).

Exile is not a bad place for a Warrior to find himself; some of the greatest liberators in history spent time in exile or jail (Jesus, Mohammed, Gandhi, King, Mandela). There they learn to fight the hardest battle of all: the struggle the Muslims call the "Greater Jihad," the spiritual warfare that rages in the soul. Media-soaked modern men can't imagine the ferocity of the secret battles that rage in prison cells and wilderness wastes — as Gerard Manley Hopkins wrote, "Oh the mind, mind has mountains, cliffs of fall, frightful, sheer, no-man fathomed. Hold them cheap may who ne'er hung there." On the moonscaped Midian mountains Moses hung until, in moments lost to us, he climbed The Mountain, conquering his fear of the mental ravines and emotional gorges below. Only then, on the holy desert summit of the soul, could Yahweh appear.

God always takes too long to show up. Perhaps on his cosmic clock, the seconds do not tick so slowly as they seem to for us, especially when we are in a desert. But suddenly, in his own good *kairos* (Greek: "appropriate time"), God will make his move, and nothing is ever the same again. So it was that on fiercely hot Horeb one day short of too late, Yahweh at last answered the groans of his people crying out in Egyptian slavery. Which is also to say that, at last, and not one day too early, Moses was ready to go to Warrior school.

Moses' encounter with Yahweh in the fiery bush on Mt. Horeb (Ex 3) is inexhaustibly rich in spiritual meaning, as nearly three thousand years of subsequent commentary proves. In addition to its being an apocalypse fraught with theological revelation, Yahweh's appearance to Moses constitutes a call to *holy war*. That term probably sends shivers of dread down our spines; human history is striped with wounds inflicted by armies who called their causes "holy." God's symbols, cross and crescent, Ark and Swastika, all too easily fall into the hands of every grubby thug, grand thief, vengeful racist, or two-bit Ayatollah who wishes to cloak his demented designs with the mantle of divine inspiration. Is "holy war" not an oxymoron?

Before we respond too quickly to that question with facile ideological certainty, we who are secured in the safety of our pacifistic philosophizing amid the most awesome array of destructive weapons ever assembled, perhaps we ought in our imaginations to address the issue to others less violently protected than we. We might ask the hopeless survivors of Auschwitz as the Allied armies rolled into their death camps in the spring of 1945; we might ask peasants terrorized by the fascist regime of El Salvador; we might ask the blacks of South Africa or, for that matter, parents in a drug-infested housing project. There are causes where holy resistance, even involving violence, is a matter of the highest duty.

Yet on Horeb the God of Moses authorizes no military crusades of conquest or conversion, no raids of revenge or retribution, no forced baptisms or theological lessons taught at the point of the sword. But make no mistake. Neither does this God remain blissfully safe in his heaven, committed to lofty principles of divine pacifism while real people die in their traces under Egypt's lash. No, Yahweh hears the cry of his people groaning in slavery, he hurts for them, and he acts. Yahweh flames with fiery anger from his Sinai bush, his Voice blazing with the command that will sear Moses' heart forever: let my people go!

Yahweh's command from Sinai is the only justification for a war that can be called "holy," that is, to let people go. Today we call this concern by its modern name "liberation theology," which is the belief that God is actively involved in freeing oppressed people from whatever pharaohs victimize them.[10] This theology causes some prim First World theologians, safe beneath the nuclear umbrella, to fret and dither over theological fine points and doctrinal niceties. But to *campesinos* in El Salvador or black activists in South Africa, liberation theology announces a firm denial that God is unmoved by their plight or cooperates in any way in their victimization. The Moses story proclaims that a terribly partisan biblical Yahweh intends to pull the mighty down from their thrones and plunk their chariots into the sea. Yahweh will do all this in his own way, according to his own holy agenda, and on his own turf. But in Egypt, in a fragile moment of history this whole divine strategy rests on the very human shoulders of an escaped felon, Moses.

The Education of a Warrior

For all his problems and weaknesses, Moses could not have had a better teacher; lest we forget, Yahweh himself is a Warrior! And now with Moses, the Old Master is about to show his stuttering student how it's done as he trains him in Fundamental Liberation Strategy 101 (Ex 3:16–20). So begins a classic mentoring relationship wherein Yahweh begins to tutor Moses personally, like a combination Marine drill instructor, Yoda the Jedi knight, and Saul Alinsky, community organizer. Moses is to become an *initiated* Warrior, a Peaceful Warrior, coached by the best.[11] Carefully and deliberately, Yahweh leads Moses through the steps necessary to win Israel's release from bondage, patiently nurturing Moses' confidence in the process (Ex 7:1–13); at every stage, there is a clear plan and a clever strategy, for the emancipation of Israel involves both a complicated community organizing task and a psychological war of wits.

One thing the Exodus does *not* require is any military violence on the part of the Hebrews. That is well worth noting; most of us tend to think of the Old Testament as a violent book, but in the Priestly writings (Genesis–Numbers), military violence is rare.[12] Moses' "arsenal" does not include a single bona fide "weapon" — no swords, spears, bows, or knives, much less chariots and horsemen. It is *Yahweh* who fights! Israel is there to fast and pray, sing Yahweh's praises, and pick up the pieces (Ex 3:21–22), but it is Yahweh who drowns the entire Egyptian army (Ex 14). The Exodus is thus the world's first instance of nonviolent resistance, and Moses' success with this tactic would impress a Gandhi or a King.

Moses the Magician

The only "weapon" Moses used in his battle with Pharaoh was his staff, symbol of the archetype of Magician. Moses warred against Pharaoh, his evil magicians, and the entire Egyptian army with a mere staff — a magic wand — by which he invoked Yahweh's Deep Magic (Ex 7–11).

The paradigm of the Magician and his wand is exceedingly ancient — it is the first of the Major Arcana of the Tarot.[13] Without access to the Magician, Moses could never have freed Israel. Nor can any of us live very heroically or accomplish our goals.[14]

In popular culture, the magician is only an entertainer who does tricks through the art of deception and sleight of hand. At the most superficial level, Moses engages this inner Houdini for use against Pharaoh, for example, when he turns his staff into a serpent (Ex 7:8–13); unfortunately, Pharaoh's magicians can also do tricks of this kind. Such trickery is also a skill that oppressed or disadvantaged people *must* learn, often enough just to survive, since they live in a world where the cards are always stacked against them; Jacob is a figure who survives by chicanery of this kind (Gen 30–31). The ability to conjure up the illusions of one's inner Magician is an important survival skill and an indication that a man has outgrown the naiveté that thinks the world is a fair and above-board place. Jesus, for example, counselled his disciples to be as cunning as serpents (Mt 10:16). In other words, one is never wise to become vulnerable to enemies or liars by telling them the whole truth; better to create the illusion of strength than advertise one's own weaknesses.

At a deeper level, however, the Magician is also the archetype that engages the resources of a man's inner psychic consciousness. Many modern men are appallingly unaware of the tremendous psychic potential that lies within them unused; educated in a left-brain/materialistic worldview, they insist that things are just what they appear, that what you see is what you get, and that any other viewpoint is just superstition and religious hocus-pocus. Other men, however, in developing an interior prayer and meditation life, begin to conjure their inner Merlin and experience the enhanced ability to "know" through a sixth sense. We call this psychic function intuition, and it is involved in such phenomena as extrasensory perception (ESP) and clairvoyance.

Intuition is a function just like thinking: it needs to be valued, developed, and practiced if it is to do anyone any good. Ancient hunters and warriors depended for survival on intuition to a high degree; one still finds in primal cultures such as the natives of Australia amazing psychic perceptual powers. Much of this ability has been forgotten among modern men, but a number of training exercises exist that can develop it: Tarot cards,[15] I Ching,[16] Medicine Cards,[17] and numerous workshops and methods that employ and exploit intuitive powers. Men who have begun to develop their inner Magician often report an increased ability to follow "hunches" that pay off in business, to detect subtle emotional changes in their spouses, or to notice how uncanny coincidences create "lucky" opportunities in their personal lives. One way to read the account of the ten plagues (Ex 7–11), for example, is to assume that Moses created his own luck, intuited the onslaught of various natural disasters in Egypt, and magically presented them to Pharaoh as divine signs of Yahweh's wrath. But we can only guess this; a true Magician will never tell.

At the deepest level of all the Magician is the archetype that connects us to the Deep Magic of the universe, that subtle but pervasive Force that guides all creation — including ourselves — according to a provident plan. Rich and powerful people, bubbling away in their hot tubs and munching their brie, like to dismiss this sort of idea as mumbo-jumbo. The poor, the weak, and the sick, however, can't afford to scoff; often enough, the only thing that keeps them afloat and alive is their humble connection to the wisdom of this Deep Magic. This is frequently the experience of people in the Twelve Step programs who are learning to turn their lives over to a Higher Power; it is true of cancer patients who are alive by the sheer force of faith alone; it is true of every man whose inner Magician learns to reach out for help, whether to St. Jude or St. Anthony, the *tao* or one's ancestors, guardian angels, ancient guides, or God himself.

Christians call this Deep Magic *grace*, a word whose root (Latin: *gratia*) means an unmerited gift. Grace is God's unexpected and gratuitous help that, to uninitiated and unaware people, seems like blind luck or good fortune, but to Magicians it is the secret force that unfolds our lives in love and wisdom. Grace is God's magic that heals our diseases, reconciles our friends, turns around our defeats, and washes away our sins; grace is that "extra" force that ought, by rights, *not* be there for us, but is — if only we will accept it.

Grace is the Deep Magic that Moses conjures up for the impossible deliverance of Israel from Egypt's dungeon. The Exodus story describes how Yahweh the High Magician teaches Moses the secrets of this force field, how to harmonize and align himself with it, how to respect its powers, and how to bring it into battle in the holy war of Israel's liberation. When Moses obeys this Force, magic things begin to happen. The primal righteousness of Israel's plea for freedom seems to strike a harmonious chord with nature herself; heaven and earth join Moses' demand: "Let my people go!" His magic staff conducting nature's orchestra, Moses calls forth ten plagues against Pharaoh: Blood. Frogs. Mosquitoes. Flies. Death of the livestock. Boils. Hail. Locusts. Darkness. Finally, the death of Egypt's firstborn sons (Ex 11; 12:29–34) capsizes Pharaoh's imperial self-composure, and he issues the royal edict, "Leave!" Their Passover meal not yet digested, Moses mobilizes Israel and leads the Great Escape. Yahweh's continual hardening of Pharaoh's heart (Ex 14:8), however, caused him to give chase to Israel, and set the fool up for a miracle so great that it still rings wherever the story is told. As Moses raises his magic staff, Israel passes through the waters of chaos (Ex 14), an everlasting symbol of the love of freedom that lies at the deepest heart of the universe. Another wave of the wand, and Pharaoh and all his chariots and charioteers were gone.

Detachment from an Archetype

After the miracle at the Reed Sea, Moses rarely led Israel into war (but see Ex 17:8–16) until the next generation began to conquer Canaan (Num 20–24). It is difficult for a man to detach himself from an archetype that has served him so well when it is no longer appropriate, but it must be done. This is especially true of the Warrior. Now Israel needed new skills; in order to craft laws, adjudicate disputes, and lead worship, Moses had to develop his inner Patriarch, Judge, and Priest. Moses knew that his Warrior would have to stand aside for awhile, that though the holy war against Pharaoh once demanded that he summon his inner Warrior, this archetype must never be allowed to possess him. The movie *Patton* ends on this theme, though; the great general could not cope with peace for he was possessed by the Warrior. This is a hard lesson: a man's whole self is always larger than any archetype.

Moses never left his Magician for long, however, because he continually encountered impossible tasks: obtaining food and water, finding a route through the wilderness, or seeking a way to rule the stiff-necked Israelites. Moses constantly had to turn to Yahweh for help; a little Deep Magic here, a little grace there. This is no surprise; couch potatoes don't need the Magician — but heroes do. And Moses developed the archetype to a high art, conjuring up quails for meat (Ex 16) or striking rocks and finding water (Ex 17). Ultimately his encounter with Yahweh on Sinai (Ex 19) led him to reveal to Israel God's secret Torah, which gives life to all who will obey. There is a great danger in developing one's Magician to this degree, for the Magician can also possess a man. All spiritual traditions stress how dangerous magic is, and the genuine Magician must learn to contain and control this magic lest it overwhelm his puny earthen vessel of a soul. Anyone who would summon the Magician in himself must take the highest precautions to detach himself from the archetype, or he will surely begin to see himself as the source of Deep Magic, rather than its instrument. Such ego-inflation is the occupational hazard of priests and psychiatrists, televangelists and New Age practitioners alike. Spiritual arrogance is perverse, and Yahweh will not tolerate it for long.

Moses learned about the dangers of pride early on; Yahweh nearly killed him one night in a bizarre incident as he first headed back to Egypt (Ex 4:24–26). Moses' wife Zipporah saved her husband from Yahweh's wrath by cutting off their son's foreskin and touching Moses' genitals with it. Only then did Yahweh spare Moses. The symbolism of this act is important; the genitals represent our most human dimension, that which ties us to the earth. When our heads begin to swell or our hearts soar dangerously high, our genitals usually restore balance by reminding us of our earthiness and sexuality. Zipporah saves Moses by reminding him of his sexual vulnerability; many other religious leaders have had to learn this lesson more publicly and painfully — often on the pages of the *New York Times* or the set of the CBS Evening News. St. Paul explained very well this process by which God saves his Magicians from becoming Sorcerers. After a spectacular mystical event that resembled an out-of-the-body experience (2 Cor 12:1–6), Paul reports that he was given a mysterious "thorn in the flesh" to keep him from getting too proud. After Paul prayed that this weakness might be taken away (2 Cor 12:8–9), God refused, but replied: "My grace is enough for you — my power is strongest in your weakness!"

Martin Luther King, Jr.: The Magic Warrior

One of the greatest men of our time was a Warrior and a Magician who, like Moses, had to learn humility through weakness: Dr. Martin Luther King, Jr. Since his birthday (January 15) became an American national holiday, a legend is beginning to develop around him that in many ways is quite misleading. In the first place, as his photograph clouds over in hazy gauze and his words are framed in Hallmark sentimentality, we are given to believe that Dr. King was mainly a mystic dreamer, rhapsodizing rhetorically on visions of racial justice and economic harmony, a figure of conventional national piety. This hagiography somehow makes him seem safe, soft, and harmless.

But Martin Luther King, Jr., was a holy Warrior. His heart beat to the drums of justice, and his blood pulsed with the righteous anger of equality too long denied. A son of relative privilege and social standing like Moses, he could have pursued a lucrative pastoring, writing, or teaching career with safe and cautious words. Or, he could have become a perfect Victim, whining at the Unfairness-of-it-all. Instead, witnessing daily the widespread devastation visited on African-American people by historic racism, Dr. King committed himself to *do something*. Quickly, he found himself at the forefront of the civil rights movement in leading the Birmingham bus boycott after a weary Rosa Parks refused to abandon her seat. Over the next decade, Dr. King led the fight for racial equality in America: leading a march here or a boycott there, organizing sit-down demonstrations and prayer services, doing civil disobedience and getting arrested, making speeches and writing books.

These activities are not those of a Dreamer, but a field marshal. His rhetoric inflamed his followers not to revenge, but to a love that did justice. His word-weapons also exposed the sickening truth of the American national lie; his strategic nonviolent raids into lunch counters and court houses enraged Pharaoh, who cowardly struck back in the only way he knew how: bombing churches, attacking children with guard dogs, and shooting men down in the night. So did Dr. King meet his fate. Dreamers aren't gunned down by enemies; Warriors are. And Dr. King fought his battles for one reason, and one reason only: to "let my people go."

Yet he never fired a shot. Martin Luther King warred as a Magician. He mastered the magic of television and produced video images out of thin air that seared deeply into America's conscience. More than one time he pulled a rabbit out of the hat, spontaneously saying the right thing to a crowd at a dangerous moment. His words themselves were magic; still after thirty years they haunt and enchant and cast their spell. Above all, Dr. King aligned himself with the Deep Magic of God, which is ever working, ever exalting the lowly and bringing down the proud, ever freeing those in bondage and dropping Pharaohs into the drink, ever bringing down Walls, whether in Jericho or in Berlin.

Martin Luther King, Jr., was no plaster saint; to prevent him from growing proud over these accomplishments, God burdened him with various weaknesses. He struggled with fear daily, knowing as he did that assassination was almost inevitable. But Dr. King tried to live each day with the courage of a warrior going into battle. Early in his civil rights campaign, he tells us, after yet another death threat to him and his family, he rose in the middle of the night in terror. As he drank a cup of coffee, he finally placed his whole life under God's authority; he immediately found a deep peace. No burning bushes here, or dividing seas — just the stillness of an Alabama night to accompany him. And on the night before his murder, this peace abided still, though he intuitively knew what fate awaited the next day. Like Moses on Mt. Nebo (Deut 34), he could promise his followers, "I may not get there with you, but I want you to know that we as a people shall get to the Promised Land."

Chapter 7

Solomon the King

The archetype of King, at first glance, would seem to provide little with which a modern man could identify. In the popular imagination, the notion of kingship connotes a certain monarchical grandiosity, an aura of royal power, and an atmosphere of regal splendor — in other words, qualities that few men could ever even hope to experience. Moreover, as democratic people, we find the idea of kingship mildly repugnant, even while we are simultaneously fascinated by its continuing mythical attraction in fairy tales, novels, and movies. Yet regardless of these conflicting attitudes, any man who finds himself in a position of power over others, whether as a political leader, religious superior, or boss of a business, needs to develop this archetype successfully if he is to govern well and keep from becoming a Tyrant. As a help in this task, we will explore the story of Solomon, the quintessential biblical king (1 Kgs 3–11), who teaches us much about the blessings and curses of this archetype.

A King Like Other Nations

We need to realize at the outset of the Solomon story that many in ancient Israel felt as conflicted about the whole idea of kingship as we do. When anyone mentioned "king," many Hebrews could only hear the word "Pharaoh"; the wounds of Egypt continued to pain Israel long after Exodus. Moreover, the Hebrews were every bit as independent-minded as most Americans; like ourselves, they didn't want "big government" nosing into their affairs, collecting their taxes, drafting their sons, and enslaving their daughters (1 Sam 8:10–18). Their traditional tribal form of government preferred patriarchal rule: small clans guided, ideally, by a beneficent and wise local ruler who knew each person by name and each family and its problems. But above all, many in Israel believed that their people already had a King — Yahweh Sabaoth — and that any earthly version of this office constituted a direct slap in the face of their God (1 Sam 8:6–9).

So widespread were these antagonisms and doubts that the largest single body of biblical literature, the Deuteronomistic History (Deuteronomy through 2 Kings) often dwells on Israel's whole tumultuous history with kings.[1] This massive work, created from earlier written traditions in the postexilic era (ca. 550 B.C.E.), even blames the demise of both kingdoms of Israel and Judah on a succession of bad kings who refused to obey the prophets. Nevertheless, even through this theological and ideological hostility, a certain awe still shines through the stories about King Solomon. A little historical review will help us understand the impact of this massive figure on Israelite life.

Late in the eleventh century B.C.E. scattered Hebrew tribes peopled the hill country of Canaan, a mountainous region stretching from the wooded peaks of Galilee to the stark desert heights of Judah. These tribes lived in constant tension and warfare with each other and their Canaanite neighbors, who lived in wealthier city-states in the fertile valleys and plains below. The invasion of the Philistines, sea peoples from the Mediterranean, dramatically changed this state of affairs. Encroaching on the Hebrew hill country from below, the Philistines threatened to dominate the whole of Canaan with their powerful military machine armed with the latest technology: iron weapons. Modern warfare had arrived; no longer could the Hebrews survive as fractious and isolated tribes led by old sheiks.

The Philistine threat presented a local Benjaminite tribal strongman, Saul son of Kish, with the opportunity of uniting the scattered clans into a Hebrew kingdom under his leadership. Saul deftly defeated the Philistines in a series of skirmishes, had himself anointed the first Hebrew king, and established his capital at the Benjaminite city of Gibeah (1 Sam 9–15).[2] But Saul's death at the hands of the Philistines at Mt. Gilboa allowed his upstart Judean rival, David son of Jesse, eventually to seize the throne, wipe out most of the surviving Saulide family, crush the Philistines, and move the Israelite capital to the newly captured city of Jerusalem (2 Sam 1–5). Victorious over all his enemies, King David established a full-fledged Israelite kingdom, complete with a military and administrative bureaucratic establishment. His ruthless success as king was not lost even on his own son, Absalom, who later led a failed rebellion that drove David into exile. Family turmoil and palace intrigues plagued the dynasty (2 Sam 9–20) until old David at last passed on the royal power to his son Solomon (who became king with a little help from his mother Bathsheba, 1 Kgs 1).[3]

Israel anointed Solomon its king about midway through the tenth century B.C.E. Though there is no doubt among scholars as to the historicity of this event, there exists real skepticism regarding the lavish descriptions of Solomon's reign found in 1 Kings.[4] No independent reference to Solomon or his kingdom, for example, has ever been found in Ancient Near Eastern records of the period; evidently, little Israel was still not politically important enough to show up on the international documentary radar screen. What then of Solomon's purported power, abundant wealth, and world-class wisdom? These literary claims are the stuff of legend, the stories that kings encourage their scribes to write about for the edification of future generations. Yet the extravagant literature about Solomon also taps deeply into the world of myth, so that the majestic narratives about the man really tell us more about the spiritual qualities of the Bible's Ideal King than political or economic conditions of tenth-century B.C.E. Israel.

The Wisdom of Solomon

Several important facets of the King archetype stand out from the Solomon story. The first and most fundamental quality relates to Solomon's mysterious night-dream at the sanctuary of Gibeon in the era before his Temple in Jerusalem had been completed (1 Kgs 3). There God tells the new king, "Whatever you ask for, I will give it to you" — a blank check, endorsed with Yahweh's handwriting! Solomon's answer flows from the core of what it means to be a king and reveals that, as is often the case with good men who pray, he already possesses what he seeks: "Give your servant a heart to govern your people, and to know right from wrong." Solomon seeks, not more political power for himself, financial resources for his family, or military hegemony for his kingdom, but the wisdom necessary to govern his people justly. Such a request Yahweh could not refuse.

Solomon knew that sacred kingship is not just a political position, but a spiritual vocation; not just a role of power, but a service of responsibility. For the Sacral King thinks of himself as an intermediary, both accountable to a High King above and responsible to his lowliest subjects beneath. He knows that, as king, he rules in the place of God himself. That is why such a great part of the Solomon literature pictures the king at prayer, seeking guidance and wisdom from Yahweh on behalf of the people (1 Kgs 3:4–15; 8:22–9:9). Obviously, this is all very heavy stuff, invested with weighty implications for the psyche of any man who would be a king. Yet it is all there in the heritage of the Sacred King, which gives the archetype such psychic gravity.

In modernity, our secular humanist philosophies have largely lopped off all psychological awareness among leaders that they are in any way responsible to God for their governance of the people. Leadership today is largely conceived as a social contract: you hire me, I deliver your goods. As logical as this arrangement might sound, it is proving to be a bankrupt one. Stripped of all sense of a *vocatio* (Latin: "call") for public service and divested of any notion of spiritual responsibility to God, many of our leaders feel themselves accountable only to the blocs who deliver their votes or PACs that fund their campaigns. This is the era of politicians beholden to the special interest groups, bosses answerable only to the stockholders, and community leaders responsible solely to the board of directors. And what of the people without political clout, the poor, the powerless, and the losers? In this framework, they do not matter, nor are they taken into account in the modern power equations of the nation without Sacred Kings. Since they sign no paychecks and deliver no votes, the little people are left with no King to care for them. And so we see them, cadging quarters on corners or ranting madly to no one in particular on city streets; the King will not hear them, and he gives them no justice.

This was the case throughout the administration of Ronald Reagan, a skillful Magician who artfully aped the trappings of the Sacred King archetype while successfully avoiding its substance. Hired by corporate interests and elected by cleverly manipulated partisans, he was employed by them to advance their interests and to help them feel good about it as he cast his spell over the media. The poor and the powerless in his realm were ignored, and no pictures of this king graced shot-gun houses in Alabama or *barrio* homes in New York. The little people knew very well he was not their King, but their Pharaoh.

Unlike Reagan, Solomon was never too great to go to the Temple and bow before Yahweh, never too important to listen to the most intimate problems of the poor of his realm (1 Kgs 3:16–28). That is why his people could sing of him in the Temple he built,

> He gives justice to poor people,
>   And saves the children of poverty.
> He frees the lowly and helpless who call on him,
>   He takes pity on the poor and the weak.
> The souls of powerless he saves...
>   Their lives are precious in his eyes.
>   Ps 72:4, 12–14

Any man who would govern people justly must access in himself something of this archetypical sacral kingship of which the Bible speaks. Whether he runs a company, represents a district, administrates a school, or leads a diocese, he must know that he acts on behalf of everyone and in the place of God (Rom 13:1–7). The litmus tests of a successful constellation of the archetype are rather simple: Do your employees trust you? Does the janitor feel free to speak with you about his concerns? Do you really care about the well-being of those in your charge?

A real King can answer yes to such questions; he is the officer who can sit down comfortably with his troops and discuss problems over C-rations, the executive concerned with equitable pay for the secretaries in the office pool, and yes, the former president who still cares enough about his people to build low-cost housing for them with his own hands.

Solomon in All His Glory

The other traits that mark Solomon, and the archetype of the Sacred King as well, are extraordinary generativity, creativity, and munificence. The biblical text lavishes extravagant and detailed attention on Solomon's sponsorship of wisdom and learning in Israel, his construction of the Great Temple in Jerusalem as a dwelling place for Yahweh, his grand palace, his building projects across the whole land, and even his pioneering maritime enterprises (1 Kgs 5–9). Nor are these descriptions purely the stuff of fantasy; archaeological findings at least partially confirm the historicity of this phenomenal building boom, and biblical scholars speak of the Solomonic Enlightenment as a period of great literary creativity that produced the Yahwist document, the Throne Succession narrative, and various collections of wisdom sayings.[5]

Psychologist Robert Moore speaks of the Sacred King as embodying the Life Principle of his realm.[6] Such a figure literally thrives on seeing his people flourish and glories when hearing of their accomplishments. The Sacred King fosters creativity, patronizes the arts, nourishes intellectual endeavors, and encourages the growth of civilization around him. The key to the psychic power of this aura of greatness is that the King takes credit for all of it under his royal auspices. He is not threatened by the successes he authors, he is glorified by them! He is Augustus Caesar, creator of the *Pax Romana;* Charlemagne of the Franks, savior of European civilization; Suleiman the Magnificent of the Turks; Frederick the Great, sponsor of the humane arts; Franklin D. Roosevelt, author of the New Deal; Lyndon Johnson, father of the Great Society; and Mikhail Gorbachev, mentor of *perestroika* and *glasnost.*

Fortunate are any of us who work under a man accessing his Sacred King in a healthy way. He is the dean who encourages his teachers to pursue their research or the professor who gives fertile leads to his graduate students; he is the pastor who rejoices in the popularity of his young assistant and the bishop who supports his priests and ministers; he is the boss who rewards his employees' new ideas for an advertising campaign or the foreman who gets bonuses for his factory workers when they devise new safety procedures. How great these men are, how large and how hearty. We have all known them and flourished under their guidance.

The Tyrant: The Shadow King

Two serious disorders relating to the King archetype can develop in men. The first is among unhealthy individuals who need to achieve power over others to possess any sense of self-worth: the all-too-familiar Tyrant. The second malady is among men who can't potentiate the King archetype at all, and who perpetually and consistently refuse to lead, make commitments, or take responsibility for anyone else: the increasingly common *Puer Aeternus*.

The aura of the Sacred King archetype is an intense magnet to threatened and emotionally insecure individuals of the first type who would compensate for their own interior psychological impotency by grasping the levers of power and donning the mantle of authority. Unable to attain any inner sense of dignity, these men allow possession by the shadow side of the King as they grasp the superficial trappings of power. Their activities are marked by intimidation, force, manipulation, pettiness, and paranoia. It is obvious that this form of narcissistic illness is one of the great scourges of human history, producing a sickening and seemingly never-ending supply of Tyrants: Herod, Nero, Caligula, Napoleon, Hitler, Khomeini, Noriega, Saddam Hussein, *ad nauseam*. Even young Solomon was capable of displaying this dark side, at least before his entreaty before Yahweh; soon after his succession to the throne, he arranged the demise of his political rivals Adonijah, Abiathar, and Joab (1 Kgs 2).

Far more common are the little Tyrants we encounter in everyday life. Full of self-doubt and disgust, they make sure no one under them flourishes or feels very good about themselves. Tyrants find fault in their underlings like heat-seeking missiles; there's always a problem with your work, and performances are never quite good enough. Under the jealousy of the Tyrant, the kingdom withers: employees learn to "cover their asses" rather than take risks, "law and order" wins out over creativity every time, and dissent is considered disloyalty. Whereas the Sacred King fosters fertility, the Tyrant is sometimes curiously asexual; ecclesiastical circles abound with this type, which achieves pseudo-intimacy with others by domination rather than the real human relationship of sharing. Tyrants and their little empires are everywhere, in libraries and emergency rooms, in government agencies and high schools — mostly places where their services are indispensable and for which the rest of us have no alternative. And so we are forced to meet their deadlines and fill out their forms, jump through their hoops and tolerate the little indignities they like to provide.

The Little Prince

An entirely opposite type to either the Great King or his Tyrant shadow is the *Puer Aeternus*, who successfully avoids all responsibility, commitment, and authority.[7] Whereas the Sacred King is a weighty figure as he sits on his throne in regal gravity, the Puer is nimble and even flighty; indeed, his tendency to flit off to new, never-ending adventures has given rise to a modern term for this classic male inability to make or keep commitments, the "Peter Pan Syndrome." The Puer is the man who would *not* be king, the man who consistently refuses ever to take responsibility for other people, sponsor or mentor anyone else, or generate any life beyond his own narrow narcissism. He is the eternal Little Prince who never grows up to be king.[8]

As Western culture shifts inevitably away from adult masculine values, instances of the Puer archetype are on the upswing. In contrast to the rugged masculinity of the Wildman, Warrior, and King archetypes, the Puer seems relatively harmless and, indeed, even a whimsical ally in the gender struggle against the "heavies" of male society: big, bad, adult men. Charming to women, the Puer is the "nice boy" raised by so many mothers and the "sensitive man" so popular with their lovers. Cute, cuddly, boyish, and gentle, the Puer archetype is also highly salable in popular culture; in his public persona, he emerges in such diverse cultural figures as Richard Simmons, Michael Jackson, Warren Beatty, Barry Manilow, and the early Beatles. Even the shadow Puer (rebellious, irresponsible, and immature) is highly marketable, as witnessed by the continuing appeal of the elderly Mick Jagger, the dead James Dean, and the appropriately named rock star Prince.

In his heterosexual avatar, the Puer is Don Juan, forever courting women — and forever leaving them. Yet according to Marie-Louise von Franz, the Puer archetype is also frequently a homosexual archetype. The claim is stereotypical, yet real; gay culture is very familiar with the effervescent Boy who floats from job to job, city to city, and relationship to relationship without ever settling down and sticking to anything or anybody save a temporarily convenient Daddy. Gay or straight, the Puer is the living embodiment of today's uninitiated male, the opposite of the Sacred King in all his substance, generativity, and dignity.

"Yes, I Am a King"

Solomon was by no means a perfect king. The Bible tells us that, toward the end of his reign, he fell away from total allegiance to Yahweh and followed other gods and goddesses. The Deuteronomist cites this sin as cause for political turmoil and military strife at the end of Solomon's life and the eventual civil schism that tore the northern kingdom of

Israel away from Judah (1 Kgs 11). Of course, historically Solomon's failures were much more complicated than mere polytheistic dalliances. It is likely that Solomon's policy of forced labor and high taxes severely alienated the northern tribes, so that when his son Rehoboam ascended the throne, the elders of Israel used the opportunity to secede from the union (1 Kgs 12).

Despite all his troubles, there is no hint that Solomon was ever devastated or destroyed as a man or as a king. The greatest test of a man's interior kingliness comes, not when courtiers scurry round the throne in sycophantic obeisance, nor when conquest follows conquest in spiraling success, nor when riches pile up in the palace. The real proof of royal mettle comes in the midst of disasters, especially those that edge one on beyond the pale. Solomon's father, David, faced such a catastrophe in the Absalom revolt (2 Sam 15–19); despite the disaster, David displayed an unmistakable quality of spiritual regality. Great kings display this royal "largeness" in the midst of their own defeats.

This royal dignity is the same quality that shines out from a descendant of Solomon, another king of the Jews. In the week that followed his triumphant entry to Jerusalem, Jesus of Nazareth, peasant preacher from Galilee, endured a succession of disasters nobly. Convicted by the courts, anathematized by the Temple, deserted by friends, mocked by cowards, tortured by thugs, executed by soldiers, and abandoned by God, he remained a king to the last: forgiving, in possession of himself, and great of spirit. The account of Jesus' passion in John's gospel, especially, captures this awesome display of dignity in the face of evil (Jn 18–19). The King is more than a social role of power; ultimately it is an archetype of the Self. This is the Self that proclaims from the hideously twisted body of the Elephant Man, "I am a man. . . . I am a human being!" This is the Self that shouts out from a ghetto youngster, "I am somebody!"

It is rare that we get to experience the King. Normally, we observe in ourselves and others painfully embarrassing petty egotism or self-loathing, even in those who are already rich, powerful, important, or famous. Yet inner royalty is completely unrelated to outer success; that is what those who intimately experience the poor or the sick keep trying to tell us. That is why those who know the poor are so often genuinely grateful to them for the opportunity to see the King. In the midst of depressing poverty, debasing destitution, or disfiguring illness, there he will stand, his throne a rocking chair or a hospital bed, his court little children or busy nurses.

I remember well my first glimpse of that inner King. He appeared in the form of an old black man, whose name I cannot remember, in a small town in Missouri in the summer of 1969. He wore coveralls. His face was lined, unshaven, his hair greying. He greeted me in his yard and answered my church census questions politely and kindly. By the end of the interview, I began to feel it — an aura of dignity and spiritual "largeness" around the gentleman. I can only imagine his life in that small southern town; whatever prejudice he faced or disasters he endured, that old man surely responded to them by finding his inner King. When I left, he fixed his eyes on mine and said, "God bless you. I guess we're brothers in the Lord." I did feel every bit like his brother, and more. For a moment, I, too, felt like something of a King.

Chapter 8

Elijah the Wildman

During the ninth century B.C.E., there lived in Israel two extraordinary prophets; the older was known as Elijah and his younger protégé was named Elisha. We know about this pair from the Elijah and Elisha Cycles (1 Kgs 17–2 Kgs 13), two fascinating pieces of literature that celebrated these two prophetic heroes. In addition to giving us historical information relating to the origins of prophecy in Israel, the Elijah and Elisha Cycles provide us with mythical lore rich in masculine spirituality. Later in chapter 9 we shall attend to the Elisha Cycle as a story about the archetypal shamanic Healer. In this present chapter, we shall explore the archetype of the Wildman as it is embodied in the story of Elijah.

A Little History

After the ten northern tribes of Israel split with Judah in about 920 B.C.E., they formed their own kingdom in Israel and anointed as king a fellow northerner named Jeroboam (1 Kgs 12). Now Israel was a large and wealthy country that extended over the most fertile plains of Canaan, including the rich Jezreel Valley and the lovely heights of Ephraim and Galilee. Despite its abundant natural resources, however, Israel had a serious problem. The Canaanite peoples whom David had subjugated decades earlier continued to live and prosper on the rich fields of the Jezreel; moreover, they held fast to their fertility religion, which featured worship of Baal and his consort Asherah. Yet the tribes of Israel, which inhabited the poorer mountainous region of the Central Highlands, stuck fast to their Yahweh religion and all its traditions. So though these Hebrews under David and Solomon had conquered the entire Canaanite area, they actually ended up in an inferior social position relative to the Canaanites after the division of the kingdoms. This situation cursed Israel with a problem that plagues modern countries even today: it had become a bi-national and bi-religious state, riven with political, religious, and class distinctions.

The Israelites, though poorer than their Canaanite neighbors, were a proud and stiff-necked people, as mountain folk tend to be. Their religion demanded stringent adherence to one God, and one God only: the Lord Yahweh, liberating warrior-deity of the Exodus. Other peoples might serve other gods, but Israel was to worship Yahweh *alone* (Deut 6:4). In return, Yahweh would protect Israel in war, bring the winter rains, and shower blessings of health, peace, and fertility on his people. When Israel pined after other gods in pursuit of these blessings, Yahweh's breath would blow hot and jealous on Israel's stiff neck as he commanded (Ex 20:3), "Thou shalt have no other gods beside me!"

The Canaanites and the Hebrews in Israel lived in uneasy religious, economic, and political tension for a number of decades after the Great Schism. Then, around 850 B.C.E., the ascension of the Israelite Ahab and his foreign wife Jezebel to the throne lit the fuse and blew hostilities sky high. In marrying the pagan Jezebel, Ahab had sinned against Yahweh by constructing altars to Baal, her Phoenician fertility god (1 Kgs 16:29–33). Ahab initially seems merely to have attempted a smart political trick: by allying himself with a neighboring king through marriage and simultaneously supporting the native Baal fertility cult through the erection of shrines, he sought to extend Israel's influence internationally while appeasing his native Canaanite constituency. The Canaanites in the kingdom probably regarded Ahab as a wise, liberal Hebrew ruler who promised to restore their freedom of religion.

The "Yahweh-alone" Israelites didn't see things that way. To them, Ahab had committed a great religious crime by officially abandoning the sole worship of Yahweh to which Israel had pledged itself under Moses and Joshua. And so it was that Yahwist religious and political circles began to foment rebellion against Ahab and Jezebel. The leaders of this grassroots insurrection were bands of Yahweh prophets, strict ascetics who lived in radical religious communities dedicated to the worship of Yahweh and the observance of his laws. We might think of these people today as religious fundamentalists, for they dreamed of the "old time religion," preached their stark morality, and attempted to transform their nation into a perfect theocracy. The leaders of this resistance movement were Elijah and his prophetic disciple Elisha, and they eventually succeeded in anointing as king the military strongman Jehu in a fundamentalist *coup d'état* that toppled and massacred the entire ruling dynasty (2 Kgs 9–10). The Elijah and Elisha Cycles, chock full of the stuff of legend (myth, folktale, miracles, and awesome natural events) celebrate these two heroes of the resistance.

Elijah hailed from Tishbe in Gilead, a mountainous region across the Jordan River from Ephraim, the Hebrew heartland. Since Gilead lay on the fringes of Israel, it rarely figures significantly in biblical history. Elijah, too, is something of a fringe figure; in fact, nothing is known about him in the Bible until he suddenly appears out of nowhere, informing Ahab that a punishing drought is about to wither Israel (1 Kgs 17:1). In opposing the king so boldly, the historical Elijah acted as a typical prophet (an archetype we shall explore in the story of Jeremiah in chapter 10). Yet the legends and stories told about Elijah in the Bible also draw heavily on the motif of the Wildman, a classic masculine archetype and source of enormous spiritual power.

Adam: The Primal Wildman

The word "Wildman" probably connotes for most people unkempt and crazy lunacy, or perhaps undisciplined social rebellion of the kind that one sees on the streets of San Francisco and Berkeley. These are indeed the disquieting characteristics of people in whom this archetype goes wrong. In fact, we are seeing this frightening shadow side of the Wildman archetype with increasing regularity in our parks and on our streets as mentally and emotionally unbalanced people flood our urban areas, choke our subways, and crowd our doorways in a kind of unconscious revenge on a society that will not care for them anymore. Unfortunately, we rarely get to encounter in the flesh nowadays the authentic Wildman, that man of raw nature who is vanishing along with the wilderness that is his home. Nevertheless, the archetype remains alive within the male psyche, buried deep beneath our modern consciousness.[1]

At one time, all men were Wildmen. At home in the jungles of Africa where humanity originated, in tune with the seasons and the movement of the stars, revering the natural forces that vivify our planet, and fearful of the great mysteries of birth, sex, life, pain, and death, every man's blood pulsed in sympathy with the wild heartbeat of nature. Wherever men later migrated, they adapted to their new environment with a harmonious spirituality that put them in touch with the natural forces without and the body's powers within. The animist nature religions of primitive humanity related men to animals in the rituals of the great hunt, to the earth in the cult of Goddess worship, and to the heavens in the mythologies of the sky gods.[2] Lest we moderns romanticize primal religion, however, we should remember that the animist cults were also brutal and indifferent to the individual, as is nature itself.

Late in the Neolithic era, remarkable changes began to appear in human culture: agriculture, the first villages and towns, and experiments in metallurgy and ceramics. Men were learning to exploit nature for their own designs, bending and breaking it for their own power, safety, and comfort. This process has never stopped, and civilization spirals upward, showering its blessings but also raining its curses on humanity. In a profound sense, the male psyche has never gotten over this break with nature, even after these many millennia. Something in men still secretly mourns the loss of all those animal species, the disappearance of the great rain forests and the virgin prairies, and the damming and fouling of the rivers. This loss is what the biblical myth of man's expulsion from the Garden of Eden (Gen 2-3) is all about.

Adam is the first biblical Wildman. Fashioned by Yahweh directly from the earth (Hebrew: *adamah* = "ground, soil"),[3] he lived in naked partnership with the wild beasts and the birds of heaven, and eventually with the woman kneaded from his own rib. But he could not resist the fruits of knowing good from evil, the chance to be like a god in creating and destroying, in knowing and analyzing and mastering nature itself. And so Yahweh expelled him from Eden, damning him with the curse that still plagues every male: banishment from the Garden onto accursed soil that yields its fruit only with great suffering and the sweat of the brow (Gen 3:17-19). Frightful monsters and a flaming sword guard the way back to that Garden, and we can never go back home again.

Mythically, this story suggests modern man's simultaneous alienation from nature and his longing for it, his exploitation and destruction of natural powers even as he desires to return to them. This conflict is the crucial issue of the century ahead as hard ecological choices determine whether man will totally curse the soil on which he labors, or learn once again to cooperate harmoniously with it. But he can never again live like Adam; Adam is lost. He can, however, gain access psychically to the Wildman remnants of Adam that still remain in him.

The Wildman Today

The Wildman is the spiritual archetype that connects men affectively to God as they experience nature in all its sheer wildness, beauty, and starkness, in the peace of the sunset as well as the sublimity of the desert on a cold, starlit night. If a man will allow himself truly to experience the awful wonder of a thunderstorm, the sickening queasiness of an earthquake, or the unimaginable terror of a solar eclipse, the most archaic remnants of his psyche will spring to life. As he watches the graceful lope of the deer or the smooth slither of the snake, this interior Wildman will remember the mythical Eden, where he once knew all the animals by name and spoke with God himself in the cool of the evening.

The Wildman is also our psychic connection to the nature of the human body, its tidal rhythms, its hungers and lusts, its energy and fatigue, and its subtle wisdom that tell us what we genuinely need and really want rather than what someone else manipulates us into needing and wanting. Modern economic, religious, and social forces, which encourage the culture of the *Puer Aeternus* and persuade grown men to feel ashamed of their hairy and bulky bodies, to feel guilty for merely being horny and lusty, and to feel somehow bad just for being rough, gruff, prickly, and rusty characters, have conspired to drive the Wildman out of the masculine consciousness and into the shadow. But access to the archetype can reconcile us to our own animality in all its beauty as well as its earthy lowliness. As Robert Bly has shown so well in his discussion of Grimm's fairy story "Iron John," which relates how a young boy discovers a rusty, hairy, and seemingly dangerous wild man in the dregs of an old pond, a modern man has to dive "down" into the pool of his unconscious in order to rediscover this wild part of himself.[4] Iron John, the scary figure he encounters there, only seems dangerous because he is so fierce and hairy. Actually, as the smooth and fearful "momma's boy" Jacob discovered when he finally worked up the courage to meet his wild and hairy brother Esau (Gen 33:1–17), the Wildman can prove a loyal, generous, and powerful ally.

I once encountered the Wildman in a vivid dream. At the time of this dream, I was a young high school religion teacher striving very hard to be "perfect," carefully preparing notes and delivering lectures, and attempting to be an upstanding model Jesuit and Christian exemplar to my students. This endeavor is the classic occupational hazard of teachers and ministers — the temptation to become a nice, co-dependent "goody-two-shoes" at the expense of one's own genuine needs and wants. In the dream, I was earnestly teaching a religion class, dressed ever-so-properly in clerical black Roman collar, when a wild, dark, and hairy figure decked out in buckskins appeared threateningly at the door, beckoning me to come outside. Compelled, I followed, then awoke. Out of my unconscious, this "dangerous" Wildman was only telling me to get back in touch with my shadow, my earthiness, my whole natural self, and not to become a cookie-cutter priest, a "nice" company man.

What is dangerous about the Wildman is his threat to cultural, political, and economic arrangements that keep men in a state of puerile domesticity or enculturated as obedient robots for the System. For to the extent that a man is in touch with his wildness, he is free from authoritarian pressures to conform, from advertisers selling him things he doesn't really need, propagandists manipulating him into thoughts he really doesn't think, and ideologists converting him to ideas he doesn't really believe. The Wildman in us isn't wooed by such false promises of security or threats of social blackmail; he knows from where his true strength comes and where his real help lies:

I lift up my eyes to the mountains,
From whence comes my help.
My help is from Yahweh,
The Creator of heaven and earth.
(Ps 121:1–2)

Jesus taught this same truth as he regarded the birds of the sky and the flowers of the field: "Don't worry," he said, "and don't say, 'What will we eat? What will we drink? What will we wear?' The pagans worry about these things. Your heavenly Father knows you need them all!" (Mt 6:25–34). The Wildman trusts in God, who made heaven and earth, not artificial rules created solely for the survival and convenience of the nearest institution. Access to the Wildman also makes us comfortable with our own natural body and free from the exploitations of the "personal care" industry that thrives only to the extent that it can continually convince men that they smell bad, that they look awful, that they are too heavy or too light, too dark or too white, or too old or too young, in order to peddle their clothes, colognes, and coiffures. The Wildman scoffs at these latest "needs" served up by Puer Culture — whether cherry-red Miatas or Club-Med getaways, hair-replacement operations, tummy-tucks, or face-lifts — whatever the latest absolute "must" is that some enterprising advertising executive tries to convince us that we can't do without.

To the extent that a man is wild, he is also unowned, unmanipulated, unbowed, unbeholden, undomesticated, unapologetic, and unashamed. Unfortunately, we see very few men so free. And yet we yearn deeply for such wildness. Our literature and cinema are filled with Wildman fantasies: *Tarzan, Robinson Crusoe, Lonely Are the Brave, Grizzly Adams, The Rainmaker, Iceman, Crocodile Dundee, The Emerald Forest, Jeremiah Johnson,* or *Dances with Wolves,* to name a few. The Bible, too, is full of Wildman stories with plenty to teach about the way this archetype connects men to God: the narratives of Adam, Ishmael, Esau, Samson, Amos, John the Baptist, and especially Jesus. Nowhere in Scripture, however, does the Wildman archetype appear more powerfully and vividly than in the legends of Elijah.

A Voice in the Wilderness

Suddenly, and out of nowhere, Elijah appears before a shocked King Ahab, proclaiming: "By the living Yahweh, the God of Israel whom I serve, there shall be no dew or rain for many years — until I say so" (1 Kgs 17:1). Wildmen are like that; they come and go freely, appearing out of the wilderness and vanishing back into it with astonishing ease.[5] Yet Ahab is more amazed by Elijah's message than his method of delivering it, for the prophet is not issuing here a long-range weather forecast predicting the probability of dry weather, but declaring bluntly that rain will cease at his own command, through the power of Yahweh!

The legends of Wildmen often speak of their mystical powers over nature — especially the ability to conjure up storms or drive them away.[6] In the Elijah legends, the punishing drought inflicted on Israel by the prophet symbolizes a fundamental disruption in the cosmic order: Israel has abandoned its worship of the one true God, and nature itself withers and languishes. Yet this story tells us something important about the Wildman archetype as well. Mythically, Elijah's ability to block rainstorms bespeaks a powerful connectedness with nature; unlike civilized men, he is not victimized by apparently freak and random acts of nature, but so unified with them as to be "at cause" with the natural forces. When the Wildman is thus constellated in a man, our Western philosophical perception of reality alters; a man no longer wars with nature — fearing it, fighting it, or trying to elude it. He goes with nature's flow, and "rides the horse the direction it is going," so to speak. Westernized and urbanized consciousness dams rivers; Wildman consciousness "causes" them to flow downstream. Ahab resists the drought and rails against it; Elijah so aligns himself with the myriad forces that bring the drought into being as to be part of its cause. One kind of consciousness alienates and enrages, the other submits and reconciles.[7]

After the confrontation, Yahweh immediately orders Elijah to flee eastward to the Great Desert. The wilderness (*midbar*), of course, is of enormous significance in the Bible. The desert is the place from which the Patriarchs came, and on the fringe of which they lived and moved and had their being. It is the place where Israel mythically became a nation during the forty years of wandering after the Exodus from Egypt. The biblical wilderness is a place of testing and tutoring, whether for Moses or for Jesus, a place where Yahweh can take his beloved to be alone with him and bring him to his senses. So it is that Elijah goes to the desert, not just to escape the wrath of Ahab, but to learn an even deeper trust in God as he prepared to confront Israel's perversity with the full fury of Yahweh's wildness.

The desert feeds Elijah. With intimate and innocent tenderness, ravens minister to him, bringing him bread by day and meat at night (1 Kgs 17:2–6). And though the land about languishes in hot drought, a cooling brook quenches the prophet's thirst. On the wilderness Elijah suckles like a baby, feeling from moment to moment and day to day his vulnerability and smallness, yet learning thereby all about humility and trust. In his daily precariousness Elijah experiences the obedient attunement of man to the universe and how the cosmos will feed him even as it teaches. In his total dependence on God, Elijah is radically free. He does not need to jump through Ahab's hoops or play Jezebel's games, for unlike the hired prophets, Elijah doesn't get his bread by delivering to Pharaoh the comfortable bromides of civil religion (Amos 7:10–16). Nor does Elijah have to jump in bed with Ahab and Jezebel like a religious whore whining for a royal kiss or a regal word of approval. The wilderness provides all the meat and drink and approval he needs.

For many modern people the wilderness, if indeed they ever go there, is somewhere to get away from it all, a picture-postcard place where they can relax before gearing up to "get back to reality." For Elijah, the wilderness *is* reality — not a vast emptiness, but a positive presence, alive with ancient spirits, tingling with mystery, steeped in deep wisdom, the place where life's forces confront him in their raw, nonnegotiable, and pristine implacability. If a modern man is to gain access to his own inner Wildman, it is to these wilds that he must go, not in ATVs with engines screaming and radios blaring, but in silence. Many modern men inflict themselves on the wilderness rather than genuinely receive anything from it, totally missing the wisdom it would provide if respected, watched, and heard. Nor does the wilderness that evokes a man's Wildman have to be the Amazon jungles or the heights of Everest; a nearby stretch of woods or even a quiet park can do it. Whatever its locale, a wild place reverently experienced can conjure the archetype, creating a consciousness-change in a man as he is freed at least for the moment from the pursuit of his most recent delusions, and challenged with the eschatological realities of life itself: birth, survival, death, and rebirth.

The Contest on Carmel

Elijah returns to Israel glowing with power; immediately he feeds a hungry widow with magic jars of meal and oil and then raises her dead son back to life (1 Kgs 17:7–24). It is significant that the biblical editors located these two miracle stories immediately after the account of the prophet's desert experience,[8] for Elijah's wilderness sojourn is not a vacation but a source of spiritual power that the prophet immediately makes available to the most vulnerable members of his society: the widow and the fatherless son. That is the great moral test of the Wildman archetype: whether its energy functions heroically — that is, on behalf of the people — or whether it is purely an egocentric mind-trip for spiritual entertainment.

Elijah next offered his Wildman energy to the whole kingdom as he sought to restore his people to the stark truth of Yahweh's sole lordship over Israel. So it was that Elijah, appearing out of nowhere as he was wont to do, directly challenged King Ahab and the prophets of Baal to a great contest — a theological Super Bowl — to determine once and for all the true God of Israel (1 Kgs 18:16–46). Each side would entreat its deity to burn as a holocaust the bull each had prepared; the God who answered with fire was God indeed. So on the appointed day, 450 prophets of Baal assembled on the heights of Mt. Carmel for the great battle against Yahweh and his lone prophet.

Men love a good contest. A tough test brings their full powers of strength, will, and spirit to the fore so that they can find out who they are and what they're really made of. A decisive game also has a way of clearing up the word-pollution that clouds disputes of all kinds; this particular match would finally cut through all the religious hot air that had steamed Israel for a generation.

Up on Carmel, the Baal prophets started out impressively enough; but though they ranted and raved, danced and shook, gashed themselves and writhed in ecstatic frenzy, nothing happened. Their impressive incantations amounted to nothing more than a lot of bull, so to speak, which was now lying cold and raw on the altar. Elijah could not resist a wisecrack, urging the Baalists to cry out even louder, since their god might be taking an afternoon nap!

Then it was Elijah's turn. In a way, the prophet could not lose. Yahweh, after all, is a storm god, a God of lightning and thunder, and a God of fire; sending a fiery sign of power is a Yahweh specialty (Ps 29). Elijah's prayer for fire was not a cheap parlor trick, however, but an invocation of Deep Magic for the purpose of demonstrating before Israel Yahweh's glory. As lightning flashed and fire fell, the bull blazed on Elijah's altar in a holy holocaust. Yahweh won, and the whole people cried out, "Yahweh is God!" Elijah, flushed hot with victory, then conjured up a storm from the implacably blue skies to the west. Suddenly, a wisp of cloud over the sea billowed into a dark storm heavy with rain; the drought was over. As Yahweh's gift fell to the earth in torrents, renewing the forests and fields of Israel with life-giving water, a stunned Ahab fled Carmel in his chariot, racing back to Jezreel and Jezebel at the highest speed. Elijah, like a young gazelle, ran after him all the way in hot pursuit.

Earth, Wind, and Fire

Back home, Ahab complained to Jezebel like a schoolyard brat whining to his momma (1 Kgs 19:1–2); someone had stood up to the royal bully at last and the little king couldn't take the heat. Jezebel was furious at this turn of events, and quickly ordered Elijah's execution. This brief vignette is noteworthy. It is an article of radical feminist dogma that political oppression and religious violence are hallmarks of male patriarchy; women are supposedly only the historic victims of this arrangement.[9] This ideological claim does not always square with the facts, either in ancient stories or modern observations. The Jezebel pericope demonstrates that the authors of the Elijah cycle are well aware that upper-class women usually profit from patriarchy and play a major role in encouraging and perpetuating economic, religious, and political injustice. A century later, the prophet Amos also realized that oppression is an equal employment opportunity when he called the aristocratic women of Israel "cows of Bashan ... oppressing the needy and grinding the poor to dust, saying to your husbands, 'Bring us drinks!' " (Amos 4:1). This ancient arrangement also holds in modern times, it seems; for every Jim has his Tammy, every Harry his Leona, and every Ferdinand his Imelda.

Hearing his death sentence, the shaken Elijah quickly flees Israel and heads south, back to the wilds of Moses' original encounter with God, Mt. Horeb.[10] The prophet's flight to this peak is more than a bid for political asylum — for that, he could have fled anywhere. Elijah's journey to Horeb is nothing less than a spiritual odyssey, a pilgrimage to the holy wilderness where Yahweh first wooed and won Israel, and where Moses first learned Deep Magic at the hands of God. Retracing the Exodus route through the Sinai for forty days and fed magically in the desert by angels, Elijah followed his inner spiritual compass unerringly to the towering Horeb, source of God's gift of holy wildness for Israel.

An increasing phenomenon among good men who struggle daily with intractable and mounting social problems is the so-called burnout syndrome. Social workers get overwhelmed with endless cases of poverty, priests get drained by the despair of the reservation or the inner-city, policemen get numbed by the growing burden of drug crimes, and so on. It is tempting for such generous men to think they have to do it all alone, that the burden lies totally on their own shoulders. So it was with Elijah; saving his entire society "alone" amounted to an enormous energy drain, and the fiery prophet was quite simply depressed and "burned out" as he trekked through the Sinai. Elijah's instincts were perfect, however, as he rightly returned to the earth to remember its ancient wisdom. That is a good lesson for those tempted to a Messiah complex: the sun rises and the sun sets, generations go and generations come, and there is nothing new under the sun (Eccl 1–2). A prominent physician friend with a large AIDS case-load, for example, heals his own burnout syndrome by working several days a week in his fruit and vegetable garden, digging into the earth, growing food and nurturing new life, and experiencing the natural rhythms of nature to balance the sorrow of watching patients drift inexorably into death.

Exhausted, depleted, and afraid as he arrives at the holy mountain, the prophet does something that bears deep mythological significance. Elijah promptly hides himself in a cave in Horeb's side and falls asleep (1 Kgs 19:9). We know now that Israel's ancestors lived in caves more than a hundred thousand years before the biblical period and that many Hebrews dwelt in house-caverns right through the time of Jesus, who was born in a cave-manger in Bethlehem, raised in a cave-dwelling in Nazareth, and buried in a cave-tomb in Jerusalem. When Elijah descends into the darkest bowels of the earth, he puts himself in direct touch there not only with his Hebrew ancestors, but powerful masculine spiritual forces of the most ancient kind.

A widespread misconception engendered by advocates of Goddess religion holds that the earth is the exclusive domain of *Gaia* and the feminine deities. This notion ignores male mythology as well as archaeological evidence of an ancient masculine religiosity that once related men to the "chthonic" (Greek: *chthon* = "earth"). Indeed, scientists uncovered the oldest evidence of man's religiosity in Neanderthal caves: Le Mustiere and La Chapelle-aux-Saints in France, and — interestingly enough — Elijah's Mt. Carmel in Israel. The magnificent Paleolithic Temple Caves of Lascaux, decorated with awesome and hauntingly beautiful paintings of prehistoric animals, probably witnessed many millennia of manhood initiation rites and ordeals.[11] The ritual significance of these caves is apparent. From the mother's womb, a child is born as a human; but to be considered an adult male, the child must "die" in the cave and experience a *masculine* rebirth ordeal. Symbolically, the earth is the place of childhood death and manhood resurrection; the cave is the child-tomb and the male-womb.[12] That is why the male earth deities are usually gods of the underworld — Freyr, Pluto, Hades, Osiris, and Tammuz — gods who rule the land of the dead and the passageways to rebirth into new life.[13] A journey into and out of a cave is thus virtually a ritual experience of death and resurrection, a sacramental encounter deep in the earth with the wild elemental powers of annihilation and recreation.

Elijah, drained from his desert trek and defeated in his prophetic task, enters the cave on Horeb to die. In the numbing black air of the cavern, heavy with the power of death, Elijah falls asleep and descends to the land of Sheol, the mythical Hebrew underworld. He is spiritually dead, defeated, a failure. But what really died? Whatever remained of Elijah's Messiah complex, his childish hope of success, his selfish dreams of fame, and more: all his egocentric claims on society's approval, its perks, its profits, and its goodies. Elijah had failed, and like languishing prophets before and after him, he sought death, perhaps longing never to have been born. But at long last, he was finally ready to live as a fully free man.

Deep inside the earth, Elijah encountered the mighty chthonic power of God, not as a Hades or a Pluto, but in the surprising *persona* of Yahweh, that deity of thunder and lightning who ought not appear *in* the earth but *above* it, the same divine presence who so astonished the Psalmist:

> Where could I flee from your face?
> If I climb the heavens, you are there.
> Even if I lie in Sheol, you are there too!
> Ps 139:7–8

Waking the slumbering prophet in a voice that no doubt shook the grotto walls, Yahweh roared, "What are you doing here, Elijah?" and commanded him to arise and climb to the top of Horeb. Pulled from his tomb, Elijah was born again under that starry desert sky, exposed to the raw elemental forces of earth, wind, and fire. First came a mighty wind that split the rocks, then an earthquake that sent the earth reeling, and then a lightning fire — all numinous signs of divine power and specialties of Yahweh's Deep Magic. But Yahweh — wild, unpredictable, unbeholden, and unbound to previous theophanies, theologies, or myths — was in none of them. Instead, his Holy Wildness wafted in on a breeze so mild and quiet, so fresh, that Elijah covered his face and retreated once more to the cave, the tough prophet unable to bear the breath of divine gentleness. There the voice charged him with a heroic mission: return to Israel and continue his prophetic ministry of faith and justice, this time dead to his society-sensitive ego and all considerations of what others might think or say or do.

Reborn and supercharged with the divine spirit-breeze, clean as the desert air, Elijah returns to Israel with new fire, burning with righteousness for the exploited (1 Kgs 21) and scorching the wicked with judgment (2 Kgs 1). There he chooses a disciple to carry forth the torch of justice and complete his mission to Israel: Elisha ben Shaphat. Leaving Elisha the mantle of responsibility, he disappears into the heavens in a chariot of fire, born aloft by horses of fire (2 Kgs 2). Elijah vanishes as quickly as he first showed up, disappearing into the thin vapor and returning to the sky, free like the crackling desert wind.

Finding the Wildman Within

How can a modern man find an Elijah's power and freedom in himself? Knowledge of the Christian tradition can help a little, though a man must do considerable digging through layers of urbanized alienation from nature to find the secret.[14] Fortunately, Catholicism retains a few lively traditions, rituals, and stories of Wildman saints and vestiges in its worship of a primal pagan relationship to nature. Such liturgical symbols as Easter fire, holy water, baptismal salts, Easter eggs, and Christmas trees revere the sacramentality of natural objects themselves and suggest a deeper holiness within all creation. Rites such as the blessing of animals and fields remind us of our dependence on and relatedness to the natural world. Festivals such as Halloween and Mardi Gras or liturgical seasons like Advent and Lent put us in touch with the mysterious death/resurrection rhythms of nature in which we share. Stories and legends of the saints — Christopher and Patrick, Francis, Anthony and the Desert Fathers — exemplify what the classical Christian Wildman looks like.

One such Wildman story relates the life of the greatest and most beloved saint of the Catholic tradition, Francis of Assisi. As a youth, Francis stripped himself nude in the city square before shocked fellow townsmen and church officials, renouncing the lure of possessions forever to embrace Lady Poverty. He is still renowned for his intimate familiarity with nature, his relatedness to Brother Sun and Sister Moon, and his friendship with ravenous wolves and darting birds alike. Yet Francis did not wallow in nature like a pining Romantic, but brought this free and refreshing wildness directly back to the world of men, whether in his tender care for leprous beggars, his concern for the poor, or his brotherly conversation with his captor, a Muslim caliph. Francis's close relatedness to nature afforded him an awesome freedom from the greed of materialistic pursuits and fear of "what other people might think," and he still stands out as an inspiration, guide, and model for Christians nearly a thousand years later.

It is not realistic or even necessarily desirable that modern men live out the Wildman archetype to the extent that Elijah or Francis of Assisi did; what is crucial is that they learn to get access to it when appropriate. A number of programs such as Outward Bound, various Christian Wilderness Retreat experiences, and Wildman Weekends exist to help men vivify this wizened archetype in themselves. Most men, however, like to re-create the Wildman on their own. For them, weekend fishing trips, autumn hunting expeditions, or summer backpacking treks aren't finally so much about catching the limit of trout, bagging a deer, or getting some exercise, but about resurrecting a moribund and atrophying part of themselves that they cherish dearly and need badly.

Ultimately, a man can find his Wildman only through his own unique spiritual hero journey, seeking Yahweh now in earthquakes, now in small breezes, now in quiet meditation, now in keen watching, letting ravens feed him and small brooks quench his thirst. In their own ways, many men have found this secret path; they are our fathers and grandfathers, brothers and sons. They tell us that they find God, not so much in church, but out under the open sky; there they pray well and truthfully. If only they would return, like Elijah, to the people of God with their wild boon! If only they would bring back to our suburbanized and Izod-shod church their earthy, windy, and fiery wildness.

Chapter 9

Elisha the Healer

The Elisha Cycle (2 Kgs 2–13) relates folktales and legends about Elisha ben Shaphat, the designated prophetic successor of Elijah. It is likely that such a historical person named Elisha did succeed Elijah from the prophetic ranks, and that he accomplished what his mentor could not: the destruction of the Ahab regime through the instigation of a *coup d'état* led by the military strongman Jehu (2 Kgs 9). The folklore surrounding Elisha, however, suggests a rather more pacific personality than we might expect. Whereas the Elijah stories are charged with symbols of fire and conflict, the Elisha Cycle is permeated with images of water and tales of healing. The archetype of the Healer that emerges from the Elisha myths illustrates the surprising potential within every man to cure illness, restore wholeness, and heal wounds.

The Shamanic Healer

One of the most forceful spiritual figures in primary cultures, whose archetype appears in old myths and even today in the lives of many men, is a healing hero known as the shaman.[1] This character is the prototype of all male religious figures, the grandfather of the Mystic, Priest, and Magician archetypes, and the origin as well of the role of physician. It is the shaman's task to cure the physical, emotional, and spiritual illnesses of his tribe, although he himself would not make very strong distinctions between these afflictions. For the shaman regards the root cause of all sickness as spiritual, namely, as the result of an attack by evil spirits. Physical disease, madness, depression — even bodily injuries — are ultimately diagnosed as the result of affliction by various enemy demons. The only possible cure for such maladies is also spiritual: exorcising the bad spirits and allying the sufferer with good spirits stronger than the ones causing the problem.

The shaman is a kind of spiritual Warrior, and his healing power is typically agonistic and masculine: fighting and overpowering attackers by making alliances with Higher Powers. As distinct from classic feminine healing, which nurtures the ill person in a relationship of love, gentleness, and empathy, masculine healing involves power and force, conflict and alliances.[2] The shaman, who may also embody certain feminine spiritual empathetic and intuitional gifts, is quintessentially the Master of Spirits. He is a seer with keen observational powers who first discerns in the sufferer's symptoms the presence of unseen malevolent demons, then finds their weak points, and finally marshals the shaman's own familiar spirits into battle through the application of powerful herbs, magic incantations, or exorcising dances.[3]

"By His Wounds We Are Healed"

The shaman typically receives his healing powers only after a harrowing spiritual hero journey. Usually vulnerable himself early in his life to physical trials and emotional or mental problems, the shaman often suffers a life-threatening illness or a major crisis that demands a monumental fight for life against the spiritual demons that plague him. Under the tutelage and encouragement of an older, mentoring shaman, he learns to ally himself with such supernatural helpers as "spirit animals," ghosts, angels, or gods. This titanic spiritual struggle issues either in death — or life. If he survives, the shaman is thereafter protected against demons by his "familiar spirits," that is, the sponsoring personal guardians who remain close to him throughout life and to whom he may turn in ecstatic moments to cure others. For this is really the point of the whole process: a shamanic healer is cured not for himself only, but on behalf of the people; his miraculous recovery from his own illness properly issues in a lifetime of heroic service to the sick.

The Healer Within

The psychic remnants of the shaman still exist in the male soul as the Healer archetype. This is an important realization for a man to come to in the present era when masculinity is regarded primarily as wounding and violent. Men need to know that, in addition to such well-known archetypes as the Warrior and King, they also come psychically equipped with a tremendous capacity to heal wounds and bring about new wholeness in themselves and others. But in an aggressive and competitive culture such as ours, how can a man call forth this Healer in himself so as to become a source of healing for others?

A man must first learn to heal himself. To be a man is to bear wounds and wear scars, a truth once vividly symbolized in the bodily incisions and mutilations of the manhood initiation rites. Unfortunately, not many men realize until late in life, if at all, that they are indeed truly injured and that they carry psychic damage such as the father-wound, mother-guilt, dashed dreams, lost opportunities, various addictions, and career or relationship failures. Since many men are forbidden in childhood to feel and express emotions, they often live their whole lives in numbness, unaware of their own continuing pain and woundedness — until a dramatic crisis breaks and overwhelms the denial.

Often this crisis emerges in the form of a psychosomatic illness as the body physically "acts out" unconscious emotional pain in the form of an illness. A man who couldn't experience love might develop heart problems, a man who couldn't stand up to his father or anyone else might create disorders of the backbone, and a man who couldn't handle his emotions might find himself with ulcers, unable to stomach things anymore. Not that psychosomatic messages are always so clear; many ailments and diseases defy facile psychological analysis. Nevertheless, the illness inevitably provokes a crisis, a demand for decision, change, and transformation. This is the great paradox and the hidden mystery of disease: in its midst can lie hopeful new possibilities for growth and wholeness.[4] The Healer is the archetype that, when accessed, guides this transformation process according to the shamanic pattern.

Self-healing is a tricky topic and subject to tremendous abuse. Some spiritual practitioners peddle a typically American "instant" version based on a dramatic religious conversion, New Age crystals, arcane herbs, or packaged mind control. All of these objects and practices may symbolize and even assist healing, but none can solely and directly cause it. The healing process takes place in a much more mysterious, complex, and individual fashion than the spiritual salesmen would have us believe, in league with forces and on a timetable not amenable to our conscious direction. Indeed, the greatest part of self-healing is probably beyond our conscious control, consisting primarily in the simple passive openness to being healed — by time, by nature, by the love of others, and by God. There is no healing without a fundamental humility before these great forces. Yet certainly one of these forces is our own willful and conscious participation in the healing pattern, a deliberate, strategic, and shaman-like "mastery of the spirits."

"Our Name Is Legion"

At the very least, spiritual mastery at times means a bottom-line, steely, and cold-blooded ability to say no to evil spirits, a refusal to listen to their voices or entertain their promptings, a willingness to banish them from our mental-emotional stage. However one wishes to conceive of these cruel forces — as negative mental "tape-recordings" from parental voices in childhood, as inherited familial demons, as actual evil spirits, or even as Satan himself — is irrelevant to the strategy for defeating them. Whatever their ontological source, these inner voices tell us that we are bad or worthless, hopelessly sick, destined to die anyway, and unable to make it through. They tell us that all this healing business is just religious mumbo-jumbo and that things are never really going to get better anyway. These evil spirits tell us many such things, all of them lies and half-truths. One must never listen to them or make decisions under their influence.

Genuine healing requires a kind of shamanic exorcism or expulsion of these nattering spirits. It is probably more truthful to say that *many* ongoing "exorcisms" are needed as part of a long process of healing. Dramatic shamanic rituals can play an essential role in symbolizing and effecting the demonic defeat; humans are sacramental and dramatic beings, after all. Yet the outward exorcising sign must be accompanied by an inward determination, exercised frequently, not to cooperate and collude in one's own spiritual or physical demise by believing the demons. Numerous studies suggest that such gritty determination not only affects one's mental and emotional state, but even enhances the physical functioning of the body's immune system.[5]

With a Little Help from My Friends

Intrinsically linked to exorcism, or slamming the door on interior negativity, is the phenomenon of spiritual alliance. None of us is capable, entirely on his own, of defeating the bad spirits and affecting his own cure. This is an unpopular truth in individualistic America, where the belief that you always have to "do it yourself" is itself one of the evil spirits that needs exorcism. Healing requires a strong community of committed and compassionate fellow human beings who join the ill person in a bond of affection, love, physical touching, supportive conversation, hope, and prayer. The Healer, when potentiated, instinctively accepts an alliance with these "good spirits." This healing alliance is a key reason Alcoholics Anonymous and similar Twelve Step programs are so effective; regular meetings with other recovering addicts offer enormous spiritual support and encouragement to individuals who, in turn, become sources of healing and help to yet others in recovery. The relationship of a Twelve Step sponsor to another in recovery directly enacts the Healer archetype in both individuals. Similar constellations of the Healer take place in support groups with individuals battling cancer, AIDS, and other diseases.[6]

The therapeutic alliance model, by the way, is one helpful way of understanding the meaning of "church." In a world where genuine spiritual values are increasingly ignored, the church can provide a place where we link ourselves with our brothers and sisters in an alliance of spirits mutually giving and seeking the regular encouragement we need to keep on loving, hoping, worshipping, and praying. Many such religious communities — churches, synagogues, and mosques — regularly provide such spiritual help to their members; it is virtually impossible to "keep the faith" (any faith) without it. Two of the main reasons why so many American men lack much spiritual depth is that, on the one hand, the church of their experience actually offers no such fellowship, or on the other, these men often are too individualistic to accept communion with other believers.

The Goodness Deep Down

Access to the Healer archetype also offers an *entrée* into the experience of spirit-world friendship in a way that we might never have imagined. The Healer knows the helping power of objects such as crystals, herbs, statues, medals, pictures, rocks, crucifixes, holy water, and holy places. Many people might call this interest magic; it is — Deep Magic. Whether holy objects and places actually possess an elemental spirit, whether they symbolize a psychological power within us, or whether they just create the so-called placebo effect, they can help cure people. An ill person can intuitively find a spiritually powerful object or place by shamanically attending through meditation to what captures his imagination or what gives hope. Some may find a favorite place with a mystical feel or uncanny sense of power around it; for others, a certain holy picture may evoke confidence; still others may find strength in a beautiful rock or crystal. It is well known that thousands of sick people have experienced recovery through the holy waters of Lourdes. Elisha the Healer found much power from the healing effects of water, as we shall see.

One of the most striking features of shamanistic healing is the belief in the power of "spirit animals" as guides and helpers; unfortunately, this insight is almost totally lacking in modern, urbanized religions. We are ourselves animals. We are related on almost every level to other animals. Animals affect us powerfully — as pets and as friends and as symbols of strength. A trip to the zoo can work wonders in restoring our sense of connectedness to nature, our humor about ourselves, and a sense of wonder at the Architect who designs such creatures. It is also well known that a pet cat or a favorite dog can provide a unique kind of companionship that helps some people recover from illness and others live longer after retirement.

The shamanistic Healer, when conjured, might seek a "power animal" to join in his therapeutic alliance; to find it, a man might reflect intuitively on which animal most symbolizes his essence or speaks to him most about health, power, and survival. Throughout my life, I have had such an uncanny spiritual relationship to the hawk, which seems to show up at crucial times in my life, circling and hovering. For me, the hawk is a messenger from the Most High who sees all and knows all; he is for me a kind of sacrament of God's presence. In a similar way, at his baptism Jesus saw a dove descending on him (Mk 1:10); Elijah the Wildman was fed by ravens, well known in the shamanistic world as bearer of magic medicine, while Elisha the Healer seems to have had a special connection to bears.[7]

All the Saints and Angels

The Healer archetype also allies us with the healing power of guardian angels and with the saints, our departed brothers and sisters who live now in glory. Belief in such a relationship with our spirit ancestors and friends is a beautiful feature of many Asian and African religions, where the shamanic Healer tradition is still strong. To its credit, Catholicism also retains a lively awareness of the "communion of saints"; every Mass remembers them, and almost every day one of their feasts is celebrated throughout the whole world. Most Catholics still pray to a special "patron saint" or even to a number of favorite spiritual helpers such as Mary, Francis, Jude, Anthony, or Therese.

In preserving the belief in spirit helpers, most of the world religions are aware that the universe is a far more mysterious and populated place than our eyes can see and that intercessory help is available from saints and Boddhisattvas and angels in the spirit world if only we will open ourselves to it. Unfortunately, many modern men are as cut off from such spirit-friendships as they are from nature and animals. Materialism insists on reducing everything to its least common denominator: matter alone, while rationalism eliminates from its purview all reality not acceptable to the left-brain. Even many theologians boil down the Christian tradition to doctrinal and ethical propositions alone and dispense theological vitamin pills to the faithful rather than invite them to feast on a rich spiritual banquet. No wonder so many modern men are, in turn, so spiritually hungry and malnourished.

When the Healer archetype is activated, however, the heart is attuned to spiritual channels that intuitively detect the presence of loving persons around us; indeed, people who have undergone out-of-the-body-experiences or "life after life" episodes often report that the spirits of departed friends and relatives float around us like clouds.[8] Many of us intuitively realize this and even instinctively know who our helping spirits are: a kindly grandfather, a favorite aunt, a parent, or a faithful friend. We can still feel from them the love and care we experienced directly in this life — a phenomenon recently portrayed so enjoyably in the film *Ghost*. Yet openness to the Healer can

also tune us into the presence of loving spirits we might not otherwise have considered. In my own experience, one such figure — a
favorite and very funny Jesuit teacher from high school — came to
my attention after numerous uncanny and synchronistic experiences
involving his funeral card, which kept showing up no matter where I
put it. Finally, I swallowed my rationalism and began consciously talking to him and acknowledging his loving presence. The "card tricks"
stopped!

Sometimes it takes the catastrophe of an illness to jar a man out of
the culturally bred rationalism that has "tuned him out" of the spirits; pain can awaken as well as hurt. Since many men often work
themselves throughout their lives into a state of hyper-independence
and alienation, access to the inner Healer can prove especially helpful to them during a health crisis. Alone at night in a hospital bed,
a man might at last admit his sense of isolation and loneliness and
find spiritual solace in the knowledge that he is surrounded by unseen loving spirits. The knowledge that we are not alone or abandoned
can transform a life; a wounded Healer can become, in turn, one
of those loving spirits for others. This is what happened with Elijah
the Wildman. Alone, wounded, and persecuted on Mt. Horeb, Yahweh sent him back to Israel to choose his faithful disciple Elisha ben
Shaphat (1 Kgs 19:16). Even after he departed this earth on chariots
of fire, Elijah remained "in the spirit" to assist Elisha in his healing
ministry.

Elisha and the Mantle of Discipleship

The story of Elisha presents a wrinkle on the classic Healer motif; unlike, for example, the shamanic prophet Ezekiel (Ezek 3–5), Elisha is
not known to have faced a life-threatening health crisis according to the
shamanic pattern. But his mentor, Elijah, did face the danger of death
on Horeb and overcame it. So perhaps when Elijah is pictured throwing
his magic mantle over his disciple Elisha immediately after returning to
Israel (1 Kgs 19:19–21), we are to understand that Elisha has now inherited in his own person the shamanic healing experience of his master.[9]
Elisha's identification with his mentor is now total; as a sign of his complete discipleship, Elisha kisses his parents goodbye and slays his dumb
oxen in a great barbecue for the people.

The mantle motif occurs again later in a dramatic farewell scene at
the Jordan River (2 Kgs 2).[10] Elisha, insisting that he inherit a *double*
portion of his master's spirit, follows the departing Elijah across the
Jordan. Suddenly, chariots of fire appear and sweep Elijah up to heaven
in a whirlwind; Elisha never saw him again. But Elisha wisely seizes his
mentor's cloak — the shaman's magic mantle that will hereafter confer

Elijah's power on the wearer — and with it strikes the waters of the Jordan. The waters divide, and Elisha crosses over dry-shod once again into the Promised Land.[11]

Immediately, the people of Jericho ask the prophet to heal their city's water supply — a fortunate request since Elisha will hereafter prove himself an expert at water miracles! Whereas Elijah worked miraculous signs involving earth, wind, and fire (1 Kgs 19:10–14), Elisha becomes adept at conjuring up wonders with the fourth natural element, water. In typically shamanic fashion, he requests a bowl and salt — a purifying magic potion — and heals Jericho's spring water for all time (2 Kgs 2:19–22). Elisha's first miracle story is a psychologically significant one: the shamanic Healer, once summoned and energized, cures the wounds in the earth that bring death and miscarriage; the Healer brings about new life for the whole people.

The Danger of Sorcery

The Elisha narrative next delivers a bizarre folkloric account picturing the misuse of the Healer, a typical feature of biblical literature that alerts readers to the shadow side of each archetype. Like a new Joshua fresh from his astonishing miracle at Jericho (see Josh 7), the victorious Elisha begins his climb up the road to Bethel and the hill country of Ephraim (2 Kgs 2:23–25). Full of himself and puffed up with power, the prophet promptly stumbles into tragedy and evil. On his path, gangs of bratty little boys taunt the traveller (as they are still wont to do in Palestine!) with shouts of "Get lost, baldy!" Angry, Elisha allows his healing power to turn demonic, and he goes over to the "dark side of the Force." Cursing the rascals with his shamanic power, Elisha summons his spirit-animals from the woods; two she-bears roar out of the forest and maul the youthful miscreants.

This is sorcery — the use of spiritual powers to harm rather than heal; Elisha misuses his shamanic connection with animal-spirits as an act of revenge.[12] But how relevant is this example of spiritual abuse for modern men? In the strictest sense, sorcery is not a common phenomenon, although as a priest I have encountered persons with voodoo and witchcraft entanglements — especially in the South — more often than I would have ever expected. But in a more extended sense, the Sorcerer is a negative archetype that describes men who exploit their spiritual powers for egotistical or jealous reasons: for medical profits rather than the holistic healing of patients, for ecclesiastical power rather than pastoral ministry, or for revenge on a co-worker rather than advancement of a common cause. The she-bear story reminds us that it is all too easy to consider one's spiritual powers as personal possessions to be used however one pleases; they are not so. Shamanic power is created for the healing of the people, not the power and convenience of the Healer.

Cleansing the Leper and Raising the Dead

After his close encounter with evil sorcery, which he overcame and never again experienced, still more water miracles flowed from Elisha. During a war against Moab, the allied kings of Israel, Judah, and Edom pleaded with the prophet to find their troops water; a reluctant Elisha fell into ecstasy and produced the needed pool (2 Kgs 3:12–20). At Gilgal he purified some poisoned soup on behalf of his fellow prophets (4:38–41) and later floated a valuable iron axe-head that one of these same prophets had dropped into the Jordan (6:1–7). But Elisha's greatest water-miracle healed, not one of his own colleagues or even one of his own countrymen, but the enemy Syrian general Naaman, stricken with leprosy, whom Elisha ordered to wash seven times in the Jordan (5:1–14). The story is a famous one, and its meaning clear: the Healer is called beyond the bounds of his own petty self-interest and beyond all political beliefs and religious ideologies as well.[13] The Healer ultimately is the archetype by which men reconcile themselves to their former enemies by experiencing with them our common need for healing and life.

None of these tests could match Elisha's greatest challenge: the son of the great lady of Shunem lying stone-cold dead on his bed (2 Kgs 4). No water tricks possible here, and at last Elijah seemed out of his depths. So we can well imagine to whom Elisha turned at this moment: his "spirit-guide" and shamanic master Elijah, who had raised another dead youth to life once before (1 Kgs 17). As the prophet came in person to the deathly room, he lay down upon the child, pressing mouth to mouth, eyes to eyes, and hands to hands. Elisha seven times breathed into the boy the breath of life. When the child's eyes blinked open, the prophet returned the boy to his mother. It was Elisha's greatest moment, and a healing experience for himself as well. Only a short while earlier he had used his shamanic powers as a Sorcerer to injure little boys; now he used those powers as a Healer to raise one of them to new life.

The Wounding and Wounded Healer

One may rightly wonder why the biblical authors would portray such a supposed Healer as Elisha as the instigator of the Jehu uprising that wiped out the entire Ahab regime and violently ushered in a fundamentalist Yahwist regime (2 Kgs 9–10). The answer lies in the mythology of the Shaman archetype itself. Masculine healing, remember, is not especially nurturing, gentle, or nice. On the contrary, the male Healer often must act as a Warrior wielding a blade, typically harsh, cold, and antagonistic to evil spirits and all life-threatening enemies. He is the surgeon, willing to slice into a frail body and bloodily cut out a cancerous growth to save the whole person; he is the dentist willing to drill painfully into a tooth to save it; and he is the psychotherapist who insists that we face our most painful memories in order to heal them. The artists who composed the Elisha Cycle saw their hero in exactly that way. The prophet saved individuals with shamanic magic; he saved Israel with a painful operation that sliced out the cancer of the sinful Ahab regime.

This is the Healer that men must at times call upon if they are to bring about wholeness: the destructive Shiva who annihilates the dying world so he can recreate anew, who burns the field so that new crops can grow, and who amputates a limb to save the body. He is the man who knows well his own wounds and his own vulnerabilities, who humbly admits his need for help, and who cooperates with his spiritual friends in a mutually healing therapeutic alliance. He is the recovering alcoholic who becomes a source of compassion and encouragement for other drunks, the hopeful Person with AIDS who teaches those around him gratitude for life, and the cancer patient whose fight for life ennobles all who know him. If we would stop for a moment, we might realize how many of these humble Healers we have in our midst: the man in the office, face lined with wrinkles, who's "been there" and has the wisdom to show for it; the loveable janitor you somehow want to talk to, but don't know exactly why; or the teacher who says more by the way he looks at you compassionately in the eye than in any lecture he ever delivers. Our world is full of many such men, and they make us a little more human and a little more wise. The force of a healing person heals.

A Final Water-Miracle

Healing language and rhetoric are frequently inflating, grandiose, and unrealistic; starry-eyed enthusiasts often speak of "total" healing and "complete recovery" so frenetically that they create in us a sense of unease. Televangelists and New Age practitioners alike still sell their products like snake oil. In my experience, the actual healing miracles that occur in men's lives are subtle and sometimes take the eye of a hawk to see. They are no less gracious for all that.

My father struggled in the last ten years of his life with increasingly serious alcoholism. I remember all too well as a child observing his possession by the demons of Irish-Catholic guilt, his devilish suicidal feelings, fears of failure, and what other evil spirits I can only imagine. Throughout it all, he allied himself with friends in AA, tried to pray, kept hoping and working on recovery. He never really recovered; you could say too easily that he failed. But my father had a lot of heart. He was a man loyal to his friends, and he helped many, many people in small but meaningful ways. He did not let his own woundedness prevent him from caring for other people.

My father also had an extraordinary pride and joy in our roguish little hometown of Deadwood, South Dakota, with its bars and gambling and prostitution. In the summer of 1961, just a few months before he died, our water taps in Deadwood literally ran dry after a third year of drought. The city reservoirs were completely empty. A drought like that can drive a man to drink! But in his love for Deadwood, my father refused his demons and instead searched out an abandoned gold-mining shaft in the Black Hills above Deadwood where he had played as a child. He had remembered that this mine always seemed to have water in it. Like Elisha in Moab, he found a great pool in the shaft, even in the midst of the drought. Working night and day that summer, he mobilized the city council to tap the source, procure the legal rights, obtain the piping, and direct the flow into Deadwood's reservoirs. In a few days, we once again had water to drink. In the spring of the next year, still proud of his accomplishment, my father died. Wounds remained. But a little humble healing had taken place in my father's soul. The man had overcome his own alcoholic thirstiness long enough to bring a drink of water to the people he loved so much. Even today, almost thirty years later, Deadwood drinks its healing water from the pool of the Cutting Mine. I think I know who watches over it, still.

Chapter 10

Jeremiah the Prophet

The prophetic struggles begun by Elijah and Elisha against the royal regime of Israel in 850 B.C.E. resumed again over a century later. At that time, the prophets Amos and Hosea began to proclaim the coming destruction of the Kingdom of Israel as punishment for its long, sinful history of idolatry, militarism, and social injustice. Their frightening eschatological judgments were fulfilled shortly thereafter in the catastrophic destruction of the capital city of Samaria and the rest of Ephraim by Assyrian forces under Sargon II in 722 B.C.E. Israel was no more, its ten tribes lost to history.

In the south, the Kingdom of Judah survived the Assyrian onslaught in 701 B.C.E., though its hated King Manasseh capitulated to vicious colonial rule for over half a century (2 Kgs 21). In reaction to Assyrian oppression, fiercely nationalist and fundamentalist Jewish forces known as "the people of the land" seem to have engineered a murderous *coup* against Manasseh's son Amon in 740 B.C.E. and then placed Amon's nine-year-old son Josiah on the throne as a Davidic figurehead. As Assyrian power disintegrated during the next two decades Josiah, in cohorts with his patriotic Yahwist patrons, began to restore native political and religious control over Judah. The so-called Josian Reform of 622 expunged all signs of Assyrian influence from the kingdom, and with them the old native Canaanite fertility gods, symbols, priests, and high-places that had dotted the landscape. Josiah would tolerate only one cult, one priesthood, one law, one God — and at only one place: the Temple in Jerusalem.

The Prophet of the End

During these heady days there grew up in a small village near Jerusalem one Jeremiah ben Hilkiah. It seems that the youth, son of an old priestly family, strongly identified with the Josian Restoration as it rebirthed

Judean pride and religiosity all around him. In a powerful mystical encounter in 627, the boy experienced a call from Yahweh to become a "prophet to the nations" (Jer 1). This vocation was an astonishing one: with it, God gave young Jeremiah power over nations and kingdoms "to uproot and knock down, to annihilate and to destroy, to build and to plant" (Jer 1:10). As Jeremiah grew to manhood during Josiah's Jewish renaissance, the greatest era since the Golden Age of David and Solomon, his future seemed bright. God himself had promised the young man great power, awesome authority, and untold success. Or so Jeremiah thought.

Then disaster struck. Intercepting the Egyptian Pharaoh Necho at Har Megiddo as he marched to help prop up the faltering Assyrian Empire in 609 B.C.E., King Josiah was killed (2 Kgs 23:29). The event proved a spiritual Armageddon for the Jewish people and for the young prophet Jeremiah especially. From that day on Egypt ruled Judean affairs through its puppet King Jehoiakim, the reform was over and its confidence smashed, and Jews once again shuffled about under colonial rule. Jeremiah could not accept these changes. At about this time, he began prophesying in long, rolling oracles that scorched the quisling Jewish king with charges of political cowardice and cultic laxity. More ominously, Jeremiah began "to uproot and knock down, annihilate and destroy": the end of Judah, he proclaimed, loomed on the horizon. Jeremiah's exciting childhood call had now become a terrible and bitter burden: to announce a fatal prognosis over his own nation. Jeremiah prophesied that Judah's long experience as a free kingdom neared its end, that Jerusalem's inviolable status as the City of God was expiring, and that the Temple's days were numbered. The time was up.

Like a terminally ill patient who can't face the diagnosis, Jerusalem danced on in denial, accepting no bouquets, taking no visitors, and allowing no funeral arrangements. Everything was all right! No problem! Peace! But there was to be no peace. And Jeremiah insisted on saying so, repeatedly claiming that the end had come — so much so that his countrymen could hear only this eschatological part of his message. What they could not hear until long after Jeremiah trudged off to Egyptian exile were his words about a new beginning, a new way, and a New Heart (Jer 31:31–40). Jeremiah just spoke too much painful truth too clearly for everyone to accept it. In this respect, Jeremiah was a quintessential prophet.

The Prophet

The prophet is a fascinating individual. Today we tend to think of this figure only in a very limited sense, namely, as a bizarre character who predicts the future. While it is often the case that prophets foresee hidden events, prediction is only a sidelight of the prophet's main task: delivering messages from God to the people. Sociologically, the prophet is a type of intermediary who functions in religious societies as a link between people and the supernatural realm, and vice versa.[1] Through ecstatic techniques, the classic prophet enters into an altered state of consciousness and receives messages from the deity that he in turn delivers to his followers. A prophet is a "channeller" who confronts society with supernatural realities otherwise unavailable.

Theologically, the biblical prophet is a channel of grace, an instrument of revelation through which God discloses his will to the people. Biblical theologian Walter Brueggemann speaks of a "prophetic imagination" by which an individual is gifted with the ability to perceive and articulate boldly an alternative consciousness, to present God's way of thinking, feeling, valuing, and acting as a contrast to whichever particular dreary worldview is presently in vogue.[2] In Christian terms, this alternative perception is none other than the consciousness of the Kingdom of God, a fresh and radically different perspective on the meaning of life and the purpose for our existence here on earth, as envisioned by Jesus of Nazareth. In his imagination, the genuine prophet sees things as God sees them, and in his empathy, he "feels" the emotions of God.[3] Moreover, the prophet vividly communicates these visions and these feelings to the rest of us, mired as we are in the deepening ruts of the dominant and profane consciousness. The true prophet is one who radically reminds us who we really are, what we are doing here, and what we are in God's own eyes and heart — in contrast to what we have come to believe about ourselves and our world under the hypnosis of mass ideology and culture.

The true prophet is also a very masculine spiritual figure. In the first place, he longs for the Totally Other (*totaliter aliter*), for the "separate reality" of pure holiness that elevates us out of ordinary and profane consciousness. In this penchant for otherness, the prophet is a kind of spiritual Pilgrim, ecstatically seeking new and deeper truths about the human experience than are available in our familiar domestic ruts. But it is what the prophet *does* with his visions and messages that reveals the spiritual virility of the figure. He does not, like Mary, treasure these things in his heart (Lk 2:51); on the contrary, the prophet immediately proceeds to confront society with his visions to bring about a *metanoia*, or conversion of heart. In this way, the prophet functions as a kind of spiritual Warrior, his God-given message flashing like a sword aimed directly at the heart of the nation, not to kill it, but to pierce its armor of denial and complacency and expose a truly human flesh beneath. Indicting, judging, accusing, attacking, exhorting, and exciting, his words sometimes wound and always irritate, and inevitably provoke and scandalize. Every prophet is obnoxious. To the complacent, he hurls warning; to the desperate, hope. He tells us what we do not want to hear when we do not want to hear it. That is why society is always so intent and finding ways to eliminate him from its earshot.

"Yahweh Speaks — Who Will Not Prophesy?"

The Prophet is also a strong archetype in the souls of men, although many don't consciously and wholly recognize it. A man who is accessing his inner Prophet in only a partial and unconscious way tends to become the Crank, vaguely and perpetually irritated with "the way things are" in politics, business, religion, and life in general. He seems cynical and grouchy, and, on hearing yet another boss's lie, politician's half-truth, or advertiser's phony claim, his well-tuned inner "Bullshit Detector" registers its complaint with rolling eyes and shrugging shoulders. All of us know men like this, but we don't stop to consider that, deep beneath the armor of their apparent negativity beat the hearts of frustrated idealists, dreamers who imagine how much better things could be, how much more honest and more truthful. It is in their conscious access to the Prophet that these men could transform their cranky negativity into a positive spiritual and social force.

Popular psychology is currently replete with books that warn against the dangers of denial, avoidance, and dysfunctional pretense in our relationships, families, institutions, and even society in general.[4] Many of us live in a web of lies and half-truths, spun by ourselves and by others in a misguided attempt to avoid pain or prevent scandal. Marriages limp by and dysfunctional families crawl on, struggling under the fiction that all is well when, in reality, corruption festers. Similarly, our workplaces are often riddled with pretense, our churches at times a sham, our national life commonly a charade. Psychologist Scott Peck even speaks of the "People of the Lie," individuals around us who perpetuate these sickening falsities to gain power and maintain control.[5] When potentiated, the Prophet archetype is our way out of this morass, the "truth-teller" that pops the phony illusions. "People of the Truth" who are accessing this inner Prophet in a healthy way are our only hope of ever cutting through lies and deceptions in order to face reality.

It is rare to see someone speaking truthfully and lovingly from this Prophet archetype. In a culture that demands smiling faces, wears treacly "Have a Nice Day" buttons, and connotes love with Valentine hearts and concern with Care-Bears, it is difficult even to imagine that a love could exist that criticizes, or that caring can also hurt, or that truth-telling comes before healing. The self-help community needed to invent a phrase for this kind of love that seems, in American culture at least, like an oxymoron: "tough love," that is, the willingness to tell the truth to your beloved without manipulation, and let the chips fall where they may.

The Prophet in us is the "tough lover." Invoked, it enables us to see society without illusions, without tribal chauvinism or flag-waving nationalism, without the prevailing group-think, and without the blinding ideologies that confuse denial with loyalty and dissent with treason. The Prophet energizes in us a conscience that cannot abide deliberate deafness and convenient blindness. And yet this intolerance for denial arises, not from crankiness and cynicism and negativity, but from fierce love and hopeful imagination. Our inner Prophet's tough-loving derives from an alternative consciousness, an entirely fresh awareness of God's original plan that sees how things really are in contrast to the chimera of what they now seem to be.

The true artist creates out of this inner Prophet, seeing original beauty and imagining potential in ways that escape everyone else. True art is prophetic. In poetry or music or paintings, the genuine artist presents us with a vision of reality that invites us to a new way of seeing, hearing, and feeling; the K-Mart painter or Hallmark poet, alienated from his Prophet, just sketches pretty pictures or coins cute phrases. Prophetic art tells the truth, cuts through the pretense, and exposes the lies. Prophetic imagination is the force that enlivens the acting of a Dustin Hoffman, the music of a Leonard Bernstein, the paintings of a Pablo Picasso, or the cartoons of a Gary Trudeau.

Our ability to speak "tough love" truthfully from our inner Prophet is genuinely heroic. The single worst phobia that most adults admit experiencing is the fear of speaking before a roomful of people, even if the words are harmless bromides and the listeners a bunch of pussycats. How much more courageous when the audience is an institution-in-denial or a society covering up its most painful wounds and denying its most damaging demons. Such groups will do almost anything to avoid confronting their dysfunctions and self-deceptions, including the elimination of those ungracious enough to point them out. We see the results of this repression with sickening regularity: demonstrating students crushed by tanks in Tiananmen Square, Palestinian protesters gunned down on the West Bank, advocates of social justice assassinated in El Salvador, or, less violently, artists censored by the government or theologians silenced in the Catholic Church. The price of prophesying is always high; few but the heroic summon the courage to pay it.

How fortunate indeed we are that any men love the truth enough to tell it without counting the cost. In their prickly obstinacy, these prophets won't shut up. They are the officials who blow the whistle on pork-barrel defense cost overruns, tenacious reporters who won't "spin" with the official version, and liberation theologians who won't stop writing. Our novels and films celebrate such heroes, from *Mr. Smith Goes to Washington*

and *Network* to *All the President's Men,* and from *Patton* to *A Man for
All Seasons.* We are especially privileged in our own time to witness
prophetic heroes speaking their truths and offering their visions; men
such as Teilhard de Chardin and Dag Hammarskjold, Ralph Nader and
Archibald Cox, Alexander Solzhenitsyn and Andrei Sakharov, Martin
Luther King, Jr., and Malcolm X, Nelson Mandela and Daniel Ellsberg,
Ron Kovic and Winston Churchill. All of these men spoke the truth in
the great confidence that the rest of us were big enough and man enough
to hear it; they spared us no detail and refused to pander to our fears.
True prophets honor their hearers, and because of them, we see things
a little more clearly and understand reality in a way that we never could
have without them. That is the same gratitude to Jeremiah that Judah
felt a generation after the Babylonian catastrophe of 586 B.C.E. when it
began to write down and treasure the words it could not hear while
Jeremiah still lived.

"Don't Say: 'I'm Just a Boy!'"

As a youth, Jeremiah experienced an extraordinary call. A Voice spoke
to him saying, "I am appointing you as prophet to the nations" (Jer
1:2). The Voice would brook no objections from young Jeremiah either;
overruling his protests of immaturity, God gave the boy life-and-death
prophetic authority over the kingdoms. Heady stuff, this commission —
so much so that many biblical scholars assume that this call narrative
is only an artificial creation placed at the head of Jeremiah's prophetic
oracles to sanction his rhetoric with divine authority; young boys, these
scholars assume, do not have such apocalyptic experiences.

But young boys do! Anthropological literature is very familiar with
stunning, almost traumatic "call" experiences that youths receive prior
to prophetic or shamanic careers. The Great Grandfathers, for example,
charged the nine-year-old Black Elk with life-and-death powers in the
summer of 1872 as the white invasion of the High Plains threatened to
wipe out the Lakota people.[6] In a vision, the oldest Grandfather gave
Black Elk a wooden cup: "Take this," he said. "It is the power to make
live, and it is yours." Then Black Elk received a bow: "Take this," he said.
"It is the power to destroy, and it is yours." Black Elk was burdened the
rest of his life with the blessing and curse of this commission: to save
the hoop of his people from destruction.[7]

A young man, searching to find himself and discover what he is to
do with his life, is an easy mark for this kind of psychic breaking-and-
entry by the Great Spirit. The lure of a Holy Grail on a vulnerable and
susceptible youngster is powerful. It is not fair. Once a Voice shatters
a youth's quiet little world with the promise of great adventure and
heroism, there really is no peace, no rest, and no comfort until his mission

is accomplished. It is no little thing for a Voice to choose a young man; he is haunted for the rest of his life by the call, feels burdened by its demands, and ends up sad and broken if he fails.[8] Jeremiah felt like this, as we shall soon see.

The End Is Near!

Young Jeremiah experienced insistent premonitions of Judah's coming catastrophe: a bubbling cauldron tips over in the market, and the boy sees disaster sweeping in from the north (1:13). Visions of a coming end dance in his head: enemies from the north, a scorching wind from the desert, a storm of chariots like a hurricane (4:5–18). Yet all around him lurks incomprehension, the denial of death, arrogant presumption, and faces harder than flint. Against such self-satisfied pseudo-security Jeremiah is compelled to speak; the Voice is insistent upon this: "Brace yourself Jeremiah! Get up and tell them all that I command you" (1:17). Such is the prophetic compulsion. A man wired into his inner Prophet *can't* shut up and can't turn his head from the obvious truth. He must speak out.

Jeremiah does. Drilling away with all the persistence of a dentist cleaning a cavity, the young prophet drove home his tough truths. Zeroing in on the myth of Jerusalem's indestructibility, Jeremiah taunted,

> Don't trust your slogan, "the temple of Yahweh," "the temple of Yahweh," "the temple of Yahweh." But if you change your ways, treat people with justice, if you don't exploit the weak, the orphan or the widow, if you don't shed innocent blood or follow strange gods, then I will dwell with you here.
>
> Jer 7:4–7

Comparing Jerusalem's priests and prophets to quacks, he charged: "They dress my daughter's wounds carelessly saying, 'health, health' — but there is no health" (8:11). For this disease, there was no balm in Gilead. Yet Jerusalem's prophets kept mumbling comforting words that soothed rather than awoke and that denied the illness instead of recommending a good doctor.

Jerusalem would not have Jeremiah's diagnosis. The Temple hierarchy, which like most religious bureaucracies was a "non-prophet" organization and could not abide the bald-faced truth of one courageous man, finally cracked down. Pashhur, the chief temple official, ordered Jeremiah bound and tortured for one long night of hell (20:1–2), no doubt ostensibly to "protect" the people of Jerusalem from experiencing any "confusion" on hearing prophetic contradictions to the official story that all was well. As in most ecclesiastical attempts to intimidate truth-tellers, Pashhur's reeducation of Jeremiah failed to silence the prophet;

on the contrary, Jeremiah responded to the inquisition with an explicit prediction: Judah would fall to Babylon.

"You Seduced Me!"

Any man who has ever found the guts publicly to speak an unpopular truth can probably relate to what happened next to Jeremiah: a collapse of inner confidence. For the activated Prophet archetype makes us vulnerable, not only to outer crackdown measures and overt social pressures to shut up, but to our own interior Inquisition as well. It is a special quality of Jeremiah's honesty that he even shares with us his own inner struggles and psychic conflicts that resulted from his prophetic truth-telling; indeed, no other biblical character except Paul so opens his heart for all to see. Jeremiah's confessions (20:7–18) are a remarkable account of a prophet's inner doubts, his alienation and anger even at God, and his sense of isolation from his fellow men. In their honesty, Jeremiah's words form a classic expression of male agonistic prayer.

Jeremiah's opening salvo, probably uttered while his wounds still burned from Pashhur's torture, is surely the most awful thing said to or about God in the whole Bible: "You have seduced me, Yahweh, and I let you seduce me! You overpowered me — you were stronger!" (Jer 20:7). Let us be quite clear. The prophet, in accusing God of false promises while Jeremiah was still a vulnerable young boy (Jer 1), is essentially charging Yahweh here with spiritual pederasty: manipulating, tempting, and overpowering a defenseless youth with grand visions of power in order to seduce him into a prophetic task that he would otherwise never have accepted. It is a serious charge and relates directly to the adolescent's susceptibility to the call to spiritual heroism.

The Naive Male

Yet we can't let Jeremiah off the hook on this one. The angry charge of "seduction," one version of the rhetoric of victimization and the politics of whining so popular today, needs a little cool-headed appraisal. Does Jeremiah have *any* responsibility in this matter? Is Yahweh totally to blame? And is Jeremiah's suffering entirely negative, or does it present opportunities for growth? On reflection, it would seem clear that this young man has a lot of growing up to do. First of all, his suffering presents the opportunity of curing a rather serious case of masculine naiveté.

Robert Bly speaks humorously and convincingly about the Naive Male, a common type of man stuck in an early stage of individuation that is all-too-trusting, overly vulnerable, and much too passive.[9] Dreamy-eyed and innocent, young males tend to rely too easily on other people, blissfully unaware of ulterior motives, frailties, and sinfulness.

The Naive Male is the Fool of the Tarot, gamboling through the fields but about to step off a cliff. Bly rightly claims that the only "cure" for this amazingly frequent phenomenon in a young man is betrayal! One good yank of the rug out from under his youthful credulity can do the trick; a business double-cross or a relationship betrayal, while painful, contains the only hope that such a young man will ever walk with his eyes wide open and think with his head squarely on his shoulders. Looked at in this light, Yahweh's "seduction" of Jeremiah is a betrayal only of the prophet's youthful naiveté.

Then there is the little matter of Jeremiah's super-ego. There is no more demanding, perfectionistic, or grandiose phenomenon on earth than the super-ego of an adolescent male. Until he grows out of it, no one and no thing is ever good enough, everything falls short of expectations, and everyone (including himself) is unacceptably imperfect. In his narcissism, Jeremiah apparently expects Jerusalem to drop everything and gratefully accept his message of doom! Unchecked, this is a man well on the way to Crankdom, the classic danger in a man possessed by the shadow side of the Prophet. The Crank offers opinions willy-nilly on every topic and can't understand why everyone doesn't agree with him.

By contrast, a man who is freely accessing his Prophet — rather than being possessed by it — takes responsibility for the consequences of his truth-telling. He is no longer naive; he knows exactly what is likely to happen in response to his confrontations and doesn't whine like a naive victim when the inevitable occurs. This is a trait visible clearly in Jesus during his criminal trial (see Jn 18–19); there is in him no anger, no blame, and no recriminations. Jesus knew exactly what he was doing and what the results would be. This is a lesson Jeremiah would learn painfully, as indeed we all must. When the genuine Prophet in us speaks, it is not in service of a super-ego run wild, but in witness to God's compassionate truth; not as a tool in a strategy of ego-inflation, but as an invitation to others to imagine hopeful new alternatives.

"God Damn the Day I Was Born!"

It is easy to criticize Jeremiah from our safe distance, but this psycho-analysis shouldn't prevent our compassion or blind us to the very real agony that emerges from his confessions. Like Jesus in the Garden of Gethsemane, Jeremiah not only faced physical torture, ridicule, and the abandonment of his friends, but worst of all, he had to endure the silence of God. It is a sign of his growing maturity that Jeremiah could share with us his inner doubts, his sense of failure and frustration, but above all, his prayer to a God of Light gone suddenly dark. We often think of prayer as prepackaged words of praise that we memorize and repeat over and over. It is not; true prayer is honest communication with

God. For Jeremiah, genuine prophetic prayer boldly protests Yahweh's betrayal and abandonment and lets Yahweh know in no uncertain terms of his pain.

Such complaint, indeed, is the classic prayer of Israel, a people that takes its name (*yisrael* = "he wrestles God") from the rough-and-tumble struggles of Jacob with Yahweh (Gen 32:22–32). It is also quintessentially masculine agonistic prayer, a no-holds-barred duel with God, an arguing and a *kvetching*, a griping and a beefing that takes God's promises with the utmost seriousness. Surely God cannot countenance such effrontery, such impudent challenges to his goodness and power! Yet God does. And more, God seems to have chosen Israel — and Jeremiah — precisely for this quality of prayerful *chutzpah* (Hebrew: "nerve"). It seems God chooses those who take him seriously enough to fight back once in a while. And if that means getting his divinity dusted up from time to time, well, it's a price worth paying for so lively a covenant partner as Israel. Jeremiah has learned well the meaning of the story of Jacob, the example of Moses, and the message of the Psalms: our arms are *not* too short to box with God, if he'll just bend down a little bit.

The Dark Side of God

In his prayerful confessions, Jeremiah admits to something terrible, something denied, something rarely articulated: the shadow side of God, the divine Shiva energy that must destroy rot and ruin for new life to emerge. The pain of this discovery is enough to make Jeremiah wish he'd never been born (20:14–18). But the Prophet in him must speak; the truth is a fire burning in his heart and trapped in his bones that must flame out (20:9). Jeremiah will not mouth a God-talk full of sweetness and marmalade, not purvey a facilely constructed theodicy, not mimic carefully crafted catechismal answers to every possible question. Jeremiah will have nothing to do with Judah's good-time religion. He dares to face, and to express, the destructive shadow of God he actually experiences. It is a side of God that surfaces repeatedly in the Bible — though we usually deny or ignore it. It is terrible, punishing, and dreadful, eschatologically threatening to end now a life, now a nation, now an entire globe. His servants he can use like expendable pawns in a greater strategy. There is no controlling him. Experiencing this terrible lordship in his own life, Jeremiah does what any man worth his salt would do: he complains. You seduced me! You used me! You lied to me! God damn the day I was born!

Jeremiah's inner Prophet has discovered and told the awful truth. Every religious man, no matter how rich and powerful, how busy and alive, how well-meaning and spiritually disciplined, lives in a more or less well-constructed illusion of specialness, immunity, and chosenness.

Unconsciously, he tends to think of himself as just a little different or a bit better than the rest, for he has amassed extra funds in his religious bank account, he enjoys special spiritual favors as a result of a moral life, he is a winner, a survivor — unlike those poor unfortunate wretches out there who haven't been so careful, so moral, and so special. The prayer of such a man is that of the Pharisee (Lk 18:9–14), whose song to God is not "How Great Thou Art," but "How Smart I Am."

Then the Job day — or the Jeremiah day — arrives with sickening dread. On that day, or rather on that dark *night* of the soul, the clever answers don't work anymore, the careful calculations no longer hold, and the lovely descriptions of a tender God repulse rather than soothe. God is gone. And a man is left all alone with his pain or abandonment or persecution, with his cancer or AIDS diagnosis, with an empty house or a gaping vacancy in his bed. Fortunate is the man who, at least, does not have to endure the self-righteous explanations of Job's friends, so confident in their cozy little religious world, spouting clichés about "mystery" or God's plan, and so busy peddling their pet theodicies that they never have to face the truth.

Jeremiah knows that God does not guarantee our security as a reward for a little righteousness. Jeremiah tells us that God, Creator and Lord of all things, is a relentless opponent of all our ego-centric delusions and illusions. The prophet has broken through, not only the deceptions of religiously pompous Judean society, but his own carefully nurtured and naive delusions of grandeur. He knows that, like Jerusalem, he is just clay in the potter's hand (Jer 18). As a result of this honesty, Jeremiah is now ready to love the real God of Israel, not the Big Daddy of Primetime Religion or the Santa Claus of our infantile dreams. He is ready to embrace God even with his shadow and love him even in his absence. If genuine forgiveness means letting the other be just as he is (not as we want him to be), then we might even say that Jeremiah has learned to "forgive God." Strange phrase that, but it describes well what follows every biblical lament: a reassertion of God's sovereignty in the face of it all. "Though he slays me, I will love him."

Satyagraha

Jeremiah stuck fast to God through it all. Moreover, he kept telling the truth to Jerusalem. In prophetic honesty and tough-love, that meant unflinchingly proclaiming the imminent destruction of the Temple, the city, and the nation by Babylon (Jer 21–29). All of this did occur in 586 B.C.E. as predicted. Yet after the disaster, before he disappeared into Egyptian exile, Jeremiah's truth-telling to Jerusalem entailed a new task: the promise of a new future — a new heart — to a people overcome with depression and hopelessness (Jer 30–33). Prophets are indeed contrary characters; against complacency and denial they speak judgment, and against despair, hope. Neither kind of confrontation is appreciated by the rest of us at the time. But a man who calls forth his inner Prophet is not looking for our approval anyway; his moral compass is the truth.

Such a man was Mohandas Gandhi, one of the most powerful moral voices of the twentieth century. Gandhi, who fashioned a strategy of nonviolent resistance that liberated his native India from British colonialism, created a Hindu term for his life's project. Gandhi called his endeavor *satyagraha* ("truth-grasping"), a term that implies, not a smug possession of Truth (as if it were a marketable commodity), but a humble and continual attempt to "grab" the truth and to tell the truth to the best of one's ability. *Satyagraha* is the lifestyle of one grasped by his inner Prophet and committed to the value of honesty, whether that means telling little everyday truths about ourselves and those around us, or very big truths about society and politics and religion.

I once met one man with such a commitment to *satyagraha*. He welcomed me into his homely Manhattan apartment and graciously served me tea. His leathered face, whitened hair, and gentle manner belied the fact that J. Edgar Hoover's FBI once hounded him across the United States as an escaped felon. His technical crime was destroying draft files; his actual offense: telling the truth about American militarism in the thick of the Vietnam war. This man is Daniel Berrigan, a priest and poet with an active prophetic imagination.[10]

Berrigan apparently lacks whatever human gene allows for moral subterfuge and seems compelled to tell the truth as he sees it, regardless of ideology or popularity. He has spoken out not only against America's war on Vietnam, but Israel's occupation of the West Bank, not only the Soviet Union's domination of Eastern Europe, but the Vatican's crackdown against dissent. This truth-telling has inflamed the Left as well as the Right, losing him friends and allies as they oh-so-conveniently shift allegiances. Through it all, Berrigan's tough-love consistency remains, his *satyagraha* leading him on like a moral magnet. Such a man is obnoxious to the rest of us, but through his extremism, we are saved. We badly need someone, even just one man, who will not compromise on telling the truth as best he grasps it. We desperately need someone who has a different vision, an alternative consciousness, to thrust in the face of our obfuscations and casuistry. We need a man like Daniel Berrigan, tough-lover and truth-teller and prophet, to remind us that, in the words of one of his book titles, there are indeed "no bars to manhood" when the inner Prophet is conjured.

And what of the rest of us men who aren't so great? Can we find in ourselves some vestige of the Prophet, some hint of a Jeremiah or a Berrigan? Many of us do but don't realize it. But every time a man sticks on a point of principle and won't budge, refuses to tell an organizational white lie, blows the whistle on corporate injustice, carries a protest sign, sees through the "spin-doctors" of politics and religion, points out the deception in an ad or the fallacy of an argument, can't stomach "going along to get along," resists an institutional theology foreign to his experience of God, or takes a criticism levelled at himself to heart, the archetype of Prophet springs to life, and Jeremiah lives.

Chapter 11

Jonah the Trickster

One of the most characteristic male archetypes is that of the Trickster, that source of all the irreverent, hilarious, satirical, and comic things men do. We see the Trickster at work in men such as the office clown with his gags, the salesman with the latest dirty joke, or the friend always ready with a witty quip. But we rarely today ever think of this archetype as possessing any positive spiritual value. This was not so in antiquity, which valued the Trickster figure as an important part of religion. Its absence today suggests why modern religion is so devoid of humor and lacking in fun, and why men are often so bored by church. Yet the Trickster remains an important spiritual gift and a valuable treasure that men can give to religion. The biblical storytellers knew this very well and served up for our comic pleasure such characters as Jacob, Gehazi, and even Peter.[1] But perhaps the best biblical example of this puckish contribution is the story of Jonah, penned by an anonymous satirist, himself something of a Trickster, in the fourth or third centuries B.C.E.[2]

What's Up, Doc?

Before we discuss Jonah, it would be a good idea to try to grasp something of the Trickster archetype, a task about as promising as Sylvester ever getting a hold of Tweety. For the Trickster is the most elusive figure in mythology and literature; scholars recognize him when they see him, but are hard put to define or describe very convincingly exactly what he does. And the Trickster, of course, likes it that way! As soon as you think he's pinned down, he changes shape with Protean glee and gets away, impishly eluding our grasp once again. But he leaves enough of a trail to make some guesses about why he is so important to the male psyche and such a significant figure in masculine spirituality.

Three types of trickster figures tend to appear in mythology and storytelling. The most basic example is the animal trickster, an especially popular character in American Indian mythology.[3] Among the most popular animal figures are Coyote, Hare or Rabbit, Raven, Spider, and Donkey — creatures full of gleeful duplicity, sheer animality, comic selfishness, and irrepressible impishness. While most of us modern people are not directly familiar with animal tricksters in their original mythological contexts, we know them very well in their modern guise as cartoon characters. We watch with hilarity as Wily E. Coyote, once again missing a chance to grab Roadrunner ("Beep-Beep!"), runs off a cliff and hangs in midair for a small infinity before plunging into a desert canyon and disappearing in a puff of dust (always, of course, to resurrect later). Bugs Bunny chomps on his carrot and wisecracks as he arranges for an anvil to fall on Yosemite Sam's head; and woe betide Elmer Fudd if he ever threatens that carrot supply. Roger Rabbit creates utter chaos and mayhem in the kitchen as he successfully saves Baby Herman from his pratfalls. And so on. A surprisingly large number of us adult men still faithfully watch these animal tricksters on Saturday morning television, or habitually check out the cartoon pages everyday in the newspaper. Why?

Men just love to laugh, of course; that's a good enough reason in itself. But much more is going on spiritually beneath the chuckles than we might think. For Bugs and Wily E. represent a very natural but largely repressed side of ourselves: our animal drives and instincts. Jung suggests that the typical animal trickster is a "psychologem," that is, an extremely old archetypal structure that presents our primitive animal nature into consciousness.[4] When we laugh at the mythological animal as he obsessively stalks dinner or trips foolishly over his own gigantic penis, we are actually laughing at ourselves indirectly, at our own animal drives and the vulnerability that our sexuality often visits on us. When, attempting to hide, the trickster sticks his head inside his own rectum, we too are "faced" with our own essential animality, the classic human condition of being an "angel with an anus." For no matter how much we might like consciously to think of ourselves as elevated and advanced spiritual beings, or however much we might deny our predatory impulses by adopting vegetarianism or espousing animal rights, we are each of us at one level just a Sylvester in search of his next Tweety. The greatest cultural, intellectual, and religious giants among us survive like the rest of us, by feeding on slaughtered animals or harvested plants and later defecating them. We are each of us here on the planet because our parents made love with hot animal passion and low grunts and groans. And when we inevitably slip into civilized denial and pretense about these things, about who we are and where we came from, up pops the Trickster to tease us and make us laugh at ourselves. The Trickster is the fool who makes us wise.

Could It Be...Satan?

A second type of trickster figure who emerges in myth and folklore is the wily, unscrupulous, or foolish *human* character. This trickster's base selfishness wreaks havoc with everything and everyone around him — ultimately with beneficial results! For he represents the emergence into consciousness of our shadow, everything in us that is puerile, instinctive, mean, sinful and earthy, which so many of us strive to overcome and cover up. But the Jack-in-the-box trickster won't let us delude ourselves here either. The rogue keeps showing up, cleverly hidden in literary or cinematic characters at a safe distance from ourselves, to remind us of our own baseness and ego-centricity. The big surprise is, despite his duplicity, despite his own worst efforts, the trickster usually ends up winning the day. This is the psyche's way of telling us that the shadow we had come to hate, the hidden side of ourselves that embarrasses us and that we tried to hide, can save us; *felix culpa.*

This type of trickster appears in the Bible as Jacob (Gen 27–35), the sneaky and underhanded underdog whose life of deception ultimately wins blessings for all Israel; or Gehazi, Elisha's slick sidekick out to make a fast buck (2 Kgs 4–8); or Peter, Jesus' thick friend who triumphs despite his own obstinacy; and Jonah, the surly prophet whom we shall shortly discuss. The trickster is Shakespeare's fool, whose ridiculous sayings constitute the only true wisdom in the king's court, and Puck in *A Midsummer Night's Dream.* He is Tom Thumb, Stupid Hans and Hanswurst of fairy tale fame. He is Calvin of the cartoons, or the bratty hero of *Ferris Bueller's Day Off,* the clever Axel in *Beverly Hills Cop,* the hilarious *Arthur,* or the unlikely war heroes in *Good Morning, Vietnam* and *MASH.* When we laugh at him in whatever guise, we loudly go to confession to everyone within earshot: "That's me!" And by laughter we are absolved.

That is why our inner Trickster is such an important spiritual figure. When religion puffs up and inflates, the Trickster pops these pretensions and deflates us to our proper human size. Healthy spirituality is characterized by a humor that laughs at itself, sick religiosity by sober prudishness. Hindu gurus, in many of whom the Trickster is still alive, delight their audiences with stories of deep irony and wit that help us laugh not only at our own foibles, but the whole cosmic enterprise as well. Even the Christian church, hardly a fun place to be now, once celebrated the Trickster in farcical celebrations with a delicious sense of divine humor. The medieval Catholic Church kept alive the Roman saturnalia with a New Year's festival featuring singing, dancing — and merry mockery. The *festum stultorum* (Latin: "feast of fools") featured a children's bishop decked out in episcopal robes, a fool's pope (*fatuorum papam*), mummers, clowns, and other jokesters mocking the self-importance of ecclesiastical pomposity. Vestiges of this tradition continue in Mardi Gras celebrations before Lent and Halloween parties on the eve of the Feast of All Saints. Not surprisingly, these celebrations today draw the ire of the religious Right as satanic, just one indication of how hard put one is to find humor or laughter anymore in anything connected with the church. Fundamentalism is rarely "fun."

So the Trickster springs to life. Whenever religion purveys self-righteousness, dogmatism, and self-importance, the Trickster is bound to appear, usually among those men who still find religion important enough to mock it. The moral fastidiousness of the church today fairly *begs* for mockery, and teasing it is a religious act of the highest sort, restoring human chaos to artificial order and recovering earthy humility in the face of prim pomposity. The gay "Sisters of Perpetual Indulgence," roller-skating down the street with habits flying and arms akimbo, mock the official church's obsession with sexual morality; chain-smoking comic "Father Guido Sarducci" teases the Vatican's hierarchy; but perhaps the most hilarious religious trickster of all is Dana Carvey, the super-repressed "Church Lady" of "Saturday Night Live." Suspicious that someone out there might be having *fun,* Church Lady scans the scenery with an Inquisitional Eye in search of something — anything — *sinful.* She knows the real cause behind every truly enjoyable thing we do: "Could it be...hmmmm...SATAN?"

The Divine Comedy

A third kind of mythological trickster is a god. Nigerians like to tell the story of the trickster god Edshu, who walks down the road wearing a hat colored red on one side and blue on the other. This later provokes an uproar when farmers on either side of the road get into an argument over whether the god they had seen had on a red or blue hat. In the midst of the quarrel, Edshu reappears and says, "It's my fault, I did it, and I meant to do it. Spreading strife is my greatest joy."[5] In his impishness, Edshu performs a very valuable service: confounding those who think they know exactly what God is like. Such trickster gods "pull the rug out" from under accepted divine metaphors that are taken too exclusively and seriously and that lead people to the dangerous impression that they have God all figured out and even franchised.

The God of the Bible is often just such a Trickster. Yahweh excels in surprising and confounding Israel when it gets too arrogant in its theology and too confident in its chosenness. The classic Christian theological term for this divine trickery is "scandal" (Greek: *skandalon* = "stumbling block"). Throughout the Bible, like a circus clown tripping a patsy, God scandalizes Israel whenever it steps too haughtily; the Jonah story is but one example.[6] This prankish quality reaches its classical theological apotheosis in the New Testament (1 Cor 1–2), where Paul calls Jesus a "scandal" to the Jews and a "fool" to the Greeks because of his crucifixion, the ultimate trickery of a God who "destroys the wisdom of the wise and brings to nothing the cleverness of the clever" (1 Cor 1:18). This text is the basis for the motif of Jesus as fool or clown, a favorite theme of the French painter Rouault and a leitmotif that appeared most recently in the charming musical *Godspell*.

Jonah: God's Pigeon

The biblical fable that best knows the Trickster — all three types — is the famous Jonah story, the "big fish" tale of all time. This yarn, composed by a puckish Jewish sage, is a delightful celebration of tricksterism, a biblical joy-buzzer and theological whoopee-cushion that can activate the Trickster archetype in anyone who will let it. Ironically, some twenty-two centuries after its composition, the Jonah satire is today taken with grim seriousness as an article of biblical-literalist faith by fundamentalists typically unable to see the humor in the tale.

The story is set in the eighth century B.C.E. when the horrific Assyrian Empire, ruled from its intimidating capital at Nineveh, threatened the whole Middle East. The tale purportedly relates the experiences of an Israelite prophet named Jonah ben Amittai (mentioned in 2 Kgs 14:25) as God sent him on a perilous mission to convert the Evil Empire. Actually, the narrative derives from a period five to six centuries after the Assyrian era, the anonymous satirist having selected the Assyrians as the ultimate Jewish enemy and perfect foil for Jonah's surly ministrations. It is a story about God's wonderful power to bring salvation despite stupid religious hatred and arrogance.

The tale opens with Yahweh's bolt-out-of-the-blue command to Jonah (Jon 1:1): "Get up! Go to the big city of Nineveh and tell them that their evil affronts me!" Right. And would you go to Tiananmen Square in the heart of Beijing and blast Chinese tyranny? How about denouncing Iraqi aggression in Baghdad or condemning South African apartheid in Pretoria? Well, Jonah gets up all right, but he heads west instead — the exact opposite direction from Nineveh — down to the port of Jaffa and the fastest ship to Tarshish (Spain). Jonah is nobody's fool. And despite his name (*yonah* = "pigeon") he's not going to be anyone's dupe, either — not even Yahweh's. So off flees our errant bird on a cruise ship to sunny Spain. Not that this is a problem for the Lord of the Storm; Yahweh the Trickster just as promptly conjures up a hurricane to blow his wayward pigeon off course.

Pitching up and down in the swells and retching over the side-rails, the other sailors detect a god behind all this. Sure enough, a little lot-casting reveals the culprit: Jonah fleeing from the face of Yahweh. So into the drink he goes. Yahweh relents, the sea calms, and the day is saved! But what of our Jonah? Yahweh, still doing his Hound of Heaven bit, has taken care of that, too: a big trickster fish comes up from the Abyss and swallows him! For three days in its belly, wrapped in seaweed and salmon eggs and God knows what else big fish eat, Jonah gets a little *more* time to reconsider the offer of Yahweh that he really can't refuse! After a nifty bit of prayer (Jon 2:3-10), our pigeon's got his head right again. So Yahweh speaks to the big fish, which promptly barfs its disagreeable load onto the shores of Israel, back at square one! Yahweh repeats Jonah's orders, and this time the prophet obeys.

Entering the vast Assyrian capital (three days' journey wide, the size of metropolitan Los Angeles), the curmudgeonly Jonah pronounced doom in a depressing one-liner: "In forty days Nineveh will be destroyed." No ifs, ands, or buts. It's the shortest prophetic message on record — no conditional clauses, invitations to repentance, or even glimmers of hope. Now, if you've ever spent any time reading the biblical prophets, you know that they are much given to stem-winding oratory, long indictments, lengthy accusations, and seemingly never-ending harangues. And all this verbiage never does any good — not once. The prophets hurl Yahweh's word at Israel, they threaten, cajole, embarrass, exhort, denounce, promise, and predict, but all to no avail; Israel never listens and never repents. Surely Nineveh won't either; so Jonah just mutters his gloomy prediction quickly and gets the hell out of town.

But it worked! The people of Nineveh promptly believed Jonah, and from the king on down to the cats and dogs, they repented, they fasted, they put on sackcloth and ashes, and they even prayed for forgiveness and delivery — to a foreign God! Yahweh repented; Nineveh was spared. Victory! Hooray for our side! For the first and only time in the history of the Bible, a prophet had succeeded in creating a change of heart, a repentance from evil ways among the people, and not just any people, but the worst: Assyria. The Evil Empire had just cried "uncle."

Jonah was furious. Only now do we find out that he'd been afraid this would happen all along! Jonah knows all too well that Yahweh is "gracious and compassionate, slow to anger and ever faithful, always ready to repent" (Jon 4:2). His worst fears had come true. From his ringside seat above the city, the vengeful Jonah sat in speechless rage: God had denied him the pleasure of watching the ultimate show — the evil Nineveh going up in smoke! Not finished with Jonah, however, the Divine Trickster struck again. No sooner did Yahweh sprout a castor-oil plant over the grumbling prophet to shelter him from the Assyrian sun than he withered it. When Yahweh cagily asked Jonah about his lost sun-shade, the prophet angrily took the bait and complained. Then Yahweh reeled him in: "You are sorry for the plant which you did not even grow... shouldn't I feel sorry for the great city of Nineveh... whose people can't tell their right hand from their left, not to mention the cattle?" And there the tale ends.

A God of Mercy and Compassion

What gave rise to this wonderful story? In the Dark Ages of the third century B.C.E. when Jonah was written, many Jews had evidently developed a religious superiority complex and an all-too-familiar attitude of prejudice against other peoples and faiths. It happens all the time in every religion: "no salvation outside the church," "you must accept Jesus as your personal savior," "you must be born again to be saved," etc. Every religion seems inevitably to sprout such a self-righteous Elect who believe they've got a patent on the name Catholic or the exclusive copyright on Islam, a lock on God or an absolute hold on the keys to salvation. Such ballooning arrogance always provokes the Trickster's pin. The unknown *mensch* who penned the Book of Jonah, spiritual ancestor of the Jewish humor of George Burns and Jack Benny, Lenny Bruce and Woody Allen, simply responded to the snobbish religious chauvinism around him in the best way he knew how: satiric laughter.

But the Jonah story also has a deeper meaning, something about God writing straight with crooked lines. Jonah, that churlish curmudgeon and hapless pigeon, is arguably the most successful character in the Bible despite his best efforts to thwart Yahweh's will! To win wisdom through the bumbling of the fool, to shame the strong with the victory of the weak, to bring holiness through the failings of the sinner — these things God delights in doing. The puckish author of the story knows that we are all of us Jonahs, pigeons in the hands of a tricky God.

"The Devil Made Me Do It"

The Trickster still lives on today in most males. Indeed, at times it seems to possess some of them. As a defense mechanism against pain and intimacy, these men become inveterate practical jokers and habitual wags, always yukking it up and never able to get serious. It is an immature man — the Boor — whose primary psychological archetype is the Trickster. Moreover, all of us are also susceptible to the antics of our inner Trickster when it plays unconscious pranks on us. Get a little puffed up about your career, and a blunder is bound to follow; try to impress a date with your culinary *savoir faire*, and hollandaise will surely land directly on your tie. Have you had "one of those days" recently when the bread landed on the floor butter-side down or you ran out of gas on the way to an important meeting? You-know-who was at work behind the scenes, raising havoc and tripping you up; "bdee bdee bdee that's all folks!"

Mostly, the inner Trickster works well with us, giving spice and hot pepper to our otherwise humdrum lives. He appears in the office as the prankster who keeps things hopping with his gags, in class as the teacher ever ready with a joke to lighten the lecture, in the operating room as the surgeon with a little dash of black humor to ease the tension, or just as that buddy you like so well who loves to party and play. He is also in that old friend who teases us in a way that helps us laugh at ourselves — while still getting his point. And he is in all the comics and comedians that so lighten and delight our lives: in the devilish repartee of Jay Leno, the dead-pan of Johnny Carson, the wicked zingers of George Carlin, the horse-laugh of Eddie Murphy, or the zaniness of Robin Williams. He is in all those wonderful men who have ever made us laugh: Charlie Chaplin, Groucho and Harpo Marx, Laurel and Hardy, the Three Stooges, Jerry Lewis or Danny Kaye, Red Skelton or Richard Pryor or Monty Python.

Fools for Christ's Sake

Where the Trickster doesn't get welcomed, deadly pomposity prevails, e.g., in many chanceries and churches. No clearer sign of masculine spiritual absence from religion exists than the boring atmosphere that passes for "church life" in many congregations and ecclesiastical publications. Not that this quite stops the Trickster, who is very likely to disrupt the tedious proceedings unconsciously with a preacher's *double entendre* ("Sex is a holy thing; man has his part, and women her part — but God has his finger in it, too!") or a daft spoonerism ("There will be a Peter Pull at St. Taffy's Parish") or a parishioner's untimely giggling fit. I remember once when, during the exchange of vows at a very pretentious wedding ceremony, an unwitting guest in the congregation very loudly farted. The suppressed laughter was painful for some time. But amid all the lacy frills and contrived decorum, something very human had happened despite all efforts to the contrary.

Fortunately, a few men in religion do have the audacity to let their Tricksters get into the proceedings. Blessed is the congregation whose priest or minister has a sense of humor and the irreverence to use it. Happy the audience who heard Bishop Sheen on television in the 1950s — the last time in history a televangelist was intentionally funny. Lucky those who heard the famous Indian Jesuit Anthony de Mello tell his funny spiritual stories in the classic Hindu guru style. As he poked at the pretensions and needled the uptight anal-retentivity of himself and his audience, great waves of laughter would begin to roll, and deep joy at the existential irony and absurdity of it all. A de Mello enlightenment was not only an "aha!" but a "ha ha" experience.

I have yet, however, to find anyone to match the religious humor of my high school English teacher Fr. Mike Tueth, S.J., who possesses a virtually shameless Trickster. Over the years he has developed a repertoire of characters available on almost instant demand for a theology class, a dinner party, or a parish gathering. One moment (with the help of a few sheets and pins) he is the imperious Mother Manguard, superior of the Sisters of Divine Wrath and Retribution, whose religious order abandoned the pious education of fabulously rich girls in favor of prison ministry — they run one. Then, in an instant, he is the dotty Monsignor O'Drool, answering the query of a parishioner, "What do you think of women priests?" "What do you think," he slobbers in reply, "of square circles?" Next he is the relevant Sister Judy, part-time nun and airline stewardess; then Father Luke, the guitar-playing, country-western priest who runs a fried-chicken stand in the parish. In the end, no one gets away from a Tueth performance unoffended, all bubbles are popped, and each rib thoroughly tickled. And somewhere, the wry author of the book of Jonah smiles impishly.

Chapter 12

The Lover

The Lover is the archetype of a man's connectedness with other people.[1] It is a *persona* that healthily activates only after basic individuating issues in a man's life have begun to be negotiated. In terms of psychological development, the Lover is a late-blooming archetype characterized by a maturing man's desire to give of himself to another person and to share in life's experiences, joys, and struggles with another. The healthier the man, the healthier his inner Lover. In an immature or narcissistic person, the archetypal potentialities of the Lover degenerate into the bleating romanticism of Top 40 radio, or the pathology of the dependent personality type we call the Clinger.

The Lover is difficult to access in the Bible, as it is in many men, for it always involves emotional vulnerability. Neither biblical literature nor ordinary men particularly like to open up, experience, or discuss that part of themselves that relates to intimacy, to sexuality, and to emotions. Moreover, the Lover is usually a deeply wounded archetype in which much pain throbs. Few among us have not been rejected or ignored by others whom we loved; with great pain goes great avoidance. To protect themselves from this pain, many men have so numbed themselves to the inner Lover that they are only vaguely conscious that it still exists. Yet somehow, even among the most anesthetized spirits among us, there lie memories of our most precious encounters with the potentiated Lover: the heat of romantic passion, the act of generosity to a close friend, the forgiving compassion we found for ourselves at a time of failure, or the ecstatic joy we once felt in the presence of God. The dearest memories and the deepest experiences of our lives involve the Lover.

Three Kinds of Love

"Love" is such an ambiguous and abused word in English that it has become customary to distinguish three kinds of love, based on three distinct Greek terms. All three types are involved in the Lover archetype.

The first is *eros*, the emotional and sexual attraction we experience for another person. Erotic love often — but not always — involves the phenomenon of infatuation or "falling in love." This development involves the romantic projection of our emotional needs onto another person, who then becomes seemingly responsible for our own happiness.

The second kind of love, known as *philia*, is the quality of friendliness that we share in partnership with others. Among men, it is experienced as male "bonding," fellowship, or brotherly love; team sports often engender this kind of fellowship and *esprit de corps*. In a man's relationship with a woman, it is the everyday companionship of friends. Whereas *eros* is two people encountering each other face-to-face, *philia* is two people side-by-side, sharing in a common experience.

The third type of love is called *agape*. It is the self-giving and generous love we give to others without expectation of reciprocation; it is known in Latin as *caritas*, from which we get the English word "charity." This is the love that the mature Hero enacts in deeds that contribute to other people or society.

The Lover usually involves all three of these "loves" in a given relationship, though normally one type predominates over the others. We rarely experience, of course, any of these "loves" as discreetly and separately as these distinctions suggest or as maturely as their definitions imply. The Lover archetype instead typically presents a tangled experience of generosity, neediness, sexual desire, affection, selfishness, and passion all rolled into one. It has always been so.

Christianity and the Lover

Christianity has proved primarily a blessing in the development of men's Lovers. Above all, its practices and devotions, preaching and ministry, encourage a deep love of God. Any man who has participated in a powerful liturgy has felt the passionate love of God that emerges in the music, the prayers, and the rituals of such a worship service.

No institution on earth has so fostered *agape* love as has the church. In countless ways, the church encourages and assists men to grow in this self-giving love that is compassionate to others and sensitive to the poor, the weak, and the vulnerable. At this moment, in cities big and small, in rural areas and on the missions, the church reaches out and concretely invites men to care for the homeless in soup kitchens, to educate the poor in literacy programs, to visit prisoners in jail, to aid migrants and illegal aliens, to befriend the aged and the forgotten, and to care for the sick. Men who respond to this call even in the simplest ways develop one aspect of their inner Lover and grow as genuinely humane people.

The church also encourages the growth of friendship and fellowship (*philia*) among its members. Indeed, this is among the chief purposes of the Christian religion: to create a community that provides mutual support for its members in their growth in faith, hope, and love. It is impossible to live the Christian life alone. Amid the alienation and loneliness of modern life, the church provides to all its members friendly outreach in the form of discussion groups, singles' support groups, adult classes, dinners and picnics, festivals, prayer partners, and spiritual conversation — tangible and concrete forms of fellowship.

The Sin of the Church

The problem — even the curse — of modern Christian religion relates to erotic love. Throughout its history, Christianity has proved inconsistent in helping its members handle the difficulties of their erotic feelings, thoughts, and experiences; moreover, they have often exacerbated the problems. At its best, the church honors erotic love in the context of the sacrament of marriage, teaching that the love between married partners is no less than a manifestation of God's love. Theologically, Christianity holds erotic love in high regard *if* it exists in the context of the marriage bond.

Behind the official teachings concerning marriage, however, there exists in Christianity a dark ambivalence regarding sexual love. Just as an individual can repress feelings and thoughts into the unconscious, so can a religion; in both individuals and groups, this repressed shadow will always somehow emerge in conflicted, confusing, and contradictory ways. The church's sexual shadow pops out in ecclesiastical "body language." Few among us have not been "zapped" unexpectedly and frightfully on sexual matters in a sermon, a confessional, or individual counseling precisely at a time when we were most vulnerable and struggling. Generations of boys have endured adolescence — as if it weren't difficult enough — with the added terror provided by some zealous preacher that one act of masturbation on a hot summer's night suited them for an eternity in hellfire and brimstone. The discovery later that the same preacher was sleeping with the choir director only adds to many men's sense of outrage at the hypocrisy of it all.

Many men are alienated from the church because it so badly wounded them as children in the most vulnerable aspect of their souls: the Lover archetype. Many men still carry a sense of guilt and shame in their sexuality because of the church's insensitivity. Such harshness to children and adolescents in the area of sexuality and erotic love actually constitutes a form of child abuse; many men never allow themselves to be wounded there again and avoid religion entirely. In the area of our lives where we most need to be taught gently and compassionately, the church often preaches with unaccountable harshness and even cruelty. Unlike Jesus, who repeatedly condemned greed sternly, but treated those with sexual problems with compassion (see Jn 8:1–11 or Lk 7:36–50), the church usually raises nary a feeble whimper at our culture's addiction to money, while railing loudly and repeatedly against the misnamed "sins of the flesh."[2]

The Christian Sexual Transformation

All of this is beginning to change. An understanding of the influence of psychology on sexual issues has helped many Christian theologians and moralists to create a more humane climate around the area of erotic love — an attitude much closer to that of Jesus. Most modern ministers and priests are already noticeably more understanding, sensitive, and compassionate on sexual matters than their predecessors. The church is beginning to face its sexual shadow. Yet the process is bound to take generations. In the meantime, many well-meaning Christians wonder: are the church's present attempts at a consistently positive outlook on *eros* evidence of decline, decadence, or even evil? A contemplation of the Lover archetype as it appears in biblical stories and poems might go a long way to allay these fears and restore around sexuality a sense of celebration and gratitude. The story of Solomon is a beautiful example.

Solomon the Lover

The Lover appears in the stories of many biblical characters, but nowhere more extravagantly than in the Solomon traditions. One of the primary aspects of the Sacred King archetype that Solomon embodies is its prodigious sexuality, eroticism, and generativity. "Solomon," we are told, "loved many women" (1 Kgs 11:1–8). To say the least! The biblical text records that he had something on the order of seven hundred wives and three hundred concubines.[3] The most politically important of these many marriages linked Solomon with the daughter of the Egyptian pharaoh himself (1 Kgs 3:1) — an interesting arrangement in the light of Israel's earlier experiences with pharaohs. The most famous of his romantic encounters involved the legendary Queen of Sheba, a fabulously wealthy and powerful woman so enamored of Solomon that she gave him expensive presents and extravagant praises (1 Kgs 10:1–13).

Solomon's legendary reputation as the great archetypal Lover is no doubt responsible for the attribution to him of an extraordinary biblical book of erotic love poetry known as the Song of Songs (in some traditions entitled the Song of Solomon). Set possibly in its original form as a musical stage production, the work features sensuous and erotic love songs that flow back and forth between the male Lover (identified as Solomon in 3:9) and his beautiful female Beloved, a "black and lovely daughter of Jerusalem" (1:5).[4]

Her love for the King is passionate and earthy, and her desire strong:

> On my bed at night, I sought him whom my heart loves;
>   I looked for him, but could not find him.
> I will get up and walk through the city,
>   Through the streets and squares
> I will search for him whom my heart loves.
>
> Sg 3:1–2

Her love is not unrequited; Solomon matches her passion verse for verse:

> How beautiful you are my love!
>   How very beautiful you are ...
> You ravish my heart with a single glance,
>   With one pearl of your necklace.
> What spell lies in your love?
>
> Sg 4:1, 9

Or, again:

> Your thighs curve like a necklace,
>   The work of an artisan;
> Your navel is a well-rounded bowl
>   That lacks not for wine.
> Your breasts are like two fawns,
>   Twins of a gazelle.
>
> Sg 7:2–4

And so it goes. The effect of the poems, even thousands of years after their composition, is sexually stimulating, so much so that the book still creates controversy as to its interpretation. Many observers, wary of its unfettered sexuality, claim that the poems must be understood allegorically, namely, as metaphors for the love of God for Israel or Christ for the church. They surely can be taken that way. But the first meaning of the Song of Songs is the plain one: a celebration of the joy and pain of falling into erotic love. Nor is the book specifically a paean to married union, as suggested by pious Christian commentators.[5] There is no mention whatsoever of marriage in the Songs; the mutual chase between the Lover and his Beloved takes place in the darkened streets of Jerusalem and in its surrounding fields without benefit of any marriage license.[6]

What lies behind this constant tendency to avoid the obvious meaning of the Song of Songs is not so much prudery as the unconscious assumption that *eros* somehow leads men and women away from spirituality and the love of God. It's as if God is a jealous and insecure lover who can't take the competition of a beautiful woman or a handsome man (though God himself created them that way). God in this supposition is so unattractive and unappealing that we will love him only if all other rivals are eliminated.

But God is not one object in a field, much less a competitor in a beauty contest. And erotic love does not by its nature lead men away from God. On the contrary, it draws them more closely to God. *Eros* is a grace that can open men up to a deep need for a love that only God can satisfy.

The experience of romantic infatuation as described in the Song of Songs is often deeply pleasurable as well as highly painful.[7] Not every man has this experience. For those whose Lover materializes around *eros*, however, a wealth of learning experiences await: ecstasy, joy, union — but also sadness, depression, and abandonment. *Eros* charges the Lover archetype with tremendous energy, effectively shattering the safe, self-sufficient emotional world each of us tends to create. Most men would regard this outcome as undesirable, and indeed it is frightening to lose control (or the *illusion* of control) over our emotional lives. Yet even in the wake of the spiritual earthquake brought on by passionate erotic love, a great grace is available.

Those who experience erotic infatuation with honesty and with awareness come to realize that the poor beloved objects of our affections can not possibly live up to our enormous needs, desires, and expectations of them, nor are they nearly so wonderful as our idealized projections would imagine.[8] They are just limited human beings unfortunate enough to have been chosen as screens onto which someone else has projected the imaginations of a highly activated Lover archetype. But what of these powerful desires for union and needs for love in ourselves? Are they forever to remain unrequited? Are they an absurd joke, an emotional longing for a love and a belonging that we can never have? Cynics would say so. The religious man, however, recognizes that in his high eroticism he has confused and transferred onto another fragile little human being the real desires and genuine needs that only one lover can fulfill, and that lover is God. As St. Augustine — no stranger to erotic love — once said, "You have made us for yourself, O God, and our hearts are restless until they rest in thee."[9]

How can we ever come concretely to realize this tremendous need for love — this "God-sized hole" in our psyches — without the experience of infatuation? We cannot. Falling in love is the most important clue a man can ever find to his latent spiritual needs and potentialities. And without the experience, a man's relationship to God remains largely one of obedience, respect, and will — surely a sound basis for a proper religious relationship, but one that ultimately lacks passion, heart, and soul. Love transforms mere religious propriety into spiritual passion; as St. Augustine also said, "Show me a man in love, and I will show you a man on the way to God."[10]

So it was with Solomon. Despite the biblical command virtually to fall into infatuated love with God ("You shall love Yahweh your God with all your heart, with all your soul, and with all your strength" — Dt 6:4), of only *one* person in the entire Bible is it actually said that he "loved Yahweh" (1 Kgs 3:3). That man is Solomon. His capacity to be ravished at the sight of a beautiful woman is identical with his capability to fall in love with the living God. And what of the mistakes of love? Solomon certainly made them, especially when he built pagan shrines for his wives (1 Kgs 11:7–8). But love is greater than such mistakes; as Solomon himself says in the Book of Proverbs, "love covers a multitude of sins" (10:12). Better to make mistakes in loving too much than to make no mistakes by not loving at all.

David the Beloved

Another related aspect of the Lover archetype is the capacity to *be loved* by others. Men are often uncomfortable with the passive role of "Beloved" and frequently don't respond well to the love, however imperfect, offered them. This is a waste. Love is not chopped liver. It is a precious personal gift not to be shrugged off or ignored or taken for granted. The mature Lover archetype learns to recognize, appreciate, and respond to love when it is offered. The story of David relates the growth of this aspect of the Lover in one of the greatest figures in the Bible.

David was a ruthless military and political leader who first conquered Canaan around 1000 B.C.E. and established the Davidic dynasty in Jerusalem. One does not have to read between the lines of the biblical text to discover what a brutal and cruel character he was in vanquishing military opponents and exterminating most of the competing Saulide dynasty. Yet as is surprisingly often the case, side-by-side with this fierce Warrior there existed an archetypal Lover of great sexual and personal attractiveness.

David is one of the few characters the Bible describes physically: "ruddy, with beautiful eyes and a handsome appearance" (1 Sam 16:12). This description helps explain to the reader David's intense personal *charisma*, and why virtually everyone who met David grew infatuated with him. No sooner did the red-hot young charmer from Bethlehem appear at the court of Gibeah than King Saul fell in love with him, appointing him his personal armor-bearer and private musician (1 Sam 16:17–23). This relationship hints of the classic male Lover-Beloved affiliation so common in the ancient Mediterranean world between older sponsors and their young protégés and explains why Saul later became infuriated when he felt competition for David's affections from Jonathan (see 1 Sam 20:30).[11] Saul's daughter Michal also fell in love with David (1 Sam 18:20), eventually becoming his bride. Indeed, so attractive was the young man that the biblical text twice mentions (1 Sam 18:16,28) that *all* of Israel and Judah loved David!

It is one thing to be gifted with intense natural magnetism, but quite another to transform this personal energy into love for another person. Many attractive men live in a kind of narcissism, numb to the affections of others, taking love but never giving much back. David had all the makings of such a selfish and passive man, what with everyone swooning whenever he entered a room. Fortunately for him, a surprising relationship developed that broke this narcissism and activated his Lover archetype. It involved Saul's son Jonathan, who, like practically everyone else, fell in love with David (1 Sam 18–20).

The story of the love affair between David and Jonathan is a fascinating one, filled with strong tones of homoeroticism and all the passion of adolescent boys with a mutual "crush" on one another.[12] Each lover was a famous and tested warrior in his own right, Jonathan the hero of the battle of Michmas (1 Sam 14), and David the victor in the contest with Goliath (1 Sam 17). One is reminded here of the passionate love that reportedly existed between Spartan warriors, who bonded together sexually to form fierce fighting units.

Typically, David did not take the initiative in the relationship; Jonathan acted the passionate Lover first, even giving David his personal battle gear as a love gift and swearing a covenant (Hebrew: *berit*) with his still-passive Beloved.

Jonathan's love for David proved to be more than a "crush": the young man risked his life to help his beloved escape from Saul's mounting jealousy (1 Sam 20). In a farewell scene of great humanity and tenderness, Jonathan and David kissed and shed many tears (20:41). This is the first time in the David story that its hero shows any emotion, any interiority, and any adult capacity to respond to another person. Jonathan's erotic love has helped David the *Puer* grow up, break out of his passive narcissistic shell, and begin to develop his inner Lover. The effect on David of this breakthrough — symbolized in many fairy tales as the kiss that frees a lover from a death-spell — is dramatic. When David later learns of Jonathan's tragic death on Mt. Gilboa, he composes a mourning song filled with love:

> O Jonathan! Over your death I am devastated,
>   I am desolate for you, O Jonathan my brother.
> You were very dear to me,
>   Your love was more wonderful to me
> Than the love of a woman.
>
> 2 Sam 1:25–26

How much the red-blooded youth from Bethlehem has grown in such a short time.

Like his son Solomon, the adult David made many "love mistakes." His passion got the best of him when he eyed the stunning Bathsheba bathing herself (intentionally?) just below the king's window (2 Sam 11). The old ruthlessness and brutality assert themselves in this episode — slam, bam, thank you, ma'am — and Bathsheba is out the door. But the cover-up was worse than the adulterous crime; David arranges for Bathsheba's husband Uriah to be killed in battle, and Bathsheba is now his — eventually to become the mother of Solomon. He seems to have learned from his mistake; one does not see David act erotically irresponsible again. Which is not to say that the fires of *eros* went out. As an old man, David had the stunning young Abishag (1 Kgs 1) to "keep him warm" in bed!

Like his son Solomon, the romantic adventures of David seem to have opened up his inner Lover to an affective relationship with God, a passion that comes through in the psalms of praise to Yahweh attributed to David. In fact, of all the characters in the Bible, Old Testament and New, only one person ever says "I love you" to God, and that is David (Ps 18:1). His songs to Yahweh are full of sweetness and intimacy:

> One thing I ask of Yahweh,
>   One thing I seek:
> To dwell in the house of Yahweh
>   All the days of my life,
> To enjoy the sweetness of Yahweh
> And to worship him in his Temple.
>
> Ps 27:4

The Lover in Us

David and Solomon, powerful kings both, teach us that a man is never too important, never too great, to learn how to love. The Lover archetype is ever in need of development, growth, and strengthening. This is true all the way to death. The Lover is the very condition of a man remaining connected to those around him — wife, lover, children, and friends. Without it, a man can slip easily into sterile isolation, loneliness, and disgust.

The Lover is also the archetype of a man's relationship to his *anima*. When Jesus commands us to love our neighbor *as ourselves*, surely among that which we most need to cherish is our inner woman, so often denied, projected, and abused. The tragedy of failing to develop the Lover archetype far outweighs the collected gravity of the inevitable mistakes one makes in animating it. The stories of David and Solomon teach us that there is redemption for a man, no matter his mistakes and sins, if only he can learn to love.

PART THREE

Masculine Theology

THE BIBLICAL STORIES that we have discussed show that masculine spirituality is vividly pictured and communicated by narratives containing the classic male archetypes. When we read these stories, archetypal potentialities in each of us are evoked and brought to awareness, and we begin to experience more consciously our own interior Wildman, Warrior, or King. These stories also teach us that archetypal potentialities can develop healthily but also degenerate, contribute goodness but also turn evil, give blessing as well as cause curse. Every archetype can go wrong, and it takes the guiding wisdom of the inner Hero to transform the archetypes into sources of grace. The Bible stories suggest how each of the archetypes is a genuine way to God when lived heroically. They are a road map outlining the way to become a Saint, who is a hero who has lived his archetypes purely, radically, and boldly for God in a way that genuinely touches, enlivens, and energizes other people.

The masculine archetypes also have another surprising treasure to give us. As the key spiritual psychological categories in which men live and grow, understand themselves and achieve greatness, these archetypes form a striking metaphorical "language" when used as images to describe God and communicate about him. Long before Israel ever appeared on the scene, our ancestors began to think in this language, to perceive and speak about the gods as Wildmen, Warriors, or Kings. Israel enriched and transformed this spiritual vocabulary immensely in its Bible, adding even more archetypes — not in the form of new gods — but as metaphors for the One God. Later, the New Testament writers spoke this same "language" in attempting to communicate their experience of Jesus of Nazareth.

The technical term for all this God-talk is "theology," the science of finding an adequate descriptive language in which we might speak about the things of God. Of course, theology is ultimately an impossible task: a quest to understand One who cannot be understood, an attempt to describe One who cannot be described. Nevertheless, we try; whole libraries are filled with theological attempts to understand and describe

God. Part Three of this book is one such undertaking, namely, an attempt to appreciate how the language of masculine metaphors says something about who God is for us.

A Christian masculine theology, naturally, centers on Jesus of Nazareth. It asks why God would choose to reveal himself definitively to the world in the person of a male. What kind of man was Jesus? In what ways is his masculinity a sacrament of divine love and a vehicle of revelation? We shall consider these questions, and the ultimate Christian spiritual archetype, the Christ, in chapter 13.

The final chapter of this book, "The Masculinity of God," discusses the irreplaceable and indispensable role of the masculine archetypes in providing a metaphorical language in which to speak about God. A theologian can only wonder, "Why would the biblical God reveal himself to the world almost exclusively through masculine archetypal metaphors?" We shall discuss four key archetypal metaphors for God in the Bible — the Wildman, the Warrior, the King, and the Father — and ponder what they have to say about God.

Chapter 13

Jesus the Christ

According to most objective historians, Jesus of Nazareth lived in Roman-occupied Palestine from approximately 4 B.C.E. until about 30 C.E. Ancient sources indicate that he wandered rural areas of northern Galilee preaching a message of repentance and mercy under the theme of a mysterious and wonderful "Kingdom of God." His lively parables about God's fatherhood and his electrifying message of healing forgiveness caused great crowds to gather, sick people to claim cures, and a small band of disciples to follow him. But Jesus' popularity began to threaten the political-religious coalition of Roman colonialists and Jewish religious authorities who feared that massive unrest might destabilize their hegemony over Palestine. They therefore arranged for Jesus' elimination. On his last visit to Jerusalem, Jesus was captured, quickly tried and sentenced for sedition, expeditiously executed by crucifixion, and buried. Days later, however, disciples found his tomb empty, and soon began to claim that God had raised Jesus from the dead.

Two thousand years later, nearly two billion people call themselves "Christian" as they attempt, with varying kinds of effort and debatable amounts of success, to pattern their lives after Jesus and live out his challenging preaching message. This phenomenon leads us to ask: what about this man still touches so many people after so many centuries? Why are many non-Christians and even atheists inspired by Jesus, even while they are often repelled by his fractious followers?

Answering these questions, some argue that Jesus' humanistic teachings are so extraordinarily profound that they can still evoke moral and ethical allegiance. There is some truth here; his message is indeed profound. Yet there is little that Jesus asserted that was really new or especially distinctive; other spiritual giants have said many of the same things over the centuries. Some people claim that Jesus, with his genius for storytelling, simply spoke his truths more effectively than most gurus. There is also something to this assertion; Jesus' parables really can "catch" listeners and never let them go!

Yet if one would ask most thoughtful and committed Christians, "Why do you follow Jesus?" most of us would attribute our faith neither to Jesus' doctrinal insights nor his rhetorical cleverness. Rather, most of us are attracted by the magnetism of his person — touched, challenged, and fascinated by the kind of man Jesus was. Moreover, something in us longs to be like Jesus. Something in us recognizes in him our highest human aspirations. We might say, in other words, that in Jesus we glimpse the ultimate archetype of what a man can be, the deepest expression of what living a human life means.

The Christ Archetype

The spiritual quality that surfaces so magnificently in the person of the historical Jesus is the Christ archetype. Until Jesus, this late-developing potentiality of the soul lay gestating deep in the human collective unconsciousness, unnamed and only dimly realized. Early biblical hints of its evolving presence appear in the Old Testament, in the Messianic oracles of Isaiah (Isa 9:1–7; 11:1–9), the apocalyptic visions of Daniel (Dan 7:13–14), and above all in Second Isaiah's song of the Suffering Servant (Isa 52:13–53:12). Then Jesus appeared. His life so animated and personified the archetype that it has come to be named after him. The term "Christ" as originally applied to Jesus by his followers (Greek: *christos*), simply translated the Hebrew word "Messiah" (*meshiach* = "anointed one"), an ancient title that connoted the ideal Israelite Warrior-King whom the Jews fervently hoped would overthrow the Romans and restore the House of David. But Jesus was not a Messiah of this kind. Instead, he completely transformed the military-political connotations and expectations of the appellation "Christ" and funded it with entirely new values.

What are the qualities of the Christ archetype that emerge so visibly in Jesus? Chief among them is *detachment*. Seen also in the Buddha, another version of the Christ archetype, this characteristic involves the gradual process of abandoning the ego's inevitable pursuit of aggrandizements and accoutrements such as money, power, family, and fame. It is a quality of radical psychological separation from all the comforts of domesticity, an act of total, radical, masculine spirituality. In his famous description of the birds in the sky and the lilies of the field (Mt 6:25–34), Jesus exhorted his followers to give up the ego's worries about food and clothing. Other times, in harsh and dreadful words, Jesus rhetorically brandished the sword as a symbol of his mission: his disciples were to cut all previous familial attachments and leave father, mother, and family (Mt 10:34–39) as indeed, he himself had (Mt 12:46–50). The detached

"Christ-self " makes a radical *masculine* move of freedom from one's immediate domestic attachments in order to make a *feminine* move toward reattachment to all people, who become brothers and sisters to be treated with love and kindness. Jesus did not just preach this detachment, he lived it.

Another Christ quality is that of *redemptive suffering*, the gift of one who bears in himself vicariously the suffering of the whole nation and whose self-sacrificing patience redeems lost people from their prisons. This is also the primary quality of the Avilokatasvara, a Buddhist saint (Boddhisattva) who foregoes entrance into *nirvana* to give spiritual assistance to suffering humanity. Biblically, this is the awesome healing archetype of the mysterious Servant of the Lord (*ebed yahweh*) described in Isaiah 52:13–53:12, and taken by Christians as the prototype of Christ:

> Someone despised and rejected by all,
>   A man of sorrows, familiar with suffering,
> A man from whom people hide their faces,
>   Someone hated and held in no account.
> Yet it was our own sufferings he bore,
>   Ours the sadness he carried . . .
> He was pierced for our faults,
>   beaten for our sins.
> His punishment brings us peace,
>   And by his wounds, we are healed.
>   (Isa 53:3–5)

Second Isaiah describes here the quintessential role of the Warrior-champion who engages the full fury of the enemy as the lone representative of the people, the suffering Hero who, in single-combat agonism, absorbs evil into himself lest it harm the nation. This is the image of Jesus on the cross, suffering on behalf of Israel and all humanity. But it is also Gandhi fasting until Hindu-Muslim violence should stop, the imprisoned Nelson Mandela patiently bearing the sins of South Africa, the Dalai Lama suffering exile on behalf of Tibet, or the Lakota Sundancer pierced with thongs, vicariously redeeming his people.

A final quality that shines out from the Christ is an aura of spiritual *indestructibility*. The words and actions of Jesus bespeak a soul that has transcended the ego's fear of abandonment, diminishment, and death. This is a man who can't be threatened or intimidated, one conscious of a deeper Self rooted in the life of God. Such courage enables the Christ-like person to risk himself boldly and to give himself over completely for others; this same quality appears in Sitting Bull's cry before the battle, "today is a good day to die," in the Elephant Man's proud claim in the face of inhuman brutality, "I am a man," and in the courage of countless martyrs whose lives witness to an invisible source of strength.

"Put On Christ"

The first followers of Jesus believed that, despite his cruel torture and brutal death, the risen Jesus lived on indestructibly in their hearts. Moreover, they began to call themselves "Christians" in the conviction that the spirit of Jesus had now evoked the same Christ archetype in each of them. The greatest Christian theologian, Paul of Tarsus, urged his listeners to "put on Christ" (Gal 3:27), that is, to adopt the Christ archetype and transform their own lives. Paul so thoroughly activated the new Christ archetype in himself that he could later say, in paradoxical but powerful language, that "life to me is Christ" (Phil 1:21) and even "I live now, not my own life, but Christ lives within me" (Gal 2:20).

One might say that the whole purpose of the life and worship of the Christian church originally was to help its members re-create the Christ archetype in themselves and thus experience the power of the risen Jesus in their lives. So when it gathered for the meal it called an *agape* (Greek: "self-giving love") — a sharing of bread and wine that Jesus passed on to his followers — the Christian community believed that the risen Jesus joined them together there spiritually. Moreover, the community believed that in experiencing Christ in this fashion, it experienced the very life of God. Paul went so far to say that anything in religion that did not foster this experience of Christ was just so much "rubbish" (Phil 3:8).

"No Male or Female"

Though Jesus himself was a male, according to Paul's theology the Christ archetype is not gender-specific. It relates to the deepest Self and the greatest human potential of both males and females made in the image and likeness of God (Gen 1:27). Paul makes clear that those who "put on Christ" find a unity deeper than the distinctions of Jew or Gentile, slave or free, and even male or female (Gal 3:27–28). In Jungian terms, we might say that the Christ-self is the human soul developed beyond the lines of ethnicity, class, or gender — the place where the *anima* and the *animus* join in healed unity. This religious opening to the *anima* — remarkable among people with a patriarchal religious heritage — appears in "virtue lists" such as Galatians 5:22–24, which cite such feminine relational values as love, joy, peace, kindness, and gentleness. The Christ-self is clearly as profoundly feminine as it is masculine. In terms of a spirituality for men, this means that the road to the Christ inevitably leads through the *anima*. Conversely, the task of imitating Christ (*imitatio Christi*) also means that women need to develop the healthy aspects of masculine spirituality that so mark the life of Jesus.

The Christ-self is a potential of each man and woman. As if to underscore this truth, the Christian tradition is filled with stories of women

saints who found their own distinctive ways to "put on Christ" in unique
and surprising ways: Catherine of Siena, Hildegard of Bingen, Joan of
Arc, Julian of Norwich, Thérèse of Lisieux, Elizabeth Seton, Dorothy
Day, and countless others. Indeed, the contemporary person probably
most radiant of the Christ is a woman, Mother Teresa of Calcutta: great
in compassion, willing to suffer with the poorest of the poor, courageous
and indomitable of spirit. Her professed motive for her life's work says it
all: in the faces of the poor and dying, *she* claims to find the face of Christ!

The Masculinity of Jesus

In God's impenetrable wisdom, nevertheless, the premier model of humanity's Christ potential is a male, Jesus of Nazareth. Lest men grow
proud or women offended by the maleness of the Son of God, we must
bear in mind that, in the Bible, God typically chooses the "least" to accomplish his holy will. Jesus Christ's masculinity is not an occasion for
male boasting, not a point scored in the eternal Gender Game, and still
less a reason to denigrate women or exclude them from ministry. The
definitive epiphany of the Christ in a historical male is, if anything, an act
of divine compassion and outreach to help the most vulnerable human
beings — men — on their way to God.

In Jesus, men can visualize what the Christ looks like in a man. This
imaginative task is accomplished primarily by reading the life of Jesus as
rendered in the four gospels. Ironically, we are probably quite fortunate
that Jesus himself wrote no autobiography, submitted to no interviews,
and appeared in no video profiles. Such resulting specificity and lit-
eralness would have created the worst kind of fundamentalism in the
Christian faith. Instead, the gospels written about him give us four different, contrasting, and varied spiritual impressions of Jesus as rendered
by four distinct theological artists, each of whom portrays his subject in
the mythical language of the masculine archetypes. The ensuing gospel
portraits of Jesus are more like poems than biographical data, abstract
art rather than photography.

It is astonishing how greatly the original gospel presentations of Jesus
differ from the impressions that have filtered into the popular imagination through two thousand years of Christian tradition, preaching, and
art. Many men feel vaguely unsettled by the Bearded Lady that stares
out at them from so many paintings of Christ, turned off by the "gentle
Jesus, meek and mild" lyrics of church hymnody, and alienated from the
often icky pulpit-talk about Christ that usually mentions only feminine
values. Films about Jesus often picture him as a dreamy-eyed, ethereal,
and even "spacy" character (e.g., Zefferelli's *Jesus of Nazareth*) or worse,
a whining wimp (*Jesus Christ Superstar*).[1] A quick reading of Mark's
gospel would instantly dispel these modern distortions.[2] Mark's Jesus

roars out of the desert and all hell breaks loose; throughout the rest of the work, Jesus is a man of electric power and masculine energy, a figure of great personal magnetism whom any man would be excited to follow.

The Jesus of the other gospels is no less masculine a figure. The way the evangelists achieve this effect is rather clear: they have sketched their Jesus according to the masculine archetypal motifs we have explored in the Old Testament. As each evangelist portrays his Jesus, now as a Wildman, now a Warrior, or now a King, men can identify with Jesus archetypically and thus draw nearer to an experience of the greatest archetype of all: the Christ. In the following pages, we shall explore the person of Jesus as portrayed in the masculine archetypes by the gospel writers.

Jesus the Wildman

Each of the Synoptic evangelists (Matthew, Mark, and Luke) includes the Wildman motif in his gospel portrait of Jesus; John does not. This technique probably originates with Mark's gospel, which opens with the Wildman John the Baptist preaching a baptism of repentance in the wilderness. Dressed in camel-skins, living on locusts and wild honey, and haunting the Jordan Valley with his stark message of repentance from sin, John seems like Elijah the Wildman reincarnated.[3] Jesus later makes this connection explicit: John *is* the reborn Elijah returned to prepare the way for the Son of Man (Mk 9:9–13).

The appearance of John's fiery, hoary, and primitive Wildman electrifies the atmosphere: something wonderful this way comes! Someone approaches, called by the Baptist from the primal reaches of humanity — someone wild, free, and dangerous. And in due time, Jesus arrives from Nazareth in Galilee. John's incendiary wildness, crackling from afar through the dry desert air, has inflamed a Nobody from Nowhere to journey his Hero's path. Left behind, in some poor but no doubt comfortable hovel in Nazareth, are all a young man's doubts and rationales and safe anonymity. Jesus' interior spiritual compass leads him south, to the Jordan and to John, drawn by the attractive force of the highest masculine energy. The Wildman will do this.

John promptly dunked Jesus in the dirty waters of the Jordan in a frightening initiation rite. Baptism (Greek: *baptizo* = "dunk"), now a cute ceremony of gurgling babies and cooing parents, originally connoted a drowning asphyxiation of the "old self" of a spiritual aspirant and the birth of a reborn "new man." So for a moment, the old Jesus of the comfortable domesticity of Nazareth drowned to death in the murky-brown Jordan. But what new Jesus would surface? What kind of new man would emerge from the river?

A new Wildman. As he burst out of the water, the very heavens opened above Jesus as a voice announced pleasure in his new Son. The Sky Father had spoken; Jesus belonged no longer to his mother Mary or even his mother Earth: the Sky Father claimed him now as Son. His divine manhood initiation ritual completed, the ordeal could begin. The violence of Mark's Greek is remarkable at this point (1:12); "immediately" we are told, "the spirit *threw* Jesus into the wilderness." In the Judean desert Jesus wandered, like Elijah on his journey to Horeb, for forty days. There Satan tempted him; Matthew (4:1–11) and Luke (4:1–13) insert accounts of these temptations, each of which involves the urge to renounce the terrible ordeals of Sky Father sonship (hungry emptiness, higher danger, constant powerlessness) in favor of the pleasures and graces of Mother Earth sonship (tasty bread, warm security, worldly power). Jesus refused.

Though a terrible place, the wilderness is not inhabited solely by demons. During blazing days and chilly nights, Jesus acquainted himself there with his own Wildman, that archetype of primitive oneness with nature that is a prelude to all genuine spiritual freedom. New-found friends suddenly began to appear as well. Wild beasts crept out of their wadi caves and sidled up to him, all under the protective watch of the angels (Mk 1:13). Jesus was safe and at home in the most dangerous place on earth. Now he could go anywhere. And now he could not be bought, intimidated, tempted, or domesticated. Jesus had become truly dangerous. He returned heroically to Galilee charged with this wild masculinity and in the full strength of his manhood.

Jesus never lost this wildness, and in fact his preaching is rich with it. To free his disciples from disabling worries about food, health, and clothing, he pointed to the birds in the sky and the flowers in the field (Mt 6:25–34). To describe his own total freedom, he once said almost ruefully, "Foxes have holes, and birds nests, but the Son of Man has nowhere to lay his head" (Mt 8:20). Indeed, one of Jesus' strongest — and to us, most difficult — teachings, surely flows from his Wildman. He repeatedly and unequivocally condemned what has become the highest value of modern capitalism: the pursuit of money.[4] One senses that his harsh teaching here not only reacts to the social injustice that usually follows from such greed, but the inevitable loss of free and detached spiritual wildness that such materialistic compulsiveness always entails.

The Synoptic evangelists also enrich the story of Jesus with classic tales of a Wildman's power over nature. On a stormy night, their boat about to capsize in the winds and waves, the disciples wake the sleeping Jesus with a plea for help. At his word of rebuke, the wind stops and the sea calms down (Mk 4:35–41). Later, in another windy storm, the same disciples see Jesus walking on the water toward their boat; when Jesus climbs aboard, the wind again dies (Mk 6:45–52). The evangelists also relate episodes in which Jesus displays magical powers over fish: once directing expert fishermen to a great catch (Lk 5:1–11), and another time helping Peter to pay the temple tax by catching a fish with a shekel in its mouth (Mt 17:24–27).

The gospel accounts of the tragic death of the Wildman Jesus on the tree at Golgotha contain awesome signs and wonders in nature. In sympathetic sadness, the noonday sky darkens into night while the very earth quakes in revulsion at the terrible crime just committed against Jesus and against nature itself (Mt 27:45–54). And though they buried him firmly inside a rock cave, Mother Earth cannot hold Jesus for long; he belongs to the Sky Father and it is to the sky that he must return (Lk 24:50–51). Like Elijah the Wildman of old, ascending on chariots of fire, the risen Jesus now belongs to the wind, and to the ages.

Jesus the Shamanic Healer

If the Jesus story reprises certain elements of Elijah's Wildman, it positively embodies the archetype of Elijah's shamanic successor Elisha; all four of the evangelists portray Jesus according to the motif of the Healer. The literary similarities of the gospel portrayal of Jesus to the Elisha Cycle are striking: both are disciples of fiery Wildmen, both receive their powers in dramatic events at the Jordan River, both raise dead children to life and cleanse lepers, and both show in their ministry special care for the poor and vulnerable. These accounts of Jesus' ministry are not purely literary, moreover; there is no doubt that the historical Jesus ministered to the physically and mentally diseased people in Galilee in a special way.[5]

How did Jesus cure? Like a shaman, and like a Warrior. We cannot fully understand the gospel healing stories until we realize that in them Jesus is waging eschatological warfare against Satan and the whole host of his evil demons. For Jesus, the possession, blindness, and paralysis of the people are the direct result of evil spirits, and they require the rite of shamanic exorcism and the cure of spiritual alliance. Before we dismiss all this as superstition, we need to remember that most diseases even today are psychosomatically involved. Genuine cures often involve the healing of depression and negativity through such spiritual work as visualization, laughter, reconciliation, and prayer.[6]

The Healer in Jesus is a surprisingly stern and bellicose figure. In the gospels, Jesus does not nurture the sick nor indulge the ill; he does not care for the diseased in the compassionate feminine way of a mother nursing her ailing child. He is certainly no Florence Nightingale. This surprises and even offends us. Wasn't Jesus gentle and tender with the sick? Not really — as shown in his first cure of the demoniac (Mark 1:23). After the poor madman shrieked at Jesus in the voice of the demon, Jesus barked sharply and coldly, "Be quiet! Come out of him." Immediately thereafter, Jesus cured Peter's mother-in-law with a touch of the hand,

and later a leper with the words, "Be cured!" along with a stern warning to keep quiet. And so the healing miracles go, a touch here, some spit in the ears or eyes there, usually a sharp command to get well, and the person is brusquely sent on his way: "Pick up your mat and walk!" (Jn 5:8) or "Go, your faith has saved you" (Mk 10:52). Doctor Jesus works fast.

Nowhere in the gospels do bystanders ever comment on Jesus' tenderness to the sick. What does astonish them is his *authority* (Mk 1:27; 2:10). Jesus heals, not by being nice, but by a show of pure masculine and spiritual force; he drives out the sickening spirits with all the gentleness of a Marine Corps drill instructor. He *orders* people to get well! Of course, none of his patients complained about this gruffness; they were too busy feeling well again to gripe about Jesus' abrupt "bedside manner." This brusque healing manner is important to consider for men who work in the medical and pastoral health care professions and who are often criticized as inadequate because of "insensitivity" or "poor pastoral technique" (i.e., the inability to wear their hearts on their sleeves). There are many ways to cure people, and strong, confident, and authoritative masculine energy can heal as surely as nurturing feminine care.

All of this is not to say that Jesus had no heart or feelings (see Mk 1:41), but that the Master of Spirits showed a kindly side only *after* he had won the battle. In the midst of the uproar around him after raising Jairus's child from the dead (Mk 5:41–43), for example, the first thing Jesus did was to find something to eat for the hungry girl he nicknamed *talitha* (Aramaic: "little lambkin"). But then, he had a weakness for little kids. They brought out in him an archetype that we don't realize he had.

Jesus the Patriarch

There is no evidence that Jesus ever married, much less sired offspring. Yet Jesus owned an active and manly Patriarch archetype, a quality of the psyche we have described as a man's ability to "father" people who are not necessarily his progeny. A number of stories bring out this quality in a touching way.

Jesus loved children. Now, this isn't an especially remarkable quality unless you have ever met a gang of the little miscreants that *pass* for children such as you still find in Palestine today. One of planet earth's great mysteries is how such polite and dignified Palestinian men ever develop from such obnoxious little brats. They beg, they annoy, they plague visitors, pinch women, make obscene comments and ugly faces, and run off delightedly, a band of little Calvins without any Hobbeses. Even the normally genteel Elisha couldn't keep himself from sicking she-bears on kids like this when they called him "baldy" (2 Kgs 2:24). So once when a gang of children surrounded Jesus, his disciples automatically started to shoo the little hellions away (Mk 10:13–16). But Jesus wanted to play. The gospel says he put his arms around them and blessed them, but this is probably a grown-up, theological way of saying he man-handled them a little, teased them a lot, tickled a few tummies, and maybe told them some great jokes and stories.

Jesus' Patriarch most visibly appears in the masterful mentoring job he did with his disciples, teaching, rebuking, and transforming in just a few years a bumptious bunch of fishermen, Zealots, and tax collec-tors into the leaders of the most successful mass movement in history. Jesus obviously knew how to father his followers, nurture their poten-tial, discipline their laziness, and confront their weaknesses. Like any true mentor and successful leader, Jesus held each of them in his heart and cared for each of them like a son.

Jesus' most significant fathering relationship occurs with Peter, whom many men find an appealing, fresh, and honest character so unlike many religious people. It was a bold gamble on Jesus' part to choose as a protégé this fisherman right off the docks (Lk 5:1–11). Does a genius know intu-itively what potential a disciple holds? Peter, for his part, surely knew a real guru when he saw him; responding immediately to the invitation, as he would years later at sight of the risen Jesus (Jn 21), Peter took the plunge. Dropping his nets, he followed. This gambling quality is just what Jesus looks for in a disciple: the ability to risk it all, put it on the line, and "just do it." With someone like that, you can work. And work Peter, Jesus did. In Matthew 10, Jesus sprays apostolic advice to Peter and his colleagues: "Do this," "Don't do that;" "Watch out" but "Don't be afraid!" And now that you've got that, Peter, would you walk on water, too? In one fantastic passage (Mt 14:22–33), the Wildman Jesus, like a doting father teaching his son to walk, lures Peter out of his boat, onto the waves and into the wind. Peter follows. But as he begins in his fear to drop like a stone, Jesus reaches out and saves him. I like to think that is when Jesus first teasingly began to call him *kephas*, which in Aramaic means "rock."

The sure confidence of a great mentor in his protégé explains Jesus' famous rebuke of Peter at Caesarea Philippi (Mt 16:13–23). After all the preaching and teaching, Jesus is ready to move his charges beyond Disci-pleship 101 and into graduate work in the Christian mystery. Like a wily Socrates, he asks them, "Who do you say I am?" Peter, typically, plunges: "You are the Christ!" Like a star student full of himself for having an-swered correctly, Peter glows in Jesus' commendation. But he isn't ready for the next step out onto the waters of scandal: Jesus explains that being a Christ means carrying the cross, suffering, and dying. These winds and waves are too stormy, Peter objects: "This must not happen to you!" Jesus, like a Zen *roshi*, shatters his student's ignorance of Christhood with a verbal stick to the head: "Get behind me, Satan!" Spare the rod, and spoil the child. Fatherhood must mean, at times, this: fiercely clear correction, passionate chastisement, and strong reproach. A man can take it; indeed, if he is any man at all, he is refreshed by the shocking waters of the cold truth.

Jesus guided his disciples as best he could into the final week in Jerusalem and the school of his suffering. Further, they could not then follow. Patiently, kindly, and clearly he had led them, cajoled them, and invited them to the brink of the Christ archetype. Now, he had to go it alone. A father teaches his son the greatest lessons not so much in what he says, but in what he does and how he does it. The last lesson plan of the Master taught us how to die: with courage, with dignity, and with forgiveness. It was accomplished. But Peter couldn't watch.

Later on, when the traumatic wounds of Calvary had begun to heal, the gospel of John tells us that the risen Jesus showed himself to the disciples as they fished out on the Sea of Galilee (Jn 21). When one of them recognized Jesus in the morning mists across the water and shouted out, "It's the Lord!" Peter, of course, promptly plunged into the lake and swam (not walked!) ashore. And there was Jesus, like a bachelor father, busily cooking them a fish breakfast (even the Lord can't teach a hungry disciple anything). Jesus, as it turns out, had one more lesson to teach after all. Naturally, he picked on Peter, his favorite pupil. A bit harshly, Jesus kept asking him, "Do you love me?" (this question, addressed to a grown man still shivering wet from his excited swim to shore to see his Master once more!). Disconcerted, Peter knew that Professor Jesus was at it again and he followed along, out onto new waters. Jesus, as it turns out, wanted to make absolutely sure that Peter knew (and we know) that loving him means following him all the way into the Christ archetype of sacrificial love: feeding others and abandoning the selfishness of the ego-project. His surprise lesson on the shores of Galilee in the early morning light just goes to show that even death can't shut up a teacher with one more thing to say, nor a father with one last piece of advice.

Jesus' activation of his own inner Patriarch not only fathered his followers superbly, but created a profound Christian teaching as well. For the most distinctive thing Jesus taught his disciples was to call God, the Master of the Universe and the utterly Holy One, by the tender Aramaic name *abba*, which means "daddy" or "papa." The intimacy with God of such a word was no less astonishing then than now. Now, one cannot give what one does not have, nor can one recognize in another what is not present in oneself. Jesus' ability to call the Lord of Hosts such an endearing name bespeaks a tender relationship to his own interior archetypal "Father"; his recognition of God's tender parenthood is an outcome of his own magnificent inner "abba." This was the same "abba" his disciples experienced in Jesus: energizing, fresh, and patient, with an authority that sought only to liberate and educate. His teaching, clever and winsome, shattered their old illusions and created new possibilities; his moral guidance got to the heart of things with astonishing simplicity.

Jesus: Trickster and Fool

So much of what we think about Jesus is serious and full of eschatological import. Our sermons, our art, and our theology all convey the utmost solemnity about the man. Even in his own time, the historical Jesus walked amid swirling controversy, political conflict, and deadly plots against his life. How surprising then to realize that Jesus, even in the thick of these heavy problems, sometimes played the Trickster and spoke with puckish wit, teasing playfulness, and even shameless word-play.

The evidence for Jesus' tricksterism is admittedly subtle — but then, so is dry wit. Like most tricksters, he loved to poke fun at the falsely pious, whether in mocking their inflated hypocrisy and religious showmanship (Mt 6:1–6) or characterizing their puffed-up and long-winded prayers as "babble" (Mt 6:7). The scribes and Pharisees he characterized as "blind guides," a comic term for the hypocrites who think themselves able to lead ordinary people, but who, in their nit-picking triviality, can't even master the basics of the Law (Mt 23). It will perhaps encourage incorrigible punsters (as if they needed it) to know that Jesus himself even occasionally stooped to this lowest form of humor. One brickbat against the Pharisees (Mt 23:24) said in the original Aramaic: "You strain out a *qamla* ("gnat") and swallow a *gamla* ("camel")!

His disciples fared little better from Jesus' wit: he loved to tease them, too. Whether nicknaming Simon "Rock" or James and John "the Sons of Thunder," playfully pulling a shekel from a fish like a rabbit from a hat in order to pay the temple tax (Mt 17:24–27), evaluating their worth as "several hundred sparrows" (Lk 12:7), or teasing squatty-body little Zacchaeus who had to climb a tree to see him (Lk 19:1–10), Jesus jested with his friends in the classic masculine fashion. Nor could death keep a good jokester down. Luke fashioned his wonderfully funny account of the risen Jesus' appearance to the disciples on the way to Emmaus (24:13–35) with classic comic elements. As Jesus walks unrecognized next to his gloomy and desperate disciples, he playfully plies them with theological questions; they don't understand them. But later, around the dinner table, they recognize him at the breaking of bread. No sooner do they see Jesus than, like any good trickster, POOF, he disappears!

Jesus is a Trickster unto us, as well; his teaching on the Christhood in us continually scandalizes, undermines, subverts, inverts, and turns inside out all our proper religious expectations. The greatest is the least, sinners are closest to God, we must become like little children, how happy are the poor, love your enemies, it is hard for the rich to enter heaven, the last shall be first — and on he goes, shocking us, surprising us, pulling the rug out from under us, and shattering our smug little religious worlds with his piquant parables. He is the Divine Trickster made flesh. When the unbelieving asked for a sign to authenticate his unorthodox teachings, Jesus replied that the only sign for them was the "sign of Jonah" (Mt 12:39). The wry reference here implies that Jesus, like the trickster prophet whose ministry unwittingly ended up saving Israel's worst enemy, would bypass Israel again and save the Gentiles — even the Romans![7]

Theologically, Christ was a Fool. His enemies didn't say that; his premier apostle Paul did! Against the strident and self-important seriousness of the people at Corinth, whose religious partisanship produced its predictable harvest of doctrinal dissension and competing factions, Paul proposed the metaphor of Jesus as a Fool (1 Cor 1). Unlike the "wise" and self-righteous Corinthians, so obsessed with practicing orthodox religion that they risked sundering the community, the Christ offered a self-emptying love that values unity more highly than "being right." As proof, he endures the "foolishness of the cross" on behalf of enemies as well as friends. Surely only a buffoon would do so! Everyone knows you have to destroy your religious enemies — or at least punish and silence them, humiliate and crack down on them — lest their errors succeed!

Yet such religious "wisdom" never gets us anywhere and certainly can't lead people into the life of the Christ archetype. Only the "folly of the cross" of Jesus can lead to the Christ-life, to ego-abandonment in an economy that puts a premium on capitalistic aggrandizement, to suffering love in a culture of people concerned with not getting hurt, to respect for others' beliefs in a world racked by fundamentalism. Christ the Fool doesn't even know how to take care of himself, can't master the basics of self-preservation, and gets all too wrapped up in other people's needs and problems.

God help a man who can't love a little foolishly like that — at least once in awhile.

Jesus the Warrior

One could scarcely have guessed, considering the popular impression of Jesus as a man of peace, that the first gospel portrays Jesus as a Warrior. Yet that is precisely what Mark did in employing this archetype as the leitmotif of his gospel presentation of Jesus.[8] For Mark, Jesus is the apocalyptic Divine Warrior whose appearance in Satan-occupied territory immediately causes eschatological warfare to erupt. Moreover, all who encounter Jesus are forced to choose sides in this great battle; there can be no fence-straddling: "he who is not with me is against me" (Lk 11:23).

However much we might like to make over Jesus in our own image as a benign teacher of enlightened ethics, a nineteenth-century liberal or a twentieth-century feminist, the apocalyptic Jesus of the gospels won't let us, forbidding all attempts at plastic surgery.[9] The truth is that the psycho-social world of Jesus and his contemporaries is to us a strange and distant landscape, dominated by satanic demons who ruled without mercy. Jesus' answer to the evil spiritual force around him, moreover, was not a timid modern one; he did not refer its victims to a therapist or pass their problems onto a committee for further study. Jesus made war against evil in a battle to the death.

In modern terms, what were the evil demons Jesus fought? The usual suspects of course: self-hatred, despair, and addictions. Jesus crushed these critters like bugs when they infected individuals in psychosomatic diseases. But these are garden-variety devils compared to the cosmic forces of evil Jesus also took on: militarism, colonialism, and systematic exploitation of whole populations. Liberation theologians are helping us see that the gospels concretely visualize the cruelty of Roman colonial power and its allied Jewish religious authoritarianism as the work of Satan.[10] When Jesus asked the name of the devils in a possessed man, for example, they screamed back at him in Latin the name of a Roman military unit: "Legion" (Mk 5:1–20); and when Judas betrayed Jesus to the Jewish authorities, Luke describes it as the work of Satan (Lk 22:3).

In inaugurating the Kingdom of God, Jesus struck directly at the power of Satan and all his minions to break forever the demonic lie of oppressive authoritarianism, whether it appears in economic, civil, or religious garb. People belong directly to God the King, Jesus taught, and only secondarily to any army or government, corporation or cult. In proposing this radical teaching, Jesus was not in the least bit naive about the consequences of his proclamation of the Kingdom; he knew the likely outcome, but did not whine about his task like a Victim or harbor any illusions about escaping from it unscathed. This would have to be a kamikaze attack.

After Jesus' wild sojourn in the desert, he invades Galilee on D-Day and proclaims the revolutionary new regime of the Kingdom of God for all who would follow (Mk 1:15). No longer will Satan hold sway on earth and no longer will God remain silent like an impotent leader of a government-in-exile. Jesus had come to proclaim in God's name a new spiritual order, to bring good news to the poor, to proclaim liberty to prisoners, and to let the oppressed go free (Lk 4:18). And for the People of the Lie who like their gurus meek, their preachers mild, and their religion effeminate, Jesus the Warrior minced no words: "Don't even think that I have come to bring peace on earth! It is not 'peace' I have come to bring, but the sword!" (Mt 10:34). This freedom-fighter brought

Elijah-fire, and like a soldier about to storm a beach, he couldn't wait for the fire-fight to begin (Lk 12:49).

Satan knew very well a war approached. As Jesus proclaimed his spiritual *coup d'état*, demons began to shriek out from those completely possessed by evil: "What do you want with us, Jesus of Nazareth? Have you come to destroy us?" (Mk 1:23). With the mad genius that only devils can muster, these fiends understood, as none of the sane could, *exactly* what Jesus was up to; he had indeed come to destroy Beelzebub and all his toadies. So went Jesus through Galilee like Moses through Egypt, the Warrior-Magician casting out demons and freeing their victims from disease, madness, and despair. The attack was direct and frontal. Satanic power faltered for a moment, then hardened once again its heart.

The People of the Lie, that murky coalition of enthralled bootlickers and cowardly sycophants, counterattacked. As always, they used the Law and the aura of religious righteousness as weapons to defend their tight-fisted hegemony over people's lives. So it was that the scribes and Pharisees accused Jesus of various crimes, ranging from association with sinners (he had dinner with them, Mk 2:15) to Sabbath violations deserving the death penalty (for healing a man's withered hand, Mk 3:6). These officials, like Goebbels or McCarthy after them, created about Jesus a sickening Big Lie: he was an instrument of Beelzebub, a tool of Satan (Mk 3:22–30). He deserved to die.

In response, Jesus escalated the attack against these hypocritical religious authorities, and these pitiful puppets of Rome. It is important for us to understand *how* Jesus the Warrior waged this battle, and against *whom*. Jesus did not take up weapons or join anti-Roman paramilitary terrorist groups such as the Zealots.[11] He could have. Yet to regard this deliberate refusal of the military option as evidence of Jesus' pacifism is a serious misunderstanding. In many ways, the spiritual war that he undertook against the ruling Roman/Jewish coalition represents a far more radical and effective strategy against authoritarianism than the Jewish *Sicarii* ever could have imagined, much less accomplished. Jesus actively campaigned throughout the villages of Galilee on behalf of the Kingdom of God, telling stories, expelling demons, and rousing his listeners out of their listless and depressing enthrallment to the Powers That Be.

And what of his enemies? How did Jesus treat them? Anyone who believes that by his command "love your enemies" Jesus meant smoothing over any differences with them in the interests of peace ought to read Matthew 23, a rip-roaring indictment of the Pharisees' hypocrisy. Jesus knew that the only strategy for dealing with such People of the Lie is to battle them with the truth (*satyagraha*), and to take special care in keeping oneself from falling under the disorienting and sickening spell of their Big Lies, little lies, and half-truths. He knew that one must always show the People of the Lie the Warrior's sword. The Jesus who answered genuine questions from people seeking enlightenment *never* naively answered the phony questions of the scribes and Pharisees that were designed to entrap him (e.g., Mk 11:27–33). He knew what was in their hearts. And he knew what was coming.

Inevitably, the final conflict drew near; Luke has Jesus "set his face toward Jerusalem" (9:51) like a warrior going into his last battle. In his final days, Jesus waged a nerve-wracking campaign against the authorities, which included a massive nonviolent demonstration (the triumphal entry into Jerusalem, Mk 11:1–11), limited symbolic violence (the expulsion of money-changers from the Temple, Mk 11:15–19), and revolutionary rhetoric (Mk 12). Tensions escalated ominously. When the time came for the Passover *seder*, alarming hints of Jesus' imminent arrest charged the air; it was in this air of finality and farewell that Jesus broke bread with his disciples for the last time. This motif of the Warrior's last words with his friends (Mk 14:12–25) is an ancient and poignant one, most recently portrayed in the Civil War film *Glory* as the black soldiers celebrated, prayed, and testified to each other on the eve of their final battle.

In the early morning hours of that Friday we call Good, in a Garden we call Gethsemane, Jesus faced his last decision as a Warrior: whether to stay and fight the last hopeless battle, or to flee quickly in the night down the road to Jericho to fight again another day. Luke fashions the scene in classic Warrior terms literally as an *agonia* (Lk 22:44), the painful conflict in a man as he struggles with his innate drive to survive and his heroic desire to do the Warrior's duty. Only soldiers who have known this seemingly endless night can truly understand the agony within Jesus when, at last, his "hour" came. He decided to stay.

The Warrior in Jesus on his life's last night is a powerful expression of what it means to be a man. Jesus loved life, all right; his stories are filled with zest, a joy of living. Yet he was not seduced into the ego's attachment to living at any cost. Jesus' Warrior broke through the brittle shell of his ego and allowed his Christ-self to emerge, a Self of greatness and invulnerability, a Self that heroically gives over life to the people.

> Unless a grain of wheat falls to the ground and dies,
>   It remains just a single grain;
> But if it dies,
>   It yields a rich harvest!
> Anyone who loves his life, loses it.
>
>   Jn 12:24–25

Throughout his last day, through torture, through ridicule, through phony justice and abandonment, through death itself, Jesus walked steadily, with a Warrior's courage. But in the end, his Warrior fell silent, like a Lamb led to the slaughter, and another archetype of the Christ-self emerged: the King.

Jesus the King

There are other archetypes we can find in the New Testament portrayal of Jesus: the Prophet, an archetypal role Jesus himself consciously accessed;[12] the Priest, the humble figure who learns humility through suffering and compassion through weakness (Heb 4:12–5:10); the Wiseman, a figure whose very being is suffused with the wisdom of the eternal *logos* (Jn 1), or the Lover, exemplified so beautifully in Jesus' farewell discourse to his friends (Jn 13–17). But we shall here consider only one more: the King, a time-honored title for Jesus still celebrated in Catholicism every year at the feast of Christ the King.

Throughout his preaching career, Jesus' commanding personal-charisma attracted crowds of people seeking a Messianic savior figure, a king, who would fulfill their nationalistic dreams for political and religious freedom. Jesus felt sorry for these people, these sheep without a shepherd (Mk 6:34). But he quite clearly did not acquiesce to any demands that he satisfy their political ambitions; on one occasion in fact, Jesus even fled the crowds when they tried to make him their king (Jn 6:15). This refusal of political power is extraordinary when considering in contrast, for example, today's televangelists and preachers who have cashed in their spiritual capital for a pot of political porridge, whether by running for office directly or forming Political Action Committees. In the face of adoring crowds, Jesus could not have remained unconscious of his great potential for a little P. T. Barnum evangelical hucksterism; indeed, this is precisely what Satan's third temptation is all about (Mt 4:8–10).

Jesus could also have exploited his royal potential in another way more subtle, insidious, and evil than the first. How many religious leaders, enamored with praise and adulation, eventually become fascist gurus, exercising almost hypnotic mind-control over their disciples' every thought and action? You have met their moon-eyed minions at your door and in your airport: vacant eyes, zombie looks, programmed speech, and robotic movements — what Eric Hoffer called the True Believers. It must be extremely pleasurable, in a sick kind of way, for a guru to run people's lives like that. Not that it is very difficult to do. For there is no area more vulnerable to tyranny than religion; it is astonishing and embarrassing how quickly vast numbers of otherwise intelligent people will abandon their rationality, responsibility, and autonomy to the dictates of a totalitarian religious leader.

Jesus was not a King of this kind. Though he said little on the subject of power and authority, what he did say, he said clearly. In front of his striving disciples, "on the make" for organizational power in the

Jesus movement with all the intensity of the men in a Prudential-Bache commercial, he set a child and said, "Unless you change and become like little children, you shall not enter the kingdom of heaven!" (Mt 18:1–4). In the midst of another apostolic power struggle, Jesus bluntly commanded his followers to avoid totally the pagan style of authority: lording it over people and running roughshod over their lives. Those in Christian authority, he said, ought to *serve* the community, not intimidate it (Mt 20:24–28). Jesus himself promised his followers a gentle mastery, a yoke so easy and a burden so light (Mt 11:28–30).

What kind of King is Jesus? St. Ignatius of Loyola (1491–1556), a one-time Basque warrior well familiar with royal courts and the service of kings, imagined in his *Spiritual Exercises* the address of an earthly king that no true knight could resist. Calling on his subjects to liberate the realm from infidels, this imaginary king offers to undergo the same hardships, eat the same foods, and even keep the same watches as his warriors. If such a king deserves our attention, reasons Ignatius, how much more does Christ the Eternal King?[13] Similarly, the Kingship of Jesus is reminiscent of David, whose warriors once risked their lives to bring their thirsty king a drink of water from his home well at Bethlehem (2 Sam 23:13–17). Like David, the royalty of Jesus attracts rather than forces, elicits love not fear, and leads rather than dominates. Jesus' sacral kingship grows directly out of his *charisma*, his personal life-force.

Make no mistake: King Jesus is no dithering democrat. He doesn't allow votes or table thorny issues; he doesn't take polls, build consensus, or make compromises. For people languish under befuddling bureaucrats as surely as tyrants, suffer from lack of leadership as much as groan under dictators. Jesus' authority is direct and clear; he commands, he leads, he rules, but asks of his followers nothing that he himself does not do: loving the neighbor and the self, but above all, loving God with one's whole heart, mind, and soul (Mk 12:28–31).

The King that emerges in Jesus is a quality of soul, an internal nobility, a psychic greatness popularly known as "class." And when, as so often happens, all the trappings of institutional power collapse and the props of official importance are stripped away from a man in authority, this "royal class" will remain in the authentic King. Consider David. In the midst of his son Absalom's patricidal revolt, David had to flee for his life. Yet in the middle of this personal and political disaster, something wonderful happened to David, and nothing so became him in office as his leaving of it. Abandoning Jerusalem for the wilderness, enduring the jeers of his enemies, he climbed the Mount of Olives with head covered and feet unshod, but royal dignity intact (2 Sam 15–16). Though all else failed, at the least he would walk out of Jerusalem like a King.

So it was that the catastrophic events of his last days put Jesus' inner King to the test. Riding back down the same Mount of Olives road that

David took out, Jesus initially accepted the adulation of the crowds as they shouted their *Hosannas* (Mk 11:1–11). Now, it is easy to look great when people hang on your every word and the press scribbles down each utterance. It is a totally different matter to feel and act like a King when all that praise suddenly turns to hatred. And that is exactly what happened to Jesus; less than a week after his triumphal entry into Jerusalem, everything came apart. Challenge the rabble, and they turn on you; disappoint their political machinations, and you get crucified. Jesus would not be their Messiah — only their King.

So soon the crowds jeered, they laughed, they scorned. And what of his followers and best friends? They knew a sinking ship when they saw one, and jumped overboard. To complete the abandonment, the two official powers in Jesus' world suddenly brought him to trial and judged him guilty: the synagogue for heresy, and the state for sedition. As he stood before Pontius Pilate, everything and everybody that had ever supported Jesus were gone, every outer support was stripped away, annihilated. All Jesus had left was his inner King.

The account in the gospel of John (chapters 18–19) of Jesus' trial before Pilate is one of the most dramatic stories in world literature. It is not simply about one dreadful moment in the life of Jesus, but about the life of every little man who ever finds himself up against the Powers That Be. It is about the nature of true manly greatness up against the forces of political authority and expediency that dehumanize and humiliate. In the account, John is teaching us as much about our own royal human dignity as that of Jesus.

"Are you the king of the Jews?" Pilate asks his prisoner with mock seriousness. Jesus answers the question with a question, not so much because he is a Jew as because he is a King, and Kings are not so mocked: "Did you come to this on your own or have others told you about me?" It is an adult reply in a childish game and it perplexes Pilate: no one interrogates the Roman governor of Palestine! Then Jesus says flat out, "Mine is not a kingdom of this world." At some level, one senses that Pilate understands the spirituality of the metaphor: "So you are a king, then?" "I am a king," Jesus replies, "and I came into the world to witness to the truth." Despite his mask of studied scornfulness, Pilate begins to see what the rabble cannot: this is a genuinely royal man before him. Had Pilate himself been more of a King and less of a political hack, he would have freed Jesus on the spot with a wave of the hand. But he allows the crowds to pressure and manipulate him with their reminders about Caesar and, thus, Pilate's political future. With delicious Johannine irony, the crowds finally cry out, "We have no king but Caesar!" Indeed, they do not. But in the end, something in Pilate urges him to order an inscription on Jesus' death-cross that tells the truth, after all: "Jesus of Nazareth, King of the Jews."

The Christ: God and Man

The gospel portrayals of Jesus in the language of classic masculine archetypes indicate the power of masculine spirituality to describe the ultimate spiritual archetype, the Christ. Moreover, the intensity of the masculine archetypes in the Jesus story shows once and for all that, to "put on Christ," a man does not have to "take off " his masculinity. On the contrary; the Christ archetype is the fulfillment of masculinity, the goal of mature manhood. Following Jesus into Christhood does not diminish a man, it completes him.

The Christ archetype is more than the highest goal of male potentiality, however. It is no less than the meeting place of the human and the divine. In activating his Christ potential, a man participates in the very life of God, becoming his adopted son.

Chapter 14

The Masculinity of God

God is not a male. God is not even human. God, the Source of all being, can never be truly apprehended, described, analyzed, defined, dissected, or known. God dwells in inapproachable light and inestimable darkness, outside of space and time, beyond language, and above all human conception. Why, then, do we call such a Being "he" or speak about the masculinity or femininity of such a Holy One?

Because we must. The Jewish-Christian-Muslim tradition is distinctive among all the world's religions because it simultaneously proclaims two radical teachings: God is One, and God is a Person. Against the pagan polytheistic notion of plural gods, competing with each other like so many characters in a cosmic soap opera, it teaches monotheism: the Creator and Origin of all existence is One. Against the idea that the Source of all being is an impersonal energy, like gravity or electricity, our tradition teaches that God is an Individual Person, involved in a responsible and loving way with all his creation.

Herein lies the theological gender problem. Since we cannot conceive of, much less relate to, another person without the aspect of sexuality, we cannot very well envision a personal God without sexualizing him — or her. And just as it is dehumanizing to eliminate sexuality from our interpersonal relationships, so it is depersonalizing to eradicate gender from our conception of God. Without sexuality and gender, religiosity becomes a transaction imbued with as much warmth as two computers interfacing. Sexuality gives our personal as well as our faith relationships depth, color, excitement, and vivacity. But does the choice of one gender over another to describe the deity constitute sexism and engender sexual prejudice? Is there no alternative to having either a God or a Goddess?

The Androgynous God

Sexuality and gender color and vivify our relationship with the One God. If our image of God must be sexual to be personal, why can't we regard God as perfectly androgynous, both male and female? At a theoretical level, we can — and must — do so. Indeed, the androgynous principle was first set out long ago in the Priestly creation story (Gen 1:27).[1]

The problem with the idea of divine androgyny is that in everyday practice it is a wholly unsatisfying way to relate to God. In the first place, perfect androgyny is an ideological ideal never achieved in reality; we are therefore in the position of trying to compare metaphorically one unknown being with Another. Moreover, since the actual quasi-androgynous persons of our experience often tend to represent the *least* common denominator of masculine and feminine rather than the strong presence of both genders' qualities, the metaphorical possibilities for theology are markedly reduced. The result is a "watered down" compromise deity that is neither very masculine nor very feminine. Finally, the effect of an androgynous personality on others is not always harmonious and not necessarily an attractive term in a theological metaphor. Relating to someone of indeterminable sexuality is an unsettling and disorienting experience for most people outside San Francisco; transferring this confusion onto the God of our prayer and worship hardly constitutes a step forward. So while intellectuals may sketch on their theological drawing boards a perfectly androgynous design for God, politically inoffensive in all its parts, what the people in the pews will end up experiencing is a sexually confused Hermaphrodite deity, or a drab and colorless God of undetermined gender.

The Emasculation of God

The neutering of God is already well underway in liberal and mainline Christian churches in America. The expressed purpose of this drive is to create an "inclusive" and nonsexist God to whom all can relate. In fact, the real political intention of the movement is to eliminate the traditional masculine language, metaphors, and images for God that supposedly encourage violence and offend women.[2] While rightly correcting the historic imbalance of masculine imagery in the Christian tradition by recovering feminine language and images for God in the Bible or creating new feminine theological metaphors,[3] liberal translators, theologians, and liturgists have also unwisely opted to "deconstruct" masculine God-talk in worship and theology.

By no means are all, or even most, women in favor of this project; it seems to have little support from the grassroots. It is probably no accident or coincidence, in fact, that the same liberal churches that are neutering God are also plummeting in membership and popular involvement while conservative churches holding to the traditional imagery thrive. The demasculinizing movement is thus an apt symbol not only of the impotence of God in Western culture, but of its widespread loss of masculinity.

In some liberal churches, the drive to "inclusive language" in biblical translations and worship has resulted in the virtual censorship of the most ancient masculine metaphors for God of the Judeo-Christian tradition. God is no longer King, but Sovereign; no longer Father, but Parent; and no longer Lord, but Creator. His old names are now scandalous: God, we are told, is not a Warrior, not a Champion, and not a Judge. He is too gentle to wrestle Jacob, too nice to argue with Job, and his once-strong right arm no longer saves.

The translation committees and liturgical commissions are emasculating our image of God. With proper packaging from his new self-appointed public relations experts, God is bound to look friendlier, more appealing, and most important, Politically Correct. At long last, behold: a kinder and gentler God, harmless, soft, and even cuddly, a deity William O'Malley calls a "Warm Fuzzy" and Michael Garvey "the Bill Cosby of All Being."[4] Perhaps now God will no longer embarrass us, no longer confront and command and demand; properly gelded, blow-dried, manicured, and made over, a God at last that Yuppie culture can enjoy: nice, nurturing, and neutral, and no danger to our many toys. Nietzsche was wrong. It is not necessary to kill God (besides, that wouldn't be nice); a simple sex-change operation will suffice. Modernity has triumphed and created the castrated deity humanistic egotism always really wanted: "It," the Divine Eunuch, Sovereign Parent of the Universe.

No one even filed an environmental impact statement. When it comes to theology, liberalism, which in other areas prides itself on due process, OSHA standards, ACLU litigation, and Miranda rights, can prove awfully autonomous. The people of God didn't want to castrate God — just a few blue-ribbon panels and elite scholars did. And so a few theological consultations here and some quick liturgical innovations there and *voilà*, a new God. Show up at a worship service and suddenly you're praising the "Sovereign," a word never used by ordinary people and without any metaphorical connotations whatsoever. Forget the Our Father; it is now the Our Parent, an abstract term originating not from everyday life and experience, but from sociology textbooks. Or listen to prayers that try to avoid the personal pronouns "he" or "she" for God; the resulting debacle is inevitably linguistically tangled and completely devoid of all poetry, emotion, or dignity.

Fortunately, it is not too late to prevent the traditional Christian God from becoming an endangered species; there is still time to spare the rest of the church from this demasculinizing trend. And spare it we must. For what is finally at stake here is not rhetorical elegance, nor male privilege or power, nor the needs of a mindless conservatism to hold onto traditions merely because they are old. The issue is whether the disappearing male metaphors possess indispensable and irreplaceable potentials for imaging and relating to God, which cannot be summarily dismissed without causing irreparable harm to the essentials of the Christian message. The question is whether the male perception of reality contributes anything unique to the rendering of God in our imagination and prayer. In other words, might men and women *need* a specifically masculine God?

The weight of five thousand years of religious history, innumerable ancient rituals from every tradition, and the sheer volume of myths and stories from every continent suggests an answer to these questions in the affirmative. Masculine spirituality has not led us far from God; on the contrary, it has proved itself a reliable universal vehicle of religious truth. Psychological and spiritual forces now unknown to us originally caused ancient peoples around the globe to coin their religious myth, ritual, and language with predominantly masculine values; we can dispense with their primal wisdom only at our spiritual peril. Rather than liquidate masculine theological metaphors, we ought to listen to what they are trying to say about God; rather than censor them from the church's life and worship, we might probe them for their wisdom. Perhaps the collective male psyche, vibrating sympathetically over the millennia with the energy of the Eternal One, has a music worth listening to, after all.

Masculine Metaphors for God

All positive God-talk is metaphorical.[5] It is necessarily so. Since God exists in eternity, beyond space and time, if we are to communicate about him we must use spatial and temporal language that is woefully inadequate to the task. To speak meaningfully about God, we must in some way link this utterly Unknown One with metaphorical referents or images that to us are familiar, such as King or Lover. The difficulty with this theological necessity, of course, is that we easily become so attached to our images of God that we forget that they are only metaphors. Worse, the images themselves become gods. We forget that metaphors always conceal as much as they reveal, that they lie as well as tell the truth. God is always infinitely greater than the poor language we concoct to describe him.

The biblical tradition offers a treasury of such God-metaphors, not all of them male, not all of them even human. The diversity of expression is astonishing; in one text after another, the poets, prophets, and

wisemen of Israel describe God as a lion, a destroyer, a faithful husband,
a cattleman, a fowler, a king, a father, a leopard, a bear, a physician, a
boxer, dew, a tree, a potter, a warrior, light, a judge, a vintager, a barber,
a stumbling-stone, a trap, a thief, a shelter, a shade, drought, a restaura-
teur, a rock, a farmer, a crown, a redeemer, an executioner, a bird, a strong
arm, a shepherd, a slaveowner, a hero, an archer, a savior, a consoler, a
teacher, a bridegroom, the sun, a midwife, a jealous lover, a stranger, a
fortress, a stream, wind, a seducer, an enemy, an eagle, a mace, a butcher,
a shield, a stronghold, a cup, a shopkeeper, a thunderstorm, a lamp, a
guard, a mason, and a song.

A glance at this list suggests the almost overwhelming range of
religious experiences that inspired the biblical writers to coin fresh God-
metaphors with bold honesty and spiritual freedom. Yet the variety of
theological imagery here also hints at our own modern poverty of spirit.
Modern religion is severely restricted in its available God-metaphors.
No wonder our sermons, worship services, and spiritual books are often so boring: we have confined ourselves to pitifully few metaphors —
Lover and Father, primarily. As rich as these images are, overuse dimin-
ishes their value and represses the truth that, in many ways, God is also
not a Lover or a Father.

Our list of biblical God-metaphors also reveals two other important things. First, the human images in the Bible are almost entirely
masculine;[6] second, these male metaphors are rather evenly divided
between positive images of care and salvation (king, father, physician,
shepherd) and negative images of animosity and punishment (judge,
executioner, destroyer, enemy). Each of these metaphors vibrates with
masculine spiritual energy; each says important things about the biblical
God that are not always pleasant or easy to hear. Rather than analyze
every one of the many positive and negative masculine metaphors for
God in the Bible, however, we shall select only a few; namely, four of the
key masculine archetypes discussed in Part Two of this book. We shall
ponder the meaning of each masculine archetype as applied to God
metaphorically in order to appreciate the value of masculine spirituality
to theology. We shall consider below God the Wildman, the Warrior, the
King, and the Father.

El Shaddai: God the Wildman

Nowhere in the Bible is God called or directly compared to a Wildman
(any more than Elijah, John the Baptist, or Jesus is ever actually so called).
Lurking behind a host of passages, however, is the archetype of a wildly
free male who rides on the clouds, hurls lightning shafts, rumbles the
thunder, waters the deserts, feeds the lions, and plays with the sea-
monsters.[7] Sometimes, he is explicitly called El Shaddai (Hebrew: "God

of the mountains"; cf. Gen 49:25–26), the potent Lord who brings fertility and the blessings of nature to Israel.

El Shaddai challenges the increasingly popular mythological, ecological, and theological notion that nature and fertility somehow belong exclusively to the feminine domain and that masculinity is "anti-nature." One man recently remarked that he has heard so much of this New Age Gaia ideology that he has begun to feel like a stranger on his own planet. El Shaddai reminds us that nature is also equally masculine. He takes us back to all that is chthonic and earthy and wild.

Biblical texts connected with El Shaddai remind us of the Wildman archetype: potent, prolific, and free. In them, he tells us repeatedly to "be fruitful and multiply!"[8] He himself smothers every breast with hot kisses and spurts his seed into every available womb in an outburst of life and vitality:[9]

> It is the God of your fathers who helps you,
>   El Shaddai who blesses you:
> Blessings of the sky above,
>   Blessings of the deep far below,
> Blessings of breasts and wombs,
>   Blessings of grain and flowers,
> Blessings of the ancient mountains.
>   Gen 49:25–26

Shaddai is the deity who creates life in all its wild and wonderful forms, the God we experience when we wander through a good zoo and see the shocking, breathtaking, and imaginatively promiscuous variety of life on earth: striped zebras and monstrous rhinos, dozing tree-sloths and sleek gazelles, bug-eye fish and vicious sharks and comic penguins. Shaddai, too, is the God we experience if we have ever travelled the four corners of the earth and enjoyed the colorful spectrum of humanity on our planet: the cool elegance of blond-haired and blue-eyed Europeans, the enchanting smiles of almond-eyed Thais, the dignity and bearing of blue-black Africans, the warmth and humor of the engaging Latinos, or the deep wisdom etched in the face of Native Americans. How can each of these peoples in their own ways look so beautiful? Who could think up such a wonderful variety of human races, or such mind-boggling multiplicity in the animal world? Shaddai. The Goddess may have birthed and nurtured them all, but El Shaddai created them out of his wild and fertile and outrageous imagination.

Another increasingly popular notion in mythological and theological circles — perpetrated again recently in "The Power of Myth," the otherwise excellent television interviews with Joseph Campbell — holds that the earth's ecological crisis is traceable to the dominating male God of the Hebrew Bible. In this view, the text ordering men and women to "fill the earth and subdue it" (Gen 1:28) inspires and legitimizes the West's exploitative war against nature; in the biblical tradition, we are told, "life is corrupt, and every natural impulse is sinful."[10] Purveyors of such tendentious ideas cannot have read very carefully the entirety of Genesis 1, where Elohim delights in his creation of the world, pronouncing it *tov meod*, *"very* good"; they cannot have sung the marvelous hymns to Yahweh's fecundity (e.g., Ps 8 or 19 or 104); they must not remember Shaddai's humorous, extravagant speech celebrating the life that he created on earth (Job 38–41).

El Shaddai is not only the metaphor of God's love of life, but of God's freedom. He is a God freer and wilder than nature itself, totally beyond our control, unable to be manipulated, bought off, controlled, coerced, or frightened. He does as he pleases. He is the God of Job, whose purposes we only obscure with our empty-headed words. We are contingent, alive entirely at his pleasure. We can make no claims and demand no rights before him. His is the starkest desert and highest sky; his the coldest stretch of snowy Alpine tundra and the densest tropical forest; his, too, the darkest thunderstorm and the shiniest sea, the most ominous eclipse and the brightest, starriest sky.

El Shaddai is the essence of masculinity: try to chain him up and he laughs, leaping away like a wild gazelle or a young stag. No matter how much we may want to catch and place him in our theological zoos or golden tabernacles, there to be safely visited or worshipped at our convenience, he escapes us. He is the feral God we want, as always, to domesticate, to manipulate into serving *our* needs, following *our* rules, and obeying *our* commands. But El Shaddai will have none of it. He will not let us destroy his wildness as we are destroying the earth's. He won't let us incarcerate or cage him no matter how fervently we try; lay out a net, and he disappears, a *deus absconditus*, or "hidden God" (Isa 45:15). And to each of our pleas for more blessings or greener grass, he grins and gives one exasperating answer: "Yes: life itself."

Ultimately, the masculinity of this Wild God reveals about him that which most makes him God: holiness. The root meaning of the Hebrew *qadosh* ("holy") connotes utter separateness; this is the quality of the divine Rudolf Otto long ago described as *ganz andere*: total Otherness.[11] Holiness in this sense is not an ethical category or a moral evaluation, but a spatial/temporal separation from all mundane and profane reality. Holiness is the only concept available for expressing the utter differentiation of our reality from that of the divine experience of the "other side," the supernatural. Holiness ("separation") is fundamentally a masculine category.

The human urge to separate, individuate, and divide — to make "other" — is a masculine psychological and spiritual hallmark. It is also the essence of the El Shaddai metaphor, which represents the free holiness of God. That is why the trendy project to demasculinize the biblical God endangers the most appropriate response humans can make to the Holy One of Israel: utter awe — what the ancients called "fear of the Lord." At risk is our modern sense of the fundamental separation that exists between God and humanity:

> My thoughts are not your thoughts,
> My ways are not your ways, says the Lord.
> The heavens are as high above the earth
> As my ways are above your ways.
>   Isa 55:8–9

The powerful masculine metaphor of God's wild Otherness warns us away from our own worst sin: thinking and acting as if *we* are God!

Yahweh: God the Warrior

Many people are appalled when they read the Old Testament for the first time, while it is still unfamiliar and before they have developed the unconscious screening mechanisms that filter out the myriad bits of evidence of one recurring motif: God is often portrayed in the Hebrew Scriptures as a frightening Warrior, an avenging General who leads the heavenly hosts into battle.[12] The New Testament also purveys this Divine Warrior motif in such apocalyptic passages as Mark 13, Matthew 24, Luke 21, and Revelation 19–20; whereas the Old Testament Warrior God marshals his forces merely to crush the selected enemies of Israel, the New Testament apocalyptic Avenger plans to destroy the whole planet in a massive cataclysm!

Understanding and handling these passages is notoriously difficult for believers; liberal churches tend to repress or excise them from their life, worship, and preaching, while conservative or fundamentalist churches take them too literally, creating a constant state of anxiety and doom. How, then, *do* we take the numerous biblical texts telling of God the terrible Warrior? From a masculine spirituality perspective, which appreciates the Warrior as a positive archetype, we might learn to take these passages metaphorically and listen to what they have to say.

The hardest texts in the Bible are those describing God as a Warrior who wants to attack *us*, his own people! In addition to the aforementioned New Testament passages, one finds this motif especially strong in the Hebrew prophets. From the earliest oracles of Amos through the late apocalypses of Third Isaiah, Yahweh of Hosts looms over a sinful Israel, threatening devastation and destruction as punishment for its sins.

One can hardly enumerate here all the texts that promise a fiery end or a violent Day of Yahweh, but Isaiah 5:25 is a typical example:

> Therefore, Yahweh burns with anger against his people.
>   He set his hand and struck them;
>   He killed their princes, their bodies lie
>   Like dung in the streets.
>   With all this His anger still surges
>   And His hand is yet set to strike.

Is God our enemy, then? Does he burn with wrath, and is his hand yet ready to attack? The answer is yes. God *is* our enemy, indeed, our worst enemy, and his right arm is forever poised to strike. How is this so, and in what metaphorical sense true?

Biblical texts again and again state the reason: *our sins* turn God into a fearful enemy warrior. But this fighter is not some deranged Rambo or perverted Nazi SS storm-trooper, a bloodthirsty Conan or a professional soldier of fortune lusting to enter battle. Yahweh the Warrior is as innocent as any fresh-faced kid ever shipped into battle and as honorable as any noble warrior who ever did his duty. The biblical God is a warrior who hates battle, but whose righteousness finally will not shrink from confronting forcefully the perversion of creation. Perhaps we can begin to gauge the seriousness of human sin in observing how we have turned the wildly free, joyful, and exuberantly life-giving El Shaddai into the fiercest of fighters, a frightful Shiva wielding the sword of death.

Our sins — a slick business deal here, a brief affair there — did all this? Isn't God overreacting? But our everyday mistakes, peccadilloes, and human failings are not the "sin" that the biblical texts have in mind. The biblical notion of sin refers, rather, to something much deeper: the all-pervasive tendency that lurks in each of us to make ourselves gods. The Bible teaches that we are each of us made for others, in service, responsibility, and interdependency; yet we tend to act as if reality exists purely on our own behalf. This perverse notion is only enhanced by modern consumer culture, which teaches us to think only in terms of our rights and not our responsibilities, our needs rather than our duties. Worse, in our arrogance we assume that other people exist solely for our own personal exploitation. This attitude is the most corrupt violation of human nature and God's creation imaginable.

The results of unchecked abuse of people and nature are apparent in the vastness of human poverty and the seriousness of global ecological ruin. Yet we have to look no further than our own personalities to see the wages of the sin of pride. We want things we cannot have, foolishly imagine ourselves to be what we are not, inflate our egos dangerously beyond the genuine limits of our psyche, and contradict the natural and simple boundaries of our bodies and minds. The results of our ego-deification range from mindless workaholism to crass hedonism to shop-till-you-drop materialism and worse: a maniacal assumption that we should somehow live exempt from the disease, pain, and death that is the human lot.

Something perverse inside us wars against our own deepest human nature, and God will not allow himself to be a party to it by becoming a Divine Shill in the phony religious game that this sinfulness creates after its own image. Amos and Hosea, the earliest of the classical biblical prophets, recognized nearly three thousand years ago that Feel-Good Religion easily serves as a deceptive cover-up to the voracious institutionalized egoism that consumes the lives and labor of the poor and then discards them like so many useless apple cores.[13] God is not mocked. He will not cave in to those demanding a "nice" cupid god to assuage all consciences and soothe all guilt. On the contrary; he roars with anger from Zion (Amos 1:2) and marshals his army to obliterate prideful perversity from Israel (Jer 15:5–9).

The image of God the Warrior-Enemy is the outcome, projected metaphorically onto the cosmos, of our own severe alienation from natural wisdom, our own inability to accept creaturehood, contingency, smallness, and our own denial of pain and death. To the extent that we refuse to "go with the flow" of human humility, thereby blocking the course of human nature, we create Yahweh the Warrior. He is the symbol of our alienation from wisdom. And when he appears to us, sword in hand or spear poised to strike, alarms should sound: we have strayed from the Way and rejected the eternal Tao.

Religion that easily dispenses with the Divine Warrior archetype divests itself of the most powerful possible metaphor for revealing our animosity to the Creator and the way of life he has fashioned. In eschewing the imagery of war, the bogus pacifism of such a religion only reinforces the tyranny of the ego. For Yahweh the Warrior, armed with his sharp and shiny sword, approaches us not to kill — but only to sever us, with swift and sure surgical strokes, from the millstone of our grave and deadly attachments. And by these wounds we are healed.

The positive side of the Divine Warrior archetype is a powerful and beautiful one also. For the Bible teaches that the liberating Yahweh also fights with fierce righteousness on behalf of the poor, the enslaved, and the oppressed. Nowhere is this divine metaphor expressed more mightily than in the Exodus story. There Yahweh carefully coaches Moses in the tactics of negotiations with and civil disobedience against the implacable tyranny of imperial Egypt. When hard-hearted Pharaoh breaks his agreement to let Israel go, Yahweh roars into battle, devastating the Egyptian army:

> Yahweh is a man of war; Yahweh is his name.
>   The chariot-army of Pharaoh he hurls into the sea...
> Your right hand, Yahweh, is wonderful in its power,
>   Your right hand, Yahweh, smashes the enemy.
>
> Ex 15: 3–6

The New Testament also knows Yahweh's liberating might. Mary, visiting her cousin Elizabeth in the Roman-occupied West Bank, rejoices to God at the promise of the liberator Jesus she holds in her womb:

> God has shown the power of his arm,
>   He has vanquished the arrogant.
> He pulls down princes from their thrones
>   and exalts the lowly.

Indeed, the whole Bible is laced with the motif of Yahweh's military intervention on behalf of the poor, as the liberation theologians have helped us to see in recent years.[14] The Bible insists that Yahweh is a God who hears the cry of the poor, who watches out for and listens to his lowly ones, and who intervenes on their behalf with wrathful indignation whenever Pharaohs trample on them. Yahweh is a "man of war" for the weak and vulnerable, a dreadful enemy to unjust kings, mighty emperors, and garden-variety poohbahs of all stripes.

The Divine Warrior archetype appears in those religions imbued with the tradition of a faith that does justice. Yahweh the Liberator is thus a metaphor of divine compassion for the "least" in our world. So the hermeneutics of suspicion encourages us to ask: among what groups do objections to this theological metaphor now flow? The answer is: among wealthy, educated, and elite First World members of the upper class. And which people most embrace — and need — this metaphor? The oppressed. The world is a place of violence; that those most vulnerable to it should hope for God's protection and deliverance from danger in the rough-and-tumble Divine Warrior language of the Bible is hardly unworthy of them. And that those who benefit most from class exploitation and weaponry should so facilely wish to excise precisely the metaphor for God that gives so much encouragement to their defenseless brothers and sisters is, in turn, by no means admirable.

Perhaps we could feel the power of the Psalmist's image of Yahweh as a "guard" if we lived in the danger of a drug-infested housing project or a gang-terrorized neighborhood:

> I look up to the mountains — whence comes my help?
>   My help comes from Yahweh, who made heaven and earth.
> He won't let your foot slip — this guard won't sleep.
>   The guard of Israel neither sleeps nor naps!

> Yahweh guards you from evil — he protects your life.
> Yahweh watches your leaving and return, now and always.
> Ps 121:1–4, 7–8

Perhaps if we lived under the wanton and arbitrary brutality of the police state of South Africa we could appreciate the joyous promise of Second Isaiah (41:11–12) as he reworked the old Divine Warrior language during the Babylonian Exile:

> Oh! They shall be put to shame and confusion
>   Those who conspired against you.
> They will become as nothing — utterly destroyed —
>   Those who fought against you.
> You will look for them but not find them
>   These enemies of yours;
> They shall be wiped out and brought to nothing
>   Those who battled against you.

For those genuinely endangered by physical violence or intimidated by overwhelming institutional oppression, is not God-talk bankrupt if it cannot include hope for deliverance under the protection of a Just One who is rougher and tougher than any enemy?

God Is King!

For most people on this planet, everyday life is an experience of chaos. The residents of a Latin American *barrio* might not know from day to day whether they than can find drinkable water or safe food; African villagers might wonder if they can find decent jobs in burgeoning but dangerous cities; and Filipinos might worry about the political and economic stability necessary to live productive lives. Even most of us in the supposedly safe First World experience chaos and disarray in our personal lives. Fear of crime always lurks in the backs of our minds; shifting economic conditions pose hazards to our jobs. Most of us also experience marginality and vulnerability in other ways, as well: "falling off the wagon," physical infirmities and diseases, aging, relationships that can come apart at any moment, neuroses and depressions that haunt many of us every day. A popular bumper-sticker and T-shirt slogan express all these feelings and fears in the succinct, if crude, sentence: "Shit Happens."

Who is God for us in this chaotic universe? The most ancient texts of the biblical tradition proclaim: He is King. The King is the archetype of order, authority, and generativity; applied to God, the metaphor is nothing less than a ringing statement of human hope that life is not purely random, accidental, or meaningless. For God it is who created the ordered world out of the watery chaos of the abyss (Gen 1:2), and he it is who rules the world firmly, making it a place where life and love can flourish under his royal auspices.

> Say to the nations: "Yahweh is King!"
> He makes the world safe and unshakable.
> He will judge the peoples in true justice.
>   Ps 96:10

This theme of the kingship of God is the central message of Jesus of Nazareth. In his parables and stories, Jesus invited his humble listeners to make God their personal king and to trust in his Lordship every day, even in small things. The Kingdom of God is a powerful proclamation of faith that, in the midst of the apparent chaos of our lives, a hidden authority operates secretly on our behalf.

Why, then, is the metaphor of God's kingship under such attack in our times? First, because the word "king" connotes the patriarchal, masculine power of a bygone age. Today we have no king but Elvis. Second, the God-as-King metaphor apparently carries too much "Christian baggage" for many of our contemporaries. One of the most helpful spiritualities of our day, the Twelve Step program, uses the vague term "Higher Power" for God in place of the King metaphor to include atheists and agnostics in its dynamics. It seems to work, as millions of people in Alcoholics Anonymous can attest.

Yet such substitutions also betray the impoverishment of our language, mythology, and imagination. Try to visualize a "creator" or use "sovereign" in a sentence; even the phrase "Higher Power" is cold and bloodless, connoting an algebraic equation or perhaps an electrical appliance. Nor would other modern metaphors of power help much. Is God a president? What sort of campaign commercials did he use to get elected? Or would you place your life in the hands of a divine CEO, an eternal Chairperson?

But a King! Now that is a metaphor that captures the imagination. Out of the archetypal memories of the collective unconscious, we envision his lordly head crowned with gold, his bearded face gazing wisely and benevolently at his court. He is Arthur, ruling Camelot with firm justice and kindly law, always looking out for the welfare of his subjects. He is the saintly Louis or the brave Henry V or the noble Chief Joseph, a regal figure of great power and great goodness. The King is the ancient ruler of myth and legend whose visage still conjures in us images of might and right, of order and mercy, under whose powerful reign we can flourish.

Does my fate then, and the fate of the world, rest in the hands of such a godly King? Easy enough to answer yes when the checkbook balances and the blood tests come back negative. But is God still our King when chemotherapy fails and the marriage falters? Is he Lord over our lives in unemployment lines and soup kitchens? Is he Master of the Universe when our business fails or a parent develops Alzheimer's? These are precisely the times when we most need the powerful metaphor of God the King, and not some cleverly contrived substitute. These are the moments we need to reach back into our ancient memories and join Israel in its monumental act of faith that enthrones Yahweh and proclaims "Our God *is* King!"

Abba: God the Father

Each of the God-metaphors that we have considered says something essential about God. For the biblical writers who concocted them and the scores of generations of faithful who held them in prayerful reverence, these images bespeak long, sometimes painful, but always intense relationships of prayer, suffering, and worship. Yet one metaphor above all others captured the imagination of Christians because it claimed such centrality in the prayer-life and personal identity of Jesus: God the Father. In his genuine intimacy with God, Jesus dared to call the King of the Universe *Abba*, an Aramaic word meaning "daddy" or "papa." So central is this name to Jesus' faith that Paul could later claim that anyone who so addressed the deity clearly possessed the Spirit and became with Jesus a child of God (Rom 8:14–17).

But is God's fatherhood a sexist expression, deeply offensive to women and in need of replacement?[15] Or does the father metaphor possess a unique and indispensable truth about God that is not available in a generic term like "Parent"? In his excellent study *Biblical Faith and Fathering*, John W. Miller argues on behalf of the Father metaphor.[16] Miller reminds us that human fathering is not an automatic "given" nor something that can be taken for granted.[17] Biologically, males are relatively marginal to the reproductive process; after the moment of conception, the growth of the fetus is entirely the concern of the mother. Primitive societies may not even have understood the link between a biological father and his offspring; thus, deliberate fathering as we now know it is probably a historically recent cultural achievement, one greatly enhanced by patriarchal religion.[18]

The force of Miller's observation is apparent when one reflects for a moment on dysfunctional families in which the father is either physically or emotionally distant or absent. The devastation in the psyches of young people who grow up without a strong and involved father is apparent to anyone who has worked with juvenile delinquents, prisoners, and indeed many kinds of emotionally wounded people. It is unfortunate that, at a time when millions of families so desperately need models and examples of father-involvement, religious intellectuals should argue for the annihilation of precisely the metaphor that most exemplifies and models masculine commitment and care: God the Father.

What does this image have to say about God? It is the metaphor of God's commitment to the human race. The ultimate expression of divine transcendence is the male sky god. Whether we know him as Yahweh, Zeus, or Wakan Tanka, the sky god dwells in the sublime regions of the heavens that are utterly foreign and unknown to humans: the cold reaches of the Milky Way by night and the dazzling realm of the Sun by day. The problem with the sky god, of course, is that his very transcendental overwhelmingness leaves us cold under the night sky and burnt under the noonday sun. Theologians call this deity *deus otiosus*, the sky god who grows so transcendent that he becomes irrelevant, leaving in his wake a vast human alienation from God, a widespread modern spiritual vacuum that began in Western culture as Enlightenment Deism and ended in modern atheism (e.g., the "death of God" movement).

The "Father" is the metaphor that mitigates the mystery of God's transcendence. The Father metaphor represents an evolution within the Godhead in which the male sky god abandons his divine prerogatives of celestial freedom and unspeakable otherness and freely commits himself to a nurturing, fathering affiliation with his people in an eternal relationship.[19] In theological language, the metaphor of the Father is the symbol of God's infinite condescension to humanity. As Father, God does graciously what he ought not to have done by "rights": he brings to bear the power of the universe to nurture us, his children.

Rather than weaken the metaphor of God the Father, Christian religion ought to strengthen it. For the human family is growing increasingly dysfunctional, lost, and aimless. Like the poorest family in the roughest ghetto, the human family does not need less "Father" energy — it needs more of it.

The historical movement from the supremacy of Neolithic Goddess religion to the modern preeminence of the father archetype is not a fall from grace, as the devotees of Gaia would suggest, but a spiritual evolution. The centrality of God the Father represents human psychic maturation from a feminine matrix of undifferentiated primitive religiosity into a highly masculine, individuated spirituality that values the independence of other beings and appreciates the graciousness of their free and unmerited love. The Father metaphor is an apt symbol of this reality.

In biblical faith, the triumph of the Father-metaphor over previous masculine images for God also represents a powerful spiritual development. The sweep of the biblical story from Genesis to the gospels ultimately means that God, who roams wild and free as El Shaddai, who wars terribly as Yahweh, and who rules powerfully and justly as

King, this same God freely makes all of this overwhelmingly great and tremendously good divine energy available to us, his adopted children. We need only cry out, "Abba!"

The Masculinity of God

The masculine spiritual language of the biblical archetypes vastly enriches our imagination of God, our worship, and our theology. That our God-talk is unfortunately deficient in the feminine is no fair reflection on the aptness of the masculine metaphors, and certainly no justification for their elimination from prayer and worship.

The contemporary creation of feminine theological language is no threat to masculine theology and, indeed, a necessary reminder that gender in God-talk is always purely metaphorical. Remembering this, we may nevertheless contemplate gratefully the role of masculinity in rendering unto us throughout the millennia the image of a God so great and so good.

Notes

Chapter 1: Sexuality, Gender, and Spirit

1. A listing of men's workshops and retreats and a catalogue of videos, books, and cassettes on men's topics is available from Ally Press, 524 Orleans St., St. Paul, MN 55107.

2. Interview with editors of *Time Magazine*, June 4, 1990.

3. For an indication of fundamentalism's unhealthy qualities, see my article The Reemergence of Catholic Fundamentalism" (172–91) or that of Dr. Mortimer Ostow, "The Fundamentalist Phenomenon: A Psychological Perspective" (99–125) in Norman J. Cohen, ed., *The Fundamentalism Phenomenon: A View from Within, A Response from Without* (Grand Rapids: Eerdmans, 1990). Not least among fundamentalism's typical unhealthiness is an abiding misogyny.

4. Some of the programs of outreach to men include: The Center for Contemplation and Action in Albuquerque (Catholic) under the direction of the Rev. Richard Rohr, O.F.M.; Brother House of Tulsa, A Center for Male Spirituality (an interdenominational group); and the Brotherhood Commission of Memphis (Southern Baptist).

A few books on masculine spirituality are also beginning to appear. Perhaps the best to date is *Biblical Faith and Fathering: Why We Call God "Father"* by John W. Miller (New York: Paulist, 1989), a scholarly treatment that indicates the need for biblical fathering in modern family life. *A Man and His God* by Fr. Martin Pable, O.F.M. (Notre Dame: Ave Maria, 1988) is a fine discussion of masculine spirituality directed to laymen. *The Intimate Connection* by James B. Nelson (Philadelphia: Westminster, 1988) offers a rather weak treatment of masculine spirituality, considerably watered down by a tone of apology and defensiveness. *Toward a Male Spirituality* by John Carmody (Mystic, Conn.: Twenty-Third, 1989) offers solid theological insights, but surprisingly little spirituality that actually has to do with men.

5. One notably excellent exception: "A Gathering of Men," an interview of Robert Bly by Bill Moyers, broadcast first on PBS in January 1990 (available in videocassette from Ally Press).

6. The great number of feminist books on religion makes a complete listing impossible here. Among the most influential and provocative Christian feminist works are Elisabeth Schüssler Fiorenza, *In Memory of Her* (New York: Crossroad, 1984), Phyllis Trible, *God and the Rhetoric of Sexuality* (Philadelphia: Fortress, 1978), and Letty M. Russell, ed., *Feminist Interpretation of the Bible* (Philadelphia:

Westminster, 1985). A plethora of post-Christian feminist studies on the Goddess are also appearing, some of which will be treated in chapter 3.

7. One recent example of this twisted logic is put forth by Rev. Joseph Fessio, S.J., in his article "Reasons Given against Women Acolytes and Lectors" (distributed by Catholics United for the Faith, Inc., 45 Union Ave., New Rochelle, N.Y.).

8. For a recent discussion of the historical and philosophical reasons (including Platonism) for the increasing alienation of Christians from an effective spirituality, see Bernard Cooke, *The Distancing of God: The Ambiguity of Symbol in History and Theology* (Minneapolis: Augsburg Fortress, 1990).

9. Christ's radical invitation to the life of a eunuch (Mt 19:10–12) occurs in the context of remarriage after divorce — not as a prescription of celibacy. For a scathing feminist indictment of priestly celibacy as an encouragement of psychological pathology, see Uta Ranke-Heinemann, *Eunuchs: For the Kingdom of Heaven* (New York: Doubleday, 1990).

10. For a discussion of the shortcomings of the model of Joseph as a male ideal, see James E. Dittes, *The Male Predicament: On Being a Man Today* (San Francisco: Harper & Row, 1985), especially chapter 1, "Joseph: Frozen Power." Feminists have challenged the "Mary ever-virgin" motif in Roman Catholicism as subtly hostile to female sexuality. Joseph's corresponding asexuality is no less undermining to male sexuality.

11. We shall examine this assumption, which has taken the form of a misandrist ideology in some extreme forms of feminism, in chapter 3.

12. For a discussion of androgyny and its relation to masculine psychology, see Joseph H. Pleck, *The Myth of Masculinity* (Cambridge, Mass.: MIT Press, 1983).

13. We shall discuss evidence for male distinctiveness from the female in the next chapter.

14. See, for example, Paul's doctrine of the resurrection in 1 Corinthians 15.

15. This psychosomatic approach is described in Dr. Bernie Siegel's popular book, *Love, Medicine, and Miracles* (New York: Harper & Row, 1986), and Dr. Larry Dossey's *Beyond Illness: Discovering the Experience of Health* (Boulder: Shambhala, 1984), among many other works.

16. See Rene Dubos, *So Human an Animal* (New York: Scribner's, 1968).

17. Perhaps the most readable account of the theories of Jung and his disciples is contained in the well-written and profusely illustrated book edited by Jung himself entitled *Man and His Symbols* (New York: Doubleday, 1964). The first essay by Jung memorably describes his insights regarding dreams and mythology.

18. For an excellent treatment of the implications of androgyny for healthy psychology and relationships, see John A. Sanford, *The Invisible Partners: How the Male and Female in Each of Us Affects Our Relationships* (New York: Paulist, 1980). For a very memorable account of the relationship of a male to his *anima*, see Robert Johnson, *He* (King of Prussia, Pa.: Religious Publishing, 1974).

Chapter 2: Masculine Spirituality

1. See, for example, Edward O. Wilson, *Sociobiology: The New Synthesis* (Cambridge, Mass.: Belknap Press, 1975). While still controversial in scientific circles, sociobiology is a highly suggestive and fruitful approach for sexual spirituality.

2. For a wonderful discussion of male agonism, see Walter J. Ong, *Fighting for Life: Contest, Sexuality, and Consciousness* (Ithaca: Cornell University Press, 1981), especially 15–48.

3. See ibid., 59–63.

4. Carol Gilligan, *In a Different Voice: Psychological Theory and Women's Development* (Cambridge, Mass.: Harvard, 1982) 9–10 cites research that demonstrates how boys prefer competitive games more than girls, especially when rule disputes come into the play.

5. By contrast, Gilligan (ibid., 9–10) suggests that feminine psychology so values interpersonal relationships that girls in play tend to call off a game rather than engage in contentious disputes.

6. For an excellent treatment of the Warrior archetype, see Carol Pearson, *The Hero Within: Six Archetypes We Live By* (San Francisco: Harper & Row, 1986), 74–97. A recent novel that portrays a college student's discovery of his own Warrior is by Dan Millman, *The Way of the Peaceful Warrior* (Tiburon, Calif.: Kramer, 1980).

7. For an excellent discussion of masculinity as a contrast to the feminine environment, see Ong, *Fighting for Life*, 64–76. See also Sam Keen, *Fire in the Belly: On Being a Man* (New York: Bantam, 1991), especially 11–24.

8. See Carol Gilligan, *In a Different Voice*, 5–8.

9. See Gilligan, ibid., 24–63.

10. See Robert Bly, *Iron John* (Reading, Mass.: Addison-Wesley Publishing, 1990).

11. The Twelve Steps are a spiritual recovery program originally designed for members of Alcoholics Anonymous, but now used in a variety of addiction programs for drugs, overeating, sexual compulsiveness, and so forth. Most bookstores feature books on the program, such as *The Twelve Steps for Everyone Who Really Wants Them* (Minneapolis: CompCare Publications, 1975).

12. A number of powerful spiritual books for people with AIDS are now available; for example, Rev. William J. Dobbels, S.J., *An Epistle of Comfort* (Kansas City: Sheed and Ward, 1990), or Paul Reed, *Serenity: Challenging the Fear of AIDS — From Despair to Hope* (Berkeley: Celestial Arts, 1987).

13. This is the central thrust of an excellent study by John W. Miller, *Biblical Faith and Fathering: Why We Call God "Father"* (New York: Paulist, 1989), especially 13–23. Miller argues that fathering is a cultural achievement and acquisition.

14. For discussions of the principal masculine archetypes, see Robert Moore and Douglas Gillette, *King, Warrior, Magician, Lover: Rediscovering the Archetypes of the Mature Masculine* (San Francisco: HarperSanFrancisco, 1990), Carol Pearson's *The Hero Within*, or Jean Shinoda Bolen's *Gods in Everyman*.

15. This tendency is well documented in Carol Gilligan's *In a Different Voice;*

the point of her study is to show that the feminine tendency to value concrete, relational reasoning is equally valuable to humanity.

16. See, for example, Lawrence Kohlberg, *The Philosophy of Moral Development* (San Francisco: Harper & Row, 1981). But see also Gilligan's *In a Different Voice*, which demonstrates that women's moral reasoning (concrete, relational) should not be judged negatively according to standards that are, ultimately, male.

17. See Ong, *Fighting for Life*, especially 38–41 and 55–61.

18. One example is the two Catholic patron saints of the missions: St. Thérèse of Lisieux spent her life in daily prayer within the confines of a cloistered convent; St. Francis Xavier, on the other hand, travelled to the distant ends of the earth, dying on a lonely Chinese island.

19. Joseph Campbell, *The Hero with a Thousand Faces* (Princeton, N.J.: Princeton University Press, 1949). Campbell's study is a pioneering work in tracing worldwide literary motifs relating to the Hero.

20. For a superb discussion of these rites, their effect on masculinity, and ways in which modern American males are initiated, see Ray Raphael, *The Men from the Boys: Rites of Passage in Male America* (Lincoln: University of Nebraska Press, 1988).

21. The classic work on initiation rites was contributed by Arnold van Gennep, *The Rites of Passage*, trans. M. Vizedom (Chicago: University of Chicago Press, 1960). Numerous studies detailing particular cultures exist as well.

22. For an in-depth study of initiation and its relation to psychological therapy, see Joseph L. Henderson, *Thresholds of Initiation* (Middletown, Conn.: Wesleyan University Press, 1967).

23. Robert A. Johnson, *He! Understanding Masculine Psychology* (San Francisco: Harper & Row, 1983).

24. Jung, *Man and His Symbols* (New York: Doubleday, 1964), 17. For a very readable and practical discussion of *anima* issues, see John A. Sanford, *The Invisible Partners* (New York: Paulist, 1980).

25. For discussions of anima possession, see especially Sanford, ibid., 31–55; and Johnson, *He!*.

26. See Sanford, ibid., especially 3–30.

27. This concept of individuation is taken from Gareth Hill, Ph.D., "Patterns of Immaturity and Archetypal Patterns of Masculine and Feminine: A Preliminary Exploration" unpublished doctoral dissertation, Institute for Clinical Social Work, Berkeley, Calif. I am indebted to John V. Platania, Ph.D., of Berkeley for making these ideas available to me in his unpublished dissertation, "Adult Learning and Patterns of Organizational Development: As Seen at the Institute for Clinical Social Work," 29–33.

Chapter 3: Misandry: The Hatred of Men

1. Only a few dictionaries list "misandry," indicating its recent public origins. According to the Oxford Annotated Dictionary, by contrast, the word "misogyny" first appeared in the seventeenth century.

2. See reactions to my article "In Search of the Hero: Masculine Spirituality

and Liberal Christianity," *America* (October 7, 1989): 206–10, which appeared in "Responses to Patrick M. Arnold's 'In Search of the Hero,'" *America* (November 4, 1989): 304–6.

3. Mary Ann Dolan, "When Feminism Failed," *New York Times Magazine*, June 26, 1988, 21ff.

4. See, for example, Neal King and Martha McCaughey, "Rape Is All Too Thinkable for Quite the Normal Sort of Man," *Los Angeles Times*, February 17, 1990.

5. "Dear Abby," *Los Angeles Times*, June 15, 1990, E2; the woman confesses she doesn't have the "guts" to admit the lie, and incidentally blames her *father* for persuading her not to recant the charges (so it is still all finally a man's fault). The celebrated case of Gary Dotson, we should note, only achieved media status because the woman who falsely accused him of rape had the courage and integrity eventually to withdraw the charge. See also "The False Cry of Rape Should Be Dealt with Harshly," *Los Angeles Times*, December 17, 1990, B-7.

6. Eugene R. August, "'Modern Men,' or, Men's Studies in the 80s," *College English* 44 (October 1982): 587. The superb movie *Kramer vs. Kramer* illustrated the essential unfairness of automatically giving child custody to the mother.

7. See David D. Butler, "Males Get Longer Sentences," *Transitions* (January/ February 1990): 2; also see M. Zingraff and Randall Thompson, "Differential Sentencing of Women and Men in the U.S.A.," *International Journal of the Sociology of Law* 12 (1984): 401–13, which shows that for second-degree murder, for example, "the adjusted deviation between women and men is 4583 days (over twelve years), favoring women."

8. One spectacular recent exception is *Field of Dreams*, which portrayed both male and female characters sympathetically and heroically.

9. Susan Dundon, "Why Men Are Jerks," *Kansas City Star Magazine*, November 11, 1990, 14.

10. "The Punch-line: The Joke's on Men," *Los Angeles Times*, December 18, 1990, E-3.

11. *Time*, June 4, 1990, 38.

12. For example, our recent search for a theology teacher at the University of San Diego was restricted by higher administration to "women and minorities"; it became clear, however, that not even minority males were viable candidates.

13. One recent example of the kind of prejudice inflicted on males in college: a law professor featured an interview by a woman lawyer of a male who claimed to have been charged once with a sex crime. The professor berated his students for not "seeing through" the client's "game": supposedly the client's comment was an obvious example of sexual intimidation of his lawyer! In the course of the class, the professor then proceeded to forbid his male students from making any class comments while subjecting them to a lecture on sexual harassment, which the women law students were encouraged to join. See also Stanley Renner, "On the Present Imbalance of Criticism: An Exercise in Consciousness-Raising," *University of Dayton Review* 18 (1986–87): 9–15.

14. See August, "Modern Men," for his account of creating a men's studies course at the University of Dayton.

15. See my commentary, "In Academe, Misogyny Meets Its Match: Misan-

drosy [sic]," *Los Angeles Times*, May 14, 1990, B7. In support of the misandrist notion that the presence of male college students victimizes their female counterparts, Carol Tavris, a Los Angeles social psychologist, penned a column entitled "Boys Trample Girls' Turf," *Los Angeles Times*, May 7, 1990, which cites as proof only a study that claims to have found such intimidation *between the ages of three and six!*

16. Probably the most serious study of ancient Goddess religion is that of archaeologist Marija Gimbutas, *The Language of the Goddess* (San Francisco: Harper & Row, 1990). A sampling of other works includes a popular volume by Riane Eisler, *The Chalice and the Blade* (San Francisco: Harper & Row, 1987); Elinor Gadon, *The Once and Future Goddess: A Symbol for Our Time* (San Francisco: Harper & Row, 1988); Merlin Stone, *When God Was a Woman* (San Diego: Harcourt Brace Jovanovich, 1976); Carl Olson, ed., *The Book of the Goddess Past and Present* (New York: Crossroad, 1988); and Monica Sjoo and Barbara Mor, *The Great Cosmic Mother: Rediscovering the Religion of the Earth* (San Francisco: Harper & Row, 1987).

17. Since most of these ancient societies existed before written language, we do not always know the names of the Goddess; later societies preserved such appellations as Ishtar, Astarte, Demeter, Hera, Kore, Isis, Nut, Maat, and Mary.

18. See, for example, Stone, *When God Was a Woman*, 62–102.

19. See Sjoo and Mor, *The Great Cosmic Mother*, especially 2–12. One realizes this book is a sexist tirade even from the dedication page, where Sjoo has the gross insensitivity to use the death of her son Leif as an occasion to bash males; the boy "was tragically killed on the 26 of August 1985 [sic] by patriarchal technology in a road accident." See also Mary Daly, *Beyond God the Father* (Boston: Beacon, 1973), 95.

20. Sjoo and Mor, ibid., 18.

21. Mary Daly, *Beyond God the Father*, 172–73. Daly, incidentally, teaches in the theology department of Boston College; reportedly, she does not allow men in her classes to speak.

22. John Rowan, *The Horned God: Feminism and Men as Wounding and Healing* (London: Routledge & Kegan Paul, 1987). Rowan's book is a work of extraordinary male self-hatred.

23. Riane Eisler, *The Chalice and the Blade*.

24. Archaeological data from the Neolithic era probably does indicate a preference for female deities. This fact is a long way, however, from proving the existence of "feminine" cultures without violence, oppression, and the full range of social evils. Overinterpretation of archaeological data is an occupational hazard of historians.

25. Eisler, *Chalice and the Blade*, 104ff. *Gylany* is a strange hybrid of Greek and English (*gy* = "female" + *l* = "linking" + *any* = "male"); as an illustration of its egalitarian quality, notice that the male is placed in the last position.

26. Ibid., 59–77; see also Sjoo and Mor, *The Great Cosmic Mother*, 33–43; and Daly, *Beyond God the Father*, 92–97, who claims that men always steal women's ideas and claim credit for them.

27. Eisler, *Chalice and the Blade*, 63. This idea is as close as one can get to direct obsession with Gnostic myth.

28. Apparently the redress for blaming Eve for humanity's fall from grace is now to blame Adam.

29. Eisler *Chalice and the Blade*, 42–58. One typical example of Reisler's tendentious interpretation of archaeological evidence: a sword in a Kurgan cave engraving shows that men "literally worshiped" their weapons (48); in feminine cultures, objects like snakes only *symbolize* the Goddess and her powers (18). In other words, men stupidly worship objects, while women see them as only symbolic of greater realities.

30. Ibid., 85–89; symptomatic of Reisler's superficial understanding of the Hebrew Scriptures is that her primary sources for biblical literature are the *notes* to the *Dartmouth Bible*, published four decades ago. For another vicious attack on Hebrew religion, see Sjoo and Mor, *The Great Cosmic Mother*, especially 264–75. I consider such one-sided treatments of Jewish faith as anti-Semitic; they compare closely in their prejudice to Nazi tracts of the 1930s.

31. The Roman Catholic doctrine of the Immaculate Conception, officially defined by Pope Pius XII in 1954, holds that Mary the Mother of Jesus was born without stain of original sin.

32. Rowan, *The Horned God*, 54.

33. Daly, *Beyond God the Father*, 9–10.

34. Elisabeth Schüssler Fiorenza, *In Memory of Her: A Feminist Theological Reconstruction of Christian Origins* (New York: Crossroad, 1984).

35. See, for example, Susanne Heine, "The 'Male' in Feminist Theology," *Theology Digest* 36 (Spring 1989): 11–14.

36. Demetria Martinez, "No, Women Are Not Every Bit as Involved as Men in the Destruction of the Unborn," *NCR*, April 6, 1990, 20. Martinez was responding to columnist Michael Garvey's earlier assertion that "women have been every bit as involved as men in the destruction of more than 20 million unborn children in America since the Supreme Court legalized abortion" (*NCR*, March 9, 1990). In her next column, Martinez published "Sexual Violence More American Than Apple Pie" (*NCR*, October 26, 1990, 15), a typical piece on male violence against women which claims that sexual violence is somehow uniquely "American" and "male." That thought might have been challenged by the 1.3 million fetuses who were exterminated by their mothers in the U.S. last year — that is, if they had lived long enough to speak.

37. Ntozake Shange, "We All Have Immediate Cause," *NCR*, April 20, 1990, 2.

38. Sr. Joan Chittister, "Sexism in the Church: Agenda for the Next Decade," *Miriam's Song*, 4.

39. *Commonweal*, October 20, 1989.

40. Possibly connected with the sometimes intense pressures mounted against Catholic seminarians in moving towards ordination is the fascinating recent phenomenon in my own Jesuit order of many seminarians leaving the "priesthood track" in order to become unordained brothers.

41. I decline to identify the article, the official, or the institution.

Chapter 4: The Crisis of Men and the Church

1. See, for example, Salim Muwakkil, "Getting Black Males Off the Endangered Species List," *In These Times* (June 22, 1988): 7, or Robert Staples, "Black Male Genocide: A Final Solution to the Race Problem in America," *Black Scholar* (June 1987). The latter article contains an estimate that by the year 2000, 70 percent of all black men will be in jail, dead, on drugs, or in the throes of alcoholism.

2. See Jan Halper, *Quiet Desperation: The Truth about Successful Men* (New York: Warner Books, 1988).

3. See John W. Miller, *Biblical Faith and Fathering* (New York: Paulist, 1989).

4. See, for example, the Autumn 1989 issue of *Wingspan: Journal of the Male Spirit*, which handles of the topic of men and religion.

5. This point is fully developed in Elisabeth Schüssler Fiorenza, *In Memory of Her: A Feminist Theological Reconstruction of Christian Origins* (New York: Crossroad, 1984).

6. I am indebted to Sam Mackintosh of Westmont, N.J., for sharing with me the rite of initiation he created for his godson, David, on the occasion of his thirteenth birthday. The young man was truly fortunate to have such caring male elders plan such a ceremony for him.

7. Anthony de Mello, S.J., *Sadhana: A Way to God* (St. Louis: Institute of Jesuit Sources, 1978).

8. One group that offers assistance in creating men's workshops and discussion groups in local churches is Christian Focus, Inc., 15857 Deer Trail Drive, Chino Hills, CA 91709; (714) 597-4266.

Chapter 5: Abraham: Patriarch and Pilgrim

1. Perhaps the most helpful treatment of the Yahwist, Elohist, Priestly, and Deuteronomistic sources of the Pentateuch is found in Walter Brueggemann and Hans Walter Wolff, *The Vitality of Old Testament Traditions* (Atlanta: John Knox Press, 1982).

2. Twenty-five years after Vatican II, "pilgrim" is probably the last adjective most people would think of to describe the Roman Catholic Church.

3. This psychological exercise is called "active imagination." For a very helpful account of methods for dialoguing with the inner self, see Robert A. Johnson, *Inner Work: Using Dreams and Active Imagination for Personal Growth* (New York: Harper & Row, 1986).

4. Ignatius called himself "the pilgrim"; for his own account of his life, see *The Autobiography of St. Ignatius Loyola*, trans. Joseph F. O'Callaghan (New York: Harper & Row, 1974).

5. This is the chief thesis of John W. Miller, *Biblical Faith and Fathering: Why We Call God "Father"* (New York: Paulist, 1989).

6. The theme of "blessing" is the key idea in the Yahwist work that first told the Abraham story; see Hans Walter Wolff, "The Kerygma of the Yahwist," in *The Vitality of the Old Testament Traditions*, 41–66.

7. For a discussion of Jewish masculine spirituality, see Harry Brod, ed., *A Mensch among Men* (Freedom, Calif.: Crossing Press, 1988).

8. For an excellent discussion of two types of fathering (Sky Father and Earth Father), see Arthur and Libby Colman, *The Father: Mythology and Changing Roles* (Wilmette, Ill.: Chiron, 1988).

9. Interpretations of the sacrifice of Isaac are legion and go back to ancient times. The sacrifice of Isaac story may well have functioned in its earlier versions, for example, as a narrative that announced the end of child sacrifice in Israel. Certainly, in its present biblical form it demonstrates Abraham's total faith and trust in Yahweh. But on a mythical level it is all about the unconscious hostility of a father toward his son.

10. For a thorough psychological discussion of father-child tensions, see Alice Miller, *Thou Shalt Not Be Aware: Society's Betrayal of the Child*, trans. H. Hannum (New York: American Library, 1986).

11. For a discussion of religion's ability to offer health or sickness, see N. S. Xavier, *The Two Faces of Religion: A Psychiatrist's View* (Tuscaloosa, Ala.: Portals Press, 1987).

Chapter 6: Moses: Warrior and Magician

1. It is widely agreed among critical scholars that the huge corpus of biblical law found in the books of Exodus, Leviticus, Numbers, and Deuteronomy dates from the period after Moses up till the Babylonian Exile in the sixth century B.C.E. Priestly and Deuteronomic editors in that late era literarily inserted Jewish religious law back into the wilderness era under Moses' auspices in order to give these prescriptions theological legitimation.

2. For a discussion of historical issues relating to Moses and Exodus, see Norman K. Gottwald, *The Hebrew Bible: A Socio-Literary Introduction* (Philadelphia: Fortress, 1985), 190–201.

3. El, or Elohim, was the chief god in the Semitic pantheon, worshipped by Canaanites and Hebrews alike. Muslims worship him still as Allah.

4. Joshua's speech in Joshua 23–24 is arranged very much like a tent-revival sermon, proclaiming the "gospel" of Yahweh and calling for a total commitment to him.

5. It is quite likely that the term "Hebrew" was originally a class designation rather than an ethnic one. The word is probably connected to the term *habiru* or *apiru* mentioned in Egyptian records as a troublesome slave-class from which mercenaries could be purchased.

6. For discussions of the Warrior archetype, see Carol Pearson, *The Hero Within: Six Archetypes We Live By* (San Francisco: Harper & Row, 1986), 74–97; and Robert Moore and Douglas Gillette, *King, Warrior, Magician, Lover: Rediscovering the Archetypes of the Mature Masculine* (San Francisco: HarperSanFrancisco, 1990), 75–95.

7. Two great Democratic liberals liked to be called the Happy Warrior: Al Smith and Hubert Humphrey. Other great political liberals like Franklin Roosevelt and John F. Kennedy projected an air of masculine strength and confidence as they pursued the liberal agenda without an air of apology or anxiety. This type has virtually disappeared in the Democratic party.

8. See Moore and Gillette, *King, Warrior, Magician, Lover,* 75–95.

9. The patriarchs are portrayed in Genesis as basically peaceful fellows who want no fights with anyone. Only rarely do they skirmish with their Canaanite neighbors (e.g., Gen 14).

10. For the classic articulation of liberation theology, see Gustavo Gutiérrez, *A Theology of Liberation* (Maryknoll, N.Y.: Orbis, 1973); for a series of essays on the relation of the Bible to this theology, see Norman K. Gottwald, ed., *The Bible and Liberation: Political and Social Hermeneutics* (Maryknoll, N.Y.: Orbis, 1983).

11. I have discussed Yahweh as a "Pedagogue of the Oppressed" in a Spanish-language article entitled, "Yahvé, Pedagogo del oprimido," *Christus* (December 1988): 60–64. For an enjoyable novelistic account of the training and initiation of a warrior, see Dan Millman, *The Way of the Peaceful Warrior* (Tiburon, Calif.: Kramer, 1980).

12. The Priestly history, edited in the fifth century B.C.E., combines both the earlier Yahwist and Elohist sources, which also downplay military violence. It is the Deuteronomistic source (Deuteronomy–2 Kings) that readily encourages harsh violence against Israel's enemies.

13. Tarot cards, considered demonic in fundamentalist circles, are actually just "pictures" of the major psychological archetypes — especially the Major Arcana, twenty-two symbols of archetypical persons and situations. For an in-depth treatment of the relation of Christian spirituality to these Major Arcana, see the anonymous work entitled *Meditations on the Tarot* (Warwick, N.Y.: Amity House, 1985). For a Jungian approach, see Sallie Nichols, *Jung and Tarot: An Archetypal Journey* (York Beach, Maine: Samuel Weiser, 1980).

14. For other treatments of the Magician, see Carol Pearson, *The Hero Within,* 116–50; and the tapes of Robert Moore, "Rediscovering Masculine Potentials" (Ally Press, 524 Orleans St., St. Paul MN 55107).

15. Many books exist that teach the use of Tarot cards as aids to psychic development; see for example Eileen Connolly, *Tarot: A New Handbook for the Apprentice* (North Hollywood, Calif.: Newcastle, 1979).

16. The Chinese I Ching is the world's oldest form of divination and intuition training; the classic work that treats it is Richard Wilhelm, trans., *The I Ching or Book of Changes* (Princeton: Princeton University Press, 1950).

17. Jamie Sams and David Carson, *Medicine Cards: The Discovery of Power through the Ways of Animals* (Santa Fe: Bear & Co., 1988), teaches intuition through identification with our connections to various animals.

Chapter 7: Solomon the King

1. For a recent and thorough scholarly review of theories regarding the Deuteronomistic History, as well as new refinements to it, see Mark A. O'Brien, *The Deuteronomistic History Hypothesis: A Reassessment* (Freiburg: Universitats-verlag, 1989).

2. I have reconstructed these events in my recent book, *Gibeah: The Search for a Biblical City* (Sheffield: Sheffield Academic Press, 1990), 87–106. For an il-luminating psychological treatment of the Saul story from a Jungian perspective,

see John A. Sanford, *King Saul, the Tragic Hero: A Study in Individuation* (New York: Paulist, 1985).

3. It is widely thought that the fascinating literature describing the turmoil in the David family, also known as the Throne Succession Narrative (2 Sam 9–20), was composed in the reign of Solomon to explain why this particular son triumphed over his older brothers. For a very readable literary and theological treatment of this literature and the entire story of David, see Walter Brueggemann, *David's Truth: In Israel's Imagination and Memory* (Philadelphia: Fortress, 1985).

4. For a readable historical discussion of Solomon's era, see J. M. Miller and J. H. Hayes, "The Reign of Solomon," in *A History of Ancient Israel and Judah* (Philadelphia: Westminster, 1986), 189–217.

5. The account of Solomon's construction of the fortress cities of Hazor, Megiddo, and Gezer (1 Kgs 9:15) may be the first historically provable text in the Bible; archaeological excavations at these sites seem to show coordinated and systematic construction activity late in the tenth century B.C.E.

6. Robert Moore and Douglas Gillette, *King, Warrior, Magician, Lover: Rediscovering the Archetypes of the Mature Masculine* (San Francisco: HarperSanFrancisco, 1990), 47–73.

7. This archetype was identified by Jung and thoroughly studied by his disciple Marie-Louise von Franz, *Puer Aeternus*, 2d ed. (Boston: Sigo Press, 1981).

8. Von Franz's study of the Puer is based, interestingly enough, on the sentimental book of Antoine de Saint-Exupery, *The Little Prince* (New York: Harcourt Brace Jovanovich, 1943).

Chapter 8: Elijah the Wildman

1. The most fruitful work on identifying and exploring the Wildman archetype has been done by poet Robert Bly in his book *Iron John* (Reading, Mass.: Addison-Wesley Publishing, 1990). See also William Anderson, *Green Man: The Archetype of Our Oneness with the Earth* (San Francisco: Harper & Row, 1990).

2. For a detailed and illustrated treatment of primitive animist mythology and religion, see Joseph Campbell, *The Way of the Animal Powers:* Part 1, *Mythologies of the Primitive Hunters and Gatherers;* and Part 2, *Mythologies of the Great Hunt* in *The Historical Atlas of World Mythology* (New York: Harper & Row, 1988).

3. English also possesses this etymological connection of man with the soil: "human" comes from "humus."

4. See Bly, *Iron John*. The journey of a man into the psychic depths was dramatically enacted recently in the film *The Abyss;* seeking an undersea monster, the hero discovered in the depths his salvation instead.

5. The motif of the elusive Wildman who appears and vanishes at will is prominent in the novels of Carlos Castañeda as he describes his adventures with the Yaqui shaman Don Juan; see for example *A Separate Reality* (New York: Simon & Schuster, 1971) or *Journey to Ixtlan* (New York: Simon & Schuster, 1972).

6. We see the Wildman's power over weather in the Don Juan stories and other shamanistic narratives such as the famous account describing how the Lakota holy man Black Elk conjured up a rain cloud on Harney Peak in the

Black Hills of South Dakota in the midst of a drought; see John Neihardt, *Black Elk Speaks* (Lincoln: University of Nebraska Press, 1961), 277–80. This motif also appears in the gospel accounts of Jesus calming storms (cf. Mk 4:35–41) and such films as *Little Big Man*, *The Rainmaker*, and *The Emerald Forest*.

7. The discussion of Western man's alienation from nature leads naturally into Buddhist philosophical territory. Indeed, the legends of Buddha are laced with the Wildman motif. A biblical counterpart to this philosophy may to a great extent be found in the book of Ecclesiastes (Qoheleth).

8. These two miracle stories also appear later in the Elisha cycle (2 Kgs 4:1–7 and 4:18–37). On the basis of the healing motif in the Elisha cycle, as opposed to the antagonistic tone of the Elijah stories, I would argue that later editors have inserted Elisha's miracle stories into the Elijah cycle at a late date.

9. The notion that political domination is historically only a male phenomenon is central, for example, to Riane Eisler's *The Chalice and the Blade* (San Francisco: Harper & Row, 1987), as well as a host of other feminist works.

10. In the northern Israelite circles in which the Elijah stories circulated, the desert mountain of Moses' encounter with Yahweh is called Mt. Horeb; in southern Judean circles, the mountain is called Sinai.

11. See Campbell, *The Way of the Animal Powers*, Part I: *Mythologies of the Primitive Hunters and Gatherers*, 58ff.

12. The ancient cave rituals might partially explain on an unconscious level why many men are so captivated by the dangerous sport of spelunking, or cave exploration.

13. See Jean Bolen, *Gods in Everyman*, 103–23; and Arthur and Libby Colman, *The Father: Mythology and Changing Roles* (Wilmette, Ill.: Chiron, 1988), 21–31.

14. Modern Christianity has become almost completely alienated from the natural experience. Two of its harshest epithets ("pagan" = Latin *paganus*, "countryman"; and "heathen" = Middle English *heth*, "heath-dweller") suggest this contempt for nature religion.

Chapter 9: Elisha the Healer

1. The word *shaman* derives from Tungus, a Siberian language, though there may be etymological roots to the Vedic *sram*, meaning "to heal oneself or practice austerities"; see Joan Halifax, *Shamanic Voices: A Survey of Visionary Narratives* (New York: Dutton, 1979), 3.

2. In homeopathic medicine, the distinction is made between "allopathic" healing (attacking the disease — masculine) and homeopathic healing (strengthening the diseased — feminine).

3. For scholarly discussions of shamanism, see for example John A. Grim, *The Shaman* (Norman: University of Oklahoma Press, 1983); Mircea Eliade, *Shamanism: Archaic Techniques of Ecstasy* (Princeton: Princeton University Press, 1964); Shirley Nicholson, ed. *Shamanism* (Wheaton, Ill.: Theosophical Publishing, 1987); and Joan Halifax, *Shamanic Voices*.

4. One of the most hopeful books dealing with the shamanic pattern and the possibility of finding wholeness in the midst of disease is by John A. Sanford, *Healing and Wholeness* (New York: Paulist, 1977).

5. For discussions of the influence of psychology on health, see Larry Dossey, *Beyond Illness: Discovering the Experience of Health* (Boulder: Shambhala, 1984).

6. A beautiful example of the Healer archetype is a book by my friend William Josef Dobbels, S.J., *An Epistle of Comfort* (Kansas City: Sheed & Ward, 1990). Fr. Dobbels transformed his own painful struggle with AIDS into a genuinely touching and wise book that is addressed to anyone suffering from catastrophic illness. Since he has "been there," Fr. Dobbels's words bear special meaning and compassion.

7. It is my contention that Elisha abused his bear connection; see 2 Kgs 2:23–25. For a helpful New Age book on the power of psychic connection to animals, see Jamie Sams and David Carson, *Medicine Cards: The Discovery of Power through the Ways of Animals* (Santa Fe, N.M.: Bear & Co., 1988).

8. See, for example, Raymond Moody, M.D., *Life after Life* (Toronto: Bantam, 1975); or Morton T. Kelsey, *Afterlife: The Other Side of Dying* (New York: Crossroad, 1986).

9. The notion that wearing another's clothes gives access to that person's experience is present, for example, in St. Paul's invitation to "put on Christ"; (see Gal 3:27, Rom 13:14, or Col 3:10).

10. The New Testament gospel writers have obviously followed 2 Kings 2 in creating the scene of John the Baptist (the new Elijah) transferring his powers at the Jordan to his disciple Jesus (the new Elisha).

11. This scene surely suggests the classic motif of the water miracle that occurred when Joshua crossed the Jordan River prior to the conquest of Jericho (Josh 3). Whereas the Warrior Joshua destroyed Jericho after this miracle, the Healer Elisha will heal the same city's water supply.

12. Biblical law specifically prohibits such sorcery, e.g. Exodus 22:18, Leviticus 19:31, and Deuteronomy 18:10–11.

13. Jesus quotes the Naaman story in Luke 4:27 to indicate that his Messiahship extends beyond the political borders of Israel; his listeners were infuriated.

Chapter 10: Jeremiah the Prophet

1. For a thorough discussion of the prophet's social role in ancient societies as well as modern, see Robert R. Wilson, *Prophecy and Society in Ancient Israel* (Philadelphia: Fortress, 1980).

2. For an energetic and striking discussion of this alternative vision, see Walter Brueggemann, *The Prophetic Imagination* (Philadelphia: Fortress, 1978).

3. The classic work on prophetic empathy is that of Rabbi Abraham J. Heschel, *The Prophets*, 2 vols. (New York: Harper & Row, 1962).

4. See, for example, Anne Wilson Schaef, *When Society Becomes an Addict* (San Francisco: Harper & Row, 1987).

5. M. Scott Peck, *People of the Lie* (New York: Simon & Schuster, 1983). This book is a valuable but chilling account of the dynamics of lying in psychologically stunted people.

6. See John Neihardt, *Black Elk Speaks* (Lincoln: University of Nebraska Press, 1961), especially 20–47. This book is destined to become a classic in the annals of

masculine spirituality. For a thorough treatment of Black Elk, see Raymond J. De-Mallie, ed., *The Sixth Grandfather: Black Elk's Teachings Given to John G. Neihardt* (Lincoln: University of Nebraska Press, 1984).

7. See my article "Jeremiah and Black Elk," *Bible Today* (May 1985): 182–85.

8. Black Elk himself, towards the end of his life, felt that he had failed in his mission and let down the Grandfathers and the people as well (*Black Elk Speaks*, 269–76). Like Jeremiah, however, his prophecies were for another day. Today Black Elk is regarded as the chief figure in the renaissance of Lakota religion.

9. Robert Bly's tape "The Naive Male" is available from Ally Press, 524 Orleans St., St. Paul, MN 55107.

10. For an account of his life, see Daniel Berrigan, *To Dwell in Peace: An Autobiography* (San Francisco: Harper & Row, 1987).

Chapter 11: Jonah the Trickster

1. For a discussion of the Trickster in biblical literature, see Susan Niditch, *Underdogs and Tricksters: A Prelude to Biblical Folklore* (San Francisco: Harper & Row, 1987).

2. A recent book that thoroughly discusses the book of Jonah from a psychological perspective is by Andre and Pierre-Emmanuel Lacocque, *Jonah: A Psycho-Religious Approach to the Prophet* (Columbia, S.C.: University of South Carolina Press, 1990).

3. See the classic work of Paul Radin, *The Trickster: A Study in American Indian Mythology* (New York: Schocken, 1956).

4. For an essay on the psychological aspects of the trickster, see Carl Jung, "On the Psychology of the Trickster-Figure," in *Four Archetypes* (Princeton, N.J.: Princeton University Press, 1959), 135–52.

5. For a discussion of trickster gods, see *Joseph Campbell: The Power of Myth with Bill Moyers*, ed. Betty Sue Flowers (New York: Doubleday, 1988), 219–20.

6. Prophetic rhetoric frequently compares Yahweh to a snare, a trap, or a stumbling stone that trips up Israel and Judah; see, for example Isaiah 8:11–15 or 28:16–17.

Chapter 12: The Lover

1. For a treatment of the Lover archetype, see Robert Moore and Douglas Gillette, *King, Warrior, Magician, Lover: Rediscovering the Archetypes of the Mature Masculine* (San Francisco: HarperSanFrancisco, 1990), 119–41.

2. The term "sins of the flesh" is itself indicative of the problem. In popular religious parlance, the phrase today connotes only sexual sin. Originally in the New Testament, however, "flesh" (*sarx*) meant all sins of narcissism, selfishness, and rebellion against God, and included the addiction to wealth, power, wisdom, and even legalistic religion itself. For an enlightening treatment of this term, see Rudolf Bultmann, *Theology of the New Testament* (New York: Scribner's, 1951), especially 1: 227–46.

3. The Deuteronomist editor of the Solomon story seems to have had no problem with the *number* of Solomon's wives — just the fact that most of them were foreigners for whom the king built pagan shrines and high places.

4. For a new translation and discussion of the book, see Marcia Falk, *The Song of Songs* (San Francisco: Harper & Row, 1990).

5. See, for example, the introduction to the Song of Songs in the Jerusalem Bible, 991–92.

6. Phyllis Trible, *God and the Rhetoric of Sexuality* (Philadelphia: Fortress, 1978), 144–65, also points out that the female Beloved in the Songs is not a passive damsel, but is the erotic equal of her boyfriend.

7. For a wise and honest discussion of the psychology of falling in love, see Dorothy Tennov, *Love and Limerence: The Experience of Being in Love* (Chelsea, Mich.: Scarborough House, 1989).

8. For a Jungian discussion of romantic love, see Robert A. Johnson, *We: Understanding the Psychology of Romantic Love* (San Francisco: Harper & Row, 1983).

9. For a treatment of the connections between romantic love and spirituality, see Charles Williams, *Outlines of Romantic Theology* (Grand Rapids: Eerdmans, 1990), a previously unpublished work written in 1924.

10. Quoted in Alfred Corn, ed., *Incarnation: Contemporary Authors on the New Testament* (New York: Viking, 1990) 288.

11. For a thorough study of homosexual myths and stories, see *Homosexuality and Greek Myth* (Boston: Beacon, 1986).

12. I would suggest that the tradition of Jonathan's crush on David may have been invented, or at least expanded upon, by later Davidic writers in order to create the scene in which Jonathan virtually abdicates to David (1 Sam 18:1–5), thus legitimizing the Davidic dynasty's royal claims; see my book *Gibeah: The Search for a Biblical City* (Sheffield: Sheffield Academic Press, 1990), 87–106. But see also Tom Horner, *Jonathan Loved David: Homosexuality in Biblical Times* (Philadelphia: Westminster, 1977).

Chapter 13: Jesus the Christ

1. Two exceptions to the film feminization of Jesus: the Italian Communist Pier Paulo Pasolini's excellent 1964 production of *The Gospel according to Matthew*, and Martin Scorcese's recent rendering of Nikos Kazantzakis's *The Last Temptation of Christ*. The controversy surrounding the latter film is particularly illustrative of the repression of masculine sexuality in modern Christianity. Fundamentalists objected violently to a scene in the movie portraying Jesus' fantasy of marriage to Mary Magdalene. In their view, male sexuality is dirty, bad, and forbidden — and certainly not something Jesus would ever possess.

2. Also recommended: the video production of *St. Mark's Gospel* by actor Alec McCowen, an energetic, one-man staging of the gospel. Available from Palisades Institute, 153 Waverly Place, New York, NY 10014.

3. Expanding on Mark's identification of John the Baptist with Elijah, Matthew 3:7–12 and Luke 3:7–18 each adds references to fiery retribution reminiscent of Elijah.

4. Luke's gospel is particularly noteworthy in its condemnation of greed; cf. Luke 12:16–21; 14:28–33; 16:13; 16:19–31; and 18:18–27.

5. Even hostile contemporary Jewish sources acknowledge Jesus' special healing powers, explaining them away as "sorcery" and magic arts learned in Egypt.

6. For a recent discussion of the value of spirituality in healing, see Dr. Bernie Siegel, *Love, Medicine, and Miracles* (New York: Harper & Row, 1986).

7. Matthew's interpretation of the remark as a prediction of Jesus' time in the tomb (Mt 12:40) may be an early Christian interpolation of Jesus' comment. The other explanation, that the comment indicated the rejection of Israel and acceptance of the Gentiles, is surely closer to what Jesus meant (cf. Mt 12:41–42, Lk 11:30–32).

8. For a thorough analysis of this motif, see James M. Robinson, *The Problem of History in Mark* (London: SCM Press, 1957).

9. The classic scholarly caution against reading a liberal figure into the lives of Jesus was issued in 1897 by Albert Schweitzer, *The Quest of the Historical Jesus* (New York: Macmillan, 1968). Schweitzer situated Jesus firmly in the apocalyptic milieu of the first century. Despite this caution, however, Jesus continues to be a screen on which moderns project their ideologies, most recently in becoming an early "feminist" (e.g., Sandra Schneiders, quoted in "Feminism and the Churches," *Newsweek*, February 13, 1989, 61).

10. See, for example, Norman K. Gottwald, ed., *The Bible and Liberation: Political and Social Hermeneutics* (Maryknoll, N.Y.: Orbis, 1983), especially the essay by John Pairman Brown, "Techniques of Imperial Control: The Background of the Gospel Event," 357–77.

11. For a recent account of revolutionary groups in first-century Palestine, see Richard A. Horsely with John S. Hanson, *Bandits, Prophets, and Messiahs: Popular Movements at the Time of Jesus* (San Francisco: Harper & Row, 1988).

12. The sayings of the historical Jesus undoubtedly bear witness to his self-designation as prophet; when rejected in his hometown of Nazareth, for example, he said, "A prophet is hated only in his own country and in his own house" (Mt 13:57). Certainly, the people understood him as such; when entering Jerusalem on a donkey, the crowds identified him as "Jesus, the prophet from Nazareth in Galilee" (Mt 21:11).

13. This meditation on Christ the King ends the First Week of the Spiritual Exercises; see Louis J. Puhl, ed., *The Spiritual Exercises of St. Ignatius* (Chicago: Loyola, 1951), 43–45.

Chapter 14: The Masculinity of God

1. "God created humans in his own image; in the image of God he created him, male and female he created them." Though this passage appears in the first chapter of Genesis, as a product of the Priestly school, it is actually a late development of Hebrew theology (sixth–fifth centuries B.C.E.).

2. For a typical feminist statement of the notion that masculine metaphors for God are violent and oppressive, see Sallie McFague, *Models of God: Theology for an Ecological, Nuclear Age* (Philadelphia: Fortress, 1987), ix–xv.

3. A notable exception to the deconstructionist vogue is Sallie McFague's book *Models of God*, which offers alternate metaphors for God such as mother, lover, and friend. For a discussion of feminine imagery in the Bible, see Phyllis Trible, *God and the Rhetoric of Sexuality* (Philadelphia: Fortress, 1978).

4. Michael O. Garvey, "Questions to Answer before Going to Kill Arabs," *National Catholic Reporter*, December 14, 1990, 13.

5. For a discussion of the role of metaphor in theology, see Sallie McFague, *Metaphorical Theology: Models of God in Religious Language* (Philadelphia: Fortress, 1982).

6. But see Phyllis Trible's *God and the Rhetoric of Sexuality*, for example, for important exceptions.

7. The "God the Wildman" motif is especially prominent in Job 38–42, the Psalms, and Isaiah 40–55.

8. See Genesis 17:2, 28:3, 35:11, and 48:3; these passages are related to Priestly material, where the term "be fruitful and multiply" is a major theme.

9. Trible, *God and the Rhetoric of Sexuality*, 61, links the term Shaddai and Hebrew *sadayim* ("breasts") in Genesis 49:25 and supposes that the pun "connotes a maternal aspect in the divine." Trible's association is itself sexist; the last time I looked, men had breasts, too.

10. *Joseph Campbell: The Power of Myth with Bill Moyers*, ed. Betty Sue Flowers (New York: Doubleday, 1988), 47–48. On the topic of the Hebrew Scriptures, Campbell's scholarly impartiality often seems to have escaped him; see 169–71.

11. Rudolf Otto, *The Idea of the Holy* (Oxford: Oxford University Press, 1958).

12. See especially in this regard Millard C. Lind, *Yahweh Is a Warrior: The Theology of Warfare in Ancient Israel* (Scottsdale, Pa.: Herald, 1980).

13. See especially Amos 4–5 and Hosea 6–7, where the prophets rail against the counterfeit Israelite religion that masks its exploitation of the poor and its idolatrous heterodoxy with fancy feasts and lovely liturgies.

14. See especially Norman K. Gottwald, *The Bible and Liberation: Political and Social Hermeneutics* (Maryknoll, N.Y.: Orbis, 1983).

15. This idea is given perhaps its most extreme expression by Mary Daly in *Beyond God the Father: Toward a Philosophy of Women's Liberation* (Boston: Beacon, 1973), especially 13–43.

16. John W. Miller, *Biblical Faith and Fathering: Why We Call God "Father"* (New York: Paulist Press, 1989).

17. A point developed forcefully by Alexander Mitscherlich, *Society without the Father* (New York: Harcourt, Brace and World, 1963); see especially 303.

18. Miller, *Biblical Faith and Fathering*, 13–39.

19. The historical-literary form of the Old Testament *berit*, or covenant, strongly conveys the metaphor of suzerain to vassal; however, we may translate this deliberate commitment of God to his people into the father-family metaphor as a kind of legal adoption, as indeed Paul seems to have done (Gal 4:1–7).

Index of Biblical References

OLD TESTAMENT

Subject and Name Index